Colonel Thomas Pride was central to one of the English Civil War's key events: the arrest and exclusion of 140 Members of Parliament at Westminster in December 1648. Those that remained in the Commons voted to bring King Charles I to trial, resulting in the first and only execution of a British Monarch. But while this monumental episode of early modern history – Pride's Purge – is renowned, the life of the army officer behind it remains shrouded in obscurity.

Cromwell's Buffoon is a detailed and engaging account of the life of soldier and regicide, Colonel Thomas Pride, a Somerset farmer's son who fought his way through the Civil Wars to become one of the English Commonwealth's most forceful personalities. Robert Hodkinson's lively and authoritative study charts Pride's rise from London brewer, his experience of the seventeenth century battle-field, gaining command of a regiment through mutiny, to finally brushing aside accusations of hypocrisy to claim ownership of a former Royal estate and a seat in Oliver Cromwell's House of Lords.

Cromwell's Buffoon is a ground-breaking examination of why and how a former apprentice boy rose in status to challenge the ruling elite and affect the death of a monarch. The first full-length biography of its subject, it is a fascinating story of a man who, until now, had all but vanished from history.

Robert Hodkinson graduated from the University of Derby in 2010 with an MA in Humanities, winning the vice-chancellor's prize for his dissertation on contemporary poetry of the First World War. His interest in the English Civil War was sparked by the Sealed Knot battle re-enactment society, and his role as a musketeer in the parliamentarian regiments of Lord Grey and Colonel Thomas Pride. He is the author of numerous articles, both online and print, on everyday life and culture during the English Civil War. He is also the author of the prize-winning poetry pamphlet, *Malvern Gibbous* (2013).

Cromwell's Buffoon

The Life and Career of the Regicide, Thomas Pride

Robert Hodkinson

Helion & Company Limited

Helion & Company Limited
26 Willow Road
Solihull
West Midlands
B91 1UE
England
Tel. 0121 705 3393
Fax 0121 711 4075
Email: info@helion.co.uk
Website: www.helion.co.uk
Twitter: @helionbooks
Visit our blog at http://blog.helion.co.uk/

Published by Helion & Company 2017
Designed and typeset by Mach 3 Solutions Ltd (www.mach3solutions.co.uk)
Cover designed by Paul Hewitt, Battlefield Design (www.battlefield-design.co.uk)
Printed by Short Run Press, Exeter, Devon

Text © Robert Hodkinson 2017
Images from author's collection unless otherwise stated
Original maps drawn by George Anderson © Helion & Company 2017

Front cover image: 'Portrait of Colonel Pride' c 1805-1825, by Thomas Athow (Image ©
Ashmolean Museum, University of Oxford, ref. WA.Suth.C.3.374.1).

ISBN 978-1-911512-11-0

British Library Cataloguing-in-Publication Data.
A catalogue record for this book is available from the British Library.

For details of other military history titles published by Helion & Company
Limited, contact the above address, or visit our website: http://www.helion.co.uk

We always welcome receiving book proposals from prospective authors.

Contents

List of Illustrations

List of Maps

Introduction

Take down any popular history of the English Civil War from the bookshelf and turn to the index. There, under the letter P, you will find and entry for 'Pride's Purge'. It might provide you with a date: 6 December 1648. Turn to the appropriate page and your book will inform you that the purge was carried out by the New Model Army; that on the aforementioned date they prevented 140 elected Members of the House of Commons from taking their seats in the House; that those few MPs who were allowed to remain subsequently voted that King Charles I be brought to trial to face the death penalty for waging a war against his own people. You might also read that 'Pride's Purge' was named after army colonel in charge of the proceedings that day. The entry in your history book may be brief but it will be there, for Pride's Purge was a momentous event in British history, the political climax to nearly a decade of civil conflict.

In December 1648 the House of Commons decided, by 129 votes to 83, to accept Charles I's proposals for peace and proceed towards a settlement. When Parliament's army discovered this they chose to intervene. The army would not settle for peace at any price; they feared that the Commons would. The army marched on Westminster, mounted a guard on the entrances to the Commons and refused entry to all members that were opposed to their views. Only those MPs who were favourable to the army were allowed to remain sitting. A vote to bring the King to justice was subsequently carried on 1 January. On 20 January Charles I arrived at Westminster to begin his trial. He was executed ten days later.

The event is invariably referred to in the history books as "Pride's Purge" – alliteration serves as a useful *aide-mémoire* as well as being pleasing to the ear. Yet this title is something of a paradox, for while reference to the Purge be found in any book on the period the life of the man after whom it is named remains a blank.

Colonel Thomas Pride was a man who was present at many significant events of the English Civil War. He was a soldier who saw a great deal of military action, including the battles of Naseby and Dunbar; he played a prominent part in the radicalism of the New Model Army, that military force with a political voice; his role in creating the Rump Parliament was instrumental in the execution of Charles I; he had a role in maintaining law and order during the Commonwealth and the Protectorate, the only period Britain has been a republic. Yet despite the man's presence at these key points in British history our knowledge of him is virtually nil. The sparsity of facts about his life (there is no date for his birth, no record of where he is buried) means that any account of Thomas Pride's life is sketchy at best.

The only biography of Pride from his own time is a mere twenty lines long. It is to be found in William Winstanley's *The Loyall Martyrology*, a collection of biographical sketches of those men who signed Charles I's death warrant. Though published in 1665, a mere seven years after Thomas Pride's death, it reveals very little. According to its author, Pride had little education, had been a brewer before the Civil War, was successful in the conflict, active in the formation of the Rump, signed the death warrant and died shortly before the Restoration. Of other details, such as where he was born and where he lived, there is nothing. *The History of King-Killers*, published by S. Redmayne in 1719, provides the reader with similar collection of short biographies. Here the account of Pride's life is almost as brief. Printed sixty years after Pride's death, *King-Killers* merely informs us that he 'was of an original so obscure that it is not worth our searching into it.'

Further character sketches of Pride emerged following his death but these, such as *'A New Meeting of Ghosts at Tyburn'* and *'The Last Speech and Dying Words of Thomas (Lord, alias Colonel) Pride'*, contained more satire than history. The rejuvenated Monarchy that followed Cromwell's Protectorate had little sympathy for the memory of a Regicide. Restoration pamphleteers presented Pride as a caricature, little more than a jumped-up yokel who took advantage of the political upheavals of the time for self gain. Such was his reputation in the years following his death: it is a truism that history is written by the victors.

As history rolled on, the picture became obscurer still. A more detailed account of Pride's life was written by Reverend Mark Noble in his *Lives of the English Regicides* (1798), with additional material to be found in the author's earlier work *The Protectorate House of Cromwell* (1787). Noble's work is a good example of the danger that lies in attempting a biography on a subject of whom we know so little. Setting out to write a comprehensive and hostile account of his subject, Noble drew on an abundance of rumour and folk-memory, little of which could be substantiated and which succeeded only in blurring the known facts. In the one hundred and forty years between Pride's death and Noble's writing the historical truth became embellished with hearsay and inaccuracies, many of which continue to be promulgated today, as this book will demonstrate. It was Noble's conclusion that Pride had been 'a useful man to Cromwell in all his projects, and acted, it is said, also as a buffoon to him.' So exhaustive and detailed was Noble's account, however, that it became the work on which many subsequent histories drew, including it would seem C. H. Firth's entry for Thomas Pride in the Oxford History of National Biography (1896).

It is because Thomas Pride has remained a minor figure of English history that no thorough account of his life has been attempted. Two modern summaries of his life can be found in Greaves and Zallers' *The Biographical Dictionary of Seventeenth Century English Radicals* and in Ian Gentiles' entry for Pride in the 2004 edition of the *Oxford Dictionary of National Biography*. Both contain a wealth of details but neither is comprehensive. The aim of this book is to bring together what little we know of Thomas Pride and construct a more detailed account of the man's life and career than can be found elsewhere: to flesh out a life from a miscellany of rumour and legend. Above all it is an attempt to understand why a man from such an apparently obscure and humble background felt compelled to carry out the momentous event of December 1648 that have borne his name ever since. It is the story of a man's emergence through the strata of mid-seventeenth century society; of a man who grew out of humble origins and, through the upheaval of a civil war, was set on a path that was to lead him out of obscurity to considerable wealth and influence.

1

Early Life, c.1608–29

West Country Roots

Five miles to the south-west of Glastonbury, on the edge of Somerset's Polden Hills, stands Thomas Pride's birthplace. A more remote, rural backwater would be difficult to find. The hamlet of Pedwell was, and is, a scattering of houses and small-holdings at the bottom of a steep hill running down to the southwards expanse of the Somerset Levels. Before the drainage works of the eighteenth century the surrounding area was subject to regular floods. At about the time of Thomas Pride's birth, in the winter of 1607, the sea had pushed inland as far as Glastonbury, returning the steep-sided Tor to the island it had been in Roman times, as Pedwell found itself lapped by the waters of the Bristol Channel. Each spring this annual flooding would recede to leave lush feeding grounds for the livestock on the Levels. At the beginning of the 17th century the climate was still warm enough that, '...in summer time England yields apricots plentifully, musk melons in good quantity, and figs in some places, all which ripen well, and happily imitate the taste and goodness of the same fruits in Italy.'[1] It was the fertile landscape around Pedwell that had prompted the Anglo-Saxons to name this part of the country *Somer Saete* – Summer Pasture. Dairy farming and the cloth trade dominated the local economy.[2]

There is no memorial to Thomas Pride in Pedwell, nor in the neighbouring village of Ashcott, the centre of the parish. Bridgwater, only eight miles distant, makes more of its Civil War past, with a museum dedicated to its native son, Admiral Robert Blake, and a statue of him in the town. Blake, Somerset-born and a staunch Puritan, had the benefit of a university education. He rose higher and faster than Pride in Parliament's army, and he has long been considered an important figure by naval historians. Thomas Pride has had no such allies to argue for his place in the history books.

Pride's father, William, was a yeoman farmer, and likely to have been a prominent figure in his small community.[3] The family's name was 'well-known in central Somerset' by the time Pride was born,[4] with references to Prides or Prydes cropping-up in documents relating to the hamlets and villages that hug the Poldens, at Cossington in 1607 and in Glastonbury as far back as the 15th century. In the early 1500s they were tenant farmers of lands owned by the monks of Glastonbury Abbey, working the largest single holding of 65 acres. It is possible that the Prides acquired the land for themselves at the Dissolution. The family had held local office too, listed as reeves in nearby Street and at Buttleigh in the 1300s. A reference to a John Pryde of Ashcott in the subsidy assessment of 1580/81 suggests that in the 16th century the Pride family were still well-to-do owners of property.[5]

But in spite of the evidence to long-standing wealth and local influence, Thomas Pride's family background remains obscure. Any attempt to detail his childhood would be little more than guesswork. The local parish registers were destroyed by fire in the 1700s, erasing forever the date of Pride's baptism and the names and number of his immediate family.

The Prides of Pedwell can be assumed to have been a cadet branch of the long-established local family. It is tempting to think of Thomas as a younger son, having elder brothers who would in time have taken on the family farm or business, because at the beginning of 1622 Thomas himself was sent off to London to be apprenticed and to earn his living in trade.

Thomas Bradway was the man to whom the young Pride was apprenticed, a London haberdasher with a large country house in Gloucestershire and doubtlessly linked to the Cotswold wool trade.[6] Pride's father would have paid a premium for his son's training and the cost of his feeding, clothing and accommodation, a solid investment for a younger son in a period when agriculture was in decline and the cloth trade was growing in importance. More than half of haberdashers' apprentices in the early 17th century were from families headed by men who considered themselves to be either yeoman, gentlemen, or of an even higher social degree. Although fathers were apt to embroider their own credentials when presenting their sons for apprenticeship, William Pride was clearly affluent enough to send his son to the Haberdashers, one of the elite London companies, who were able to charge a higher premium for apprentices on account of their reputation.

The age of an apprentice in was not fixed, but it is more than likely that Pride was in his early to mid-teens when he began to work under Bradway. This allows us to place the date of Pride's birth at about 1608.

The London that the young Thomas encountered on his arrival in 1622 might well have been another country altogether. Growing up in a lazy Somerset backwater, the grandest buildings of Pride's childhood would have been the medieval ruins of Glastonbury Abbey, but witnessing the publication of William Harvey's treatise on circulation, the First Folio edition of Shakespeare's plays, Bacon's *Essays*, Pride's formative years as a London apprentice coincided with landmarks in science, literature and philosophy. Likely as not, he never encountered any of them first-hand: Pride's formal education was never to reach beyond the needs of his apprenticeship. Nevertheless, he would have witnessed in his youth an English Renaissance that reached new heights of innovation and perception, and which promised to sweep away the cobwebs of medieval thought.

Not the least among these new voices was that of the resurgent House of Commons, which had then recently resurrected the process of impeachment with which to prosecute businessmen who profited unfairly from monopolies. Impeachment had not been used since 1449; and its revival revealed a new assertiveness within the legislature for the benefit of London's trade. The same year Pride arrived in London the MP John Pym, a focus of parliamentary opposition against James I, was placed under house arrest for hostile remarks made in the Commons concerning the monarch. When Parliament had urged that James's heir, Charles, to marry a protestant princess, James had warned them 'not to meddle with anything concerning our deep affairs of state',[7]and Parliament's protest was removed from the pages of the *Commons Journal* at James's behest.[8] Beneath the optimism of the age ran an undercurrent of tension and suppressed freedoms by a monarchy which feared that such liberties could undermine its authority.

When Pride left Somerset for a life in London commerce, his journey was part of an increasing drift from the countryside to urban centres, the result of growth in a population that had been steadily rising since Tudor times. England's population had nearly doubled during the late 16th and early 17th centuries, with London experiencing an eight-fold increase between 1520 and 1640.[9] By the mid-17th century the problems that resulted from such a rise were beginning to be felt. There was frequent shortage of food, inflation, and high levels of unemployment due to a surplus of labour. But there were some people who thrived in such circumstances, and London tradesmen, including the young Thomas Pride, found themselves prospering.

What little schooling Pride received (and he would later be popularly regarded as 'an ignorant, illiterate fellow')[10] came solely from his apprenticeship. Indeed, some apprenticeship indentures specified that the master instruct, or ensure that apprentices were instructed, in basic reading, writing and arithmetic. Pride would have been taken into his master's household, living with the family and working for his board and education while his master was responsible for his apprentice's 'dyet, for his health, for his safety'.[11] At the beginning of his service his tasks would have been menial (young apprentices were known by the wry title of 'broom-clerks'), but it was a life that provided young people (half of apprentices were girls) not with a sense of servitude but of self-worth. It advocated self-advancement against competition from others, yet with an emphasis on business partnership, common goals and shared values. Coupled with the feeling of community of belonging to one of the fifty London livery companies, such values meant that by the early 17th century a distinct social group of young, aspirational skilled craftsmen was beginning to emerge.[12]

A word on haberdashers. It is difficult to put one's finger on the precise nature of a haberdasher's business in this period. By the late 16th century it was thought to consist of dealing in 'French or Milan caps, glasses, daggers, swords, girdles and such things'. The Elizabethan antiquary, John Stow listed 'mousetraps, bird cages, shoe horns, lanterns and Jews' trumps' among the items haberdashers sold, and a further description of wares from 1576 lists 'bells, necklaces, beads of glass, collars, points, purses, needles, girdles, thread, knives, scissors, pincers, hammers, hatchets, shirts, coifs, handkerchiefs, breeches, clothes, caps, mariners' breeches …'[13] Hats featured regularly in haberdashery, as it was from haberdashers that one would buy new linings and hat bands; the Guild of Hat-makers had amalgamated with the Haberdashers in 1502. It seems that as long as an item was ready-made and hand-sized, a haberdasher would be prepared to sell you one.

Pride served his term as an apprentice and was made free of the Haberdashers' Company on 24 April 1629.[14] While bound to a master he would not have been permitted to court and relationships with women would have been discouraged. He wasted little time once free of his indentures, however, and within four months he had married Elizabeth Thomason, the daughter of an ironmonger, at St. Anne's church Blackfriars.[15] Elizabeth was born in about the year 1609, which makes her perhaps a year or two younger than her husband, but our knowledge of her is scant.[16] Posterity (and a male-dominated culture) has allowed Elizabeth to bequeath us even less of her history than her husband.

The minister that wed Thomas and Elizabeth, William Gouge, was a noted religious nonconformist – a 'Puritan'. He had received censure some years previously for not administering communion as stipulated in the Anglican Common Prayer Book: instead of receiving the sacrament from the minister's hand, Gouge had allowed his communicants to pass the cup between themselves, placing the worshipper at the heart of communion rather than the presiding minister. Gouge had also refused to read from James I's *Book of Sports*, which licensed dancing and games on the Sabbath,[18] and it is in Gouge that we glimpse the first hints of an association with religious nonconformity that would shape Pride's faith and politics in coming years.

At some point during the 1630s (it is difficult to establish an exact date), there was a marked shift in Pride's business interests as he moved aside from haberdashery into brewing. His former master, Bradway, is known to have owned property including a brew house in St. Bride's parish and this may have been the route through which Pride entered his chosen trade. Most larger houses in this period would have had facilities for brewing, but Bradway's premises were substantial enough for its ownership to be contested in the courts following his death; it was a property in its own right.[19] Writing in 1661, Dr. George Bate claimed that Pride had once worked as 'a Servant to Mr. Hiccocks a Brewer in Southwark'.[20] There is no evidence to substantiate this, though William Hiccocks himself was real enough. Hiccocks was still alive at the time Bate was writing. He was both a brewer and a former Parliamentarian, a member of the Southwark militia and responsible for that borough's defence in the Civil War.[21] He and Pride had clearly moved in the same circles and may well have known of each other, but there is nothing to suggest that Pride ever worked as his servant. Pride, as we have seen, was a trained and skilled worker, he was not of servant class. The fact that Dr.

Bate made his claim in a work subtitled '*that horrid murder of our late pious and sacred soveraigne King Charles I*' betrays his Royalism, and the reference to Pride being a servant was undoubtedly intended to sully Pride's posthumous reputation. However, it was not unknown for a master to loan or 'turn-over' an apprentice to a master to learn aspects of another trade.[22] Bradway, a haberdasher but also owner of a substantial brew house, may have wished an apprentice of his to learn the fundamentals of brewing to help expand his own business interests, and it is possible that Pride gleaned some knowledge of brewing by working for a time under Hiccocks. Certainly the rumour of Pride having begun as a menial worker in would recur time and again during the course of his career.

Brewing was vital to London, and with an estimated 8,000 people a year migrating the capital[23] the demand for beer and ale soared. It was a necessity for a large, urban population in a period where disease could spread uncontrollably: it is a truism that everyone in 1600s London had to drink beer because the water would kill them. By this period domestic brewing had gone into decline, traditional brewing methods unable to cope with the demands of a rapidly expanding population. Ale house keepers who would have formerly brewed on their own premises were increasingly having to buy on credit from independent brewers. By the time that Pride completed his apprenticeship brewing was no longer a domestic occupation, it was big business. The money that Pride would have made was augmented by low overheads: workers' wages were increasing at a slower rate than profits because of the population rise. Unskilled workers were begging for jobs, and if they were prepared to work for less money in order to guarantee employment then it suited brewers all the better. The economic upheaval of the early 17th century was turning Pride into a rich man.

Given the eclectic nature of a haberdasher's trade, it would seem that a side-step into brewing was no great leap. Pride certainly prospered, so much so that by the early 1640s it would appear that brewing was his sole concern, and no business other than that of brewing is referred to in his will.[24] Even so, Pride was shrewd enough not to abandon his old trade entirely. In the 1650s his knowledge and contacts in haberdashery allowed him to manage lucrative contracts in supplying the English army with shoes and clothing,and he was responsible for the education of 6 apprentice haberdashers between 1635 and 1654.[25]

It is questionable how 'hands-on' Pride would have been in the process of brewing beer and ale. He was not privy to the 'brewer's mystery and trade', which a brewing apprenticeship would have provided, and his lack of an apprenticeship in this field barred him from trading as a brewer in his own right.[26] He certainly owned breweries, but it would be more accurate to describe Pride as a businessman who had an interest in brewing, rather than a brewer himself.

A contemporary account of the yeomen of Somerset describes them as: 'Wealthy and substantial men though none of the best bred … their neighbours about them are apt to slander them with the title of clowns; but they care not much for that, knowing they have money in their purses to make them gentlemen'.[27] It seems that not only were people of Pride's background and status prospering, they also formed a distinct group with a common identity. Pride may have inherited much of his character from his provincial family and rural roots. For much of his life he would be regarded by many as ill-bred *nouveau riche*, but he would always brush aside the slander with confidence (often over-confidence) in the belief that it was always within his power to achieve whatever he wanted. It was the personality of the typical Somerset yeoman that gave him the self-assurance that he needed. Pride's early rise in social status – from yeoman's son, to London apprentice, to successful businessman – was precipitated by the apprenticeship system. Importantly, though, this kind of social progression was starkly at odds with the accepted views of the time.

The popular understanding of societal order in the 17th century was one founded on the belief of the 'Great Chain of Being', a philosophy which decreed that everyone and everything had its rightful place in God's scheme. One's place in the universe was ordained, unchanging and irrefutable, from the movement of the planets and the hierarchy of angels to the relationship between monarch and subject. This was the philosophy that maintained England's social hierarchy, a relic of medieval feudalism that was increasingly out of place given the country's changing circumstances. Pride's social climb, from country lad to prospering tradesman, would have been inconceivable without the apprentice system. Believing that they had enough 'money in their purses to make them gentlemen', Pride and other London tradesmen of his time were the ancestors of what would become, in a later period, the Middle Class: upwardly mobile, buoyed on their solvency and eager to earn respectability. The very concept of such a social 'movement' was anathema to 17th century thought, predicated as it was on the idea of an ancient, rigid social hierarchy. The reactionary attitude of the Crown, seen in James' reaction to the Commons 'meddling' in his affairs, would restrict and frustrate the growth of prospering men such as Pride. The following years would see their progress hindered, independence curbed and liberties infringed. The year 1629 was a significant one for Pride: it was the year he had completed his apprenticeship, achieved independence and married Elizabeth Thomason. It was also the year that Charles I dissolved Parliament and chose to rule by his own authority.

2

London, 1630–42
Rising Among the Middling Sort

A satire of 1680, *The Last Speech and Dying Words of Thomas (Lord, Alias Colonel) Pride*, alleges that Pride's first brewery stood at Pye Corner in London, adjacent to Smithfield.[1] In the Middle Ages this had been the site of the Pye Tavern ('pye' being the older form of the word 'magpie', which graced the tavern's painted sign), and although this tavern had disappeared by the early 17th century the area retained an association with the vending of food and drink. However, Pride's link to this part of London should be accepted with some caution. Pye Corner had a nefarious reputation, having been associated with prostitution since the medieval period.. Shakespeare's tragicomic drunk, Falstaff, counts the area among his haunts and goes 'continually to Pie Corner … to buy a saddle', meaning a woman's rump[2]. The fact that Pye Corner abutted 'Cock Lane' did not help raise the tone. It is possible, then, that *The Last Speech* sought to stain Pride's reputation by association. Also evident was the Pye Tavern's continued notoriety, into the early 18th century, as a haunt of Civil War republicanism:

> See *Mag* without perch'd chattering on a Stump
> Within sit Sons of *Belial* and the Rump,
>
> …
>
> And scarce one Customer in lower Room
> But signs the M[onar]chy's and Ch[urc]hes' Doom[3]

With no direct reference to Pride, however, his link to Pye Corner's political reputation is far from certain. But although it would be wrong to rely too heavily on *The Last Speech* as a source of fact, there are many points of contact between Pride and this particular area of London, the ward of Farringdon Without.

So called because it lies outside the city walls, Farringdon Without extends from the parish of St. Bartholomew at its north east corner to Holborn in the west, and down through the liberty of Temple to the north bank of the Thames. St. Bride's parish and Fleet Street fall within its boundaries, as do the precincts of Bridewell and Whitefriars. On the north side of Pye Corner stands Saint Bartholomew's Hospital where Pride would be a governor in the 1650s and where he would oversee the services of its church, St Bartholomew-the-Less, in the more religiously tolerant period of Cromwell's Protectorate[4] To the west, at the bottom of Holborn Hill, stood the palace of the Bishop of Ely, which served as a military hospital and which Pride would also help administrate. In St. Bride's parish was Thomas Bradway's brew house, which Pride may well have had a hand in running, and the parish records of St. Bride's record the baptism of a John Pride on the 12 November 1630, the son of Thomas and Elizabeth. Finally, the 1650s pamphleteer Nathaniel Burt cited his address as being in Windmill Court, 'neer Col. Prides', at the site of Holborn Viaduct today.[5] This is an area, then, with which the newly-wed Prides are clearly associated: the site of St. Anne's church, where they were married, St. Brides and Pye Corner were all within five minutes walk of each other.

On the western extremity of Farringdon Without was the expanding area of Holborn, where new-built houses were spreading towards Westminster. Here were found the spacious houses of The Strand, the residences of lawyers and London professionals, and also Covent Garden with its fashionable, Italianate 'Piazza'. This was the respectable neighbourhood for a city gent, something of an oasis where the expansive gardens of the larger houses (replete with fig trees and morello cherries) were a contrast to the cramped streets of the city. This was where Oliver Cromwell was to move after the first Civil War, to a house on Drury Lane, where he hoped to live out his remaining days in peace as a gentleman.[6] But it is on the eastern side of Farringdon that find St. Bride's parish and Thomas Pride – closer to the City. This was where the Fleet River emptied itself into the Thames, though by this date the tributary was known as 'Fleet Ditch' and was little more than an open sewer: butchers along the Fleet cleaned entrails from the end of a wharf, polluting its lower reaches.[7] This was the filthier part of London, the site of Bridewell, a combination of hospital, workhouse and house of correction, with its ducking stool and floggings. Nearby was the debtors' prison, the Fleet, where for a small fee a legally dubious 'Fleet marriage' could be obtained from any of several defrocked clergymen.[8] It was an altogether seedier side of the capital, between the less crowded commercial areas of the City and the airy luxury of Covent Garden and the Inns of Court. On Farringdon's north side was Smithfield, which at the end of every August was host to the two-week long Cloth Fair of Saint Bartholomew's, the largest market in the country and a notorious haunt of cut-purses, pedlars and mountebanks.

Farringdon Without, then, was an area where the opposites of Stuart society merged. Its position on the main thoroughfares into London from Westminster meant that there was a continual movement to and from the commercial and political nerve centres of the capital. *Multi pertransibunt et augebitur scientia* runs the motto of Holborn's modern borough council: *'many will pass through and learning will be increased'*. Members of Parliament, City businessmen, gentlemen from their Strand residences, lawyers from the Inns of Court, the itinerants that the annual fair brought in: they all intermingled in Farringdon. All cities have similar convergences of class and population, but the variety boasted by Farringdon – from physicians to pickpockets – was particularly extreme. Holborn also had its freedoms: Temple Bar on Fleet Street marked the western most point of the City's jurisdiction, the place where London ended and Westminster began. Traditionally, the monarch could not pass this point without permission of London's Lord Mayor.[9]

John Milton declared the London of his time to be a 'city of refuge, the mansion house of liberty'.[10] Hundreds were migrating to the capital each year and London had become a crucible for different philosophies, ways of life and points of view. It was a place of relative anonymity, where minorities could find a niche for themselves among the crowds. Among the new arrivals to London in the late 1620s was Daniel Chidley, a Shrewsbury tailor and a religious separatist. Driven from his home by persecution, Chidley had fled to London with his wife and eight children and found refuge among the congregation of a lay preacher, John Duppa. Another of Duppa's small congregation was Thomas Pride.[11]

John Duppa's congregation was an offshoot of the Jacob Church, the most prominent independent church in London at the time, whose adherents are best described as semi-separatists. They diverged from the established church on many points of worship but were not severed from it entirely: the Jacob Church rejected the 'high church' liturgical reforms that were taking place in the Anglican Church, yet their services were led by ordained Church of England ministers; members were free to circulate between the small, private gatherings of the church and their own parish churches. The congregation's central tenet was that independent congregations should co-exist alongside the established church, and it offered no direct challenge the authority of the Church of England.[12] Henry Jacob, who had established the group in 1616, had himself been a moderate dissenter who sought reform of the Church of England from within. In short, it was a tolerant congregation that might have numbered as few as twenty individuals, or a handful of families.

Following Henry Jacob's death in 1624 the congregation had been led by John Lathrop, an Anglican clergyman who had renounced orders that same year.[13] But in 1630 one of its members, John Duppa, formed a splinter group whose religious attitude was quite different from the rest of the congregation. Duppa protested at the direction the parish churches of London were taking, believing them to have been tainted by the high church beliefs of William Laud (Bishop of London from 1628). After one of Lathrop's congregation had his child baptised in an Anglican church, Duppa urged the congregation to reject all the parish churches in Laud's see, critical as he was of the leniency of allowing members to practice intercommunion with other churches. It was Duppa's insistence on total separation from the Anglicanism that led to several members, including Pride, breaking away to seek a purer form of worship.[14]

It is easy to understand how Pride might have sensed a commonality with those of Duppa's congregation. Most of its members were from among the London trades.

The Shrewsbury tailor, Chidley, was, like Pride, a freeman of the Haberdasher's Company. Others members were David Brown, a Scottish teacher who taught adults to read and write; John Jerrow, a Tewkesbury glover; and Rice (properly Rhys or Reece) Boy, an itinerant preacher who had travelled in Wiltshire and Gloucestershire before gravitating to London.[15] The congregation clearly offered a welcome to those from outside the capital.

Where did Pride's separatist beliefs come from? There were dissenters in the rural backwaters of Somerset, certainly: a petition to exclude bishops from the House of Lords was circulated in the county in 1642,[16] but this was a form of

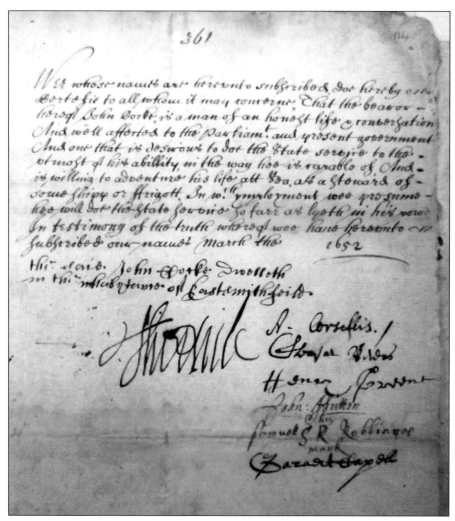

Thomas Pride's ungainly but domineering signature.

anti-Episcopalian protest rather than the more contentious brand of noncon-formity taken up by Pride. From the available evidence, Pride's religious separa-tism is likely to have been the effect of radical and compelling thinking circulating in London during the 1620s and 30s on an impressionable young man. Pride's fellow worshipper, William Kiffin, left an account of the important role religion played in his own apprenticeship:

> I began to be acquainted with several young men who diligently attended on the means of grace… And, being apprentices as well as myself, they had no opportunity of converse, but on the Lord's days. It was our constant practice to attend the morning lecture, which began at six o'clock … We also appointed to meet together an hour before service, to spend it in prayer and communicating to each other what experience we had received from the Lord.[17]

The congregation was not simply a place of worship for the apprentices, it provided an opportunity to socialise and a way of allowing disparate people to identify themselves as a distinct group. It is quite possible that Pride was one of the frater-nity that Kiffin recollects in his memoirs. They were clearly an enthusiastic bunch, although Kiffin admitted that they studied the Bible with some difficulty: 'we also read some portion of Scripture, and spake from it what it pleased God to enable us'.[18]

This brand of eager, individualistic interpretation of the Bible was problematic for those in authority. Throughout the 1630s Charles I governed through Royal edict with no recourse to an elected assembly. One aspect of Monarchy, specifi-cally the brand of absolutist, unrestrained monarchy of the Tudors and Stuarts, is that subjects are expected to worship in the manner of the sovereign. William Kiffin describes the effect this this situation had on the gathered church which he and Pride attended in the 1630s:

> It being then the heat of the Bishops' severities, we were forced to meet very early in the morning, and to continue till night … meeting one Lord's day at a house on Tower-hill, on coming out, several rude persons were about the door; and many stones were flung.[19]

Fearful of travelling in daylight, confined to the house during the day, sought by the authorities, vulnerable to attack: for Thomas Pride and others this was what reli-gious worship had been reduced to. Two years after Pride and his fellow worship-pers broke away with Duppa the Jacob Church was uncovered by William Laud's pursuivants in a determined effort to stamp out religious separatism. On 29 April 1632 the congregation was arrested *en masse* while at worship in the Blackfriars home of Humphrey Barnet, a brewer's clerk. The arrested members, charged with delinquency and schism, were uncooperative with the High Commission that tried them, many refusing to swear the oath. Most of those arrested remained in prison for up to two years. John Lathrop served two years in the Clink and was one of the last of his congregation to be released. Freed in April 1634, he subsequently left England and settled with thirty of his flock at Plymouth Colony, Massachusetts.[20]

The Jacob Church had never directly challenged the authority of Laud. Indeed, the presence of an ordained clergyman to lead its worship meant that services would have been carried out along quite conservative lines. But separatism, however slight, could not be tolerated under the rule of an absolute monarch. Any deviation from the view of the religious establishment was to question, and thus threaten, the monarch's authority as head of the church. Duppa's congregation, still active, would surely have identified themselves as part of the same family of separatist churches in London as their Jacob Church brethren. It is with their repression that we can see how Pride's beliefs were to bring him into conflict with the establishment.

We can make a reasoned assumption of Pride's religious views from what we know from his associates. Duppa's congregation remained defiantly separatist: they refused to share communion with anyone from the London parish churches and had shunned worship with the semi-separatists of their former church. They turned their backs on the very buildings where they believed idolatrous services were being conducted. It is a moot point whether Pride ever visited church at this time, tainted as he may have believed they were by Bishop Laud's high church doctrine. Duppa's 1653 pamphlet, *Thunder from the Throne of God*, advocated demolishing every church building in the country to eradicate, finally, the spectre of Medieval Catholicism.[21]

The particular brand of separatism that Pride pursued can be glimpsed in the beliefs of other members of the Duppa congregation. Katherine, the wife of Daniel Chidley, though barred from church office by her sex, would become the author of a number of radical religious tracts and pamphlets in the 1640s; her son Simon, also a pamphleteer, served as lay minister for the Duppa Church and, later, at Christ Church Newgate;[22] Samuel Eaton, a button-maker who had been among those arrested with Lathrop's congregation, was baptised by a lay preacher in prison to 'cleanse' himself of the Church of England. He joined Duppa's church on his release and was repeatedly arrested throughout the 1630s for leading illegal conventicles, eventually residing in Newgate where he was allowed to minister to a congregation of seventy inmates and occasionally allowed out to preach. He died in prison in 1639;[23] William Kiffin espoused 'believers' baptism' (i.e. the voluntary baptism of adults) over that of children. Orphaned in an outbreak of the plague of 1625, he had been a glove-maker's apprentice and was to join a Baptist congregation led by Eaton in 1638, the year he was made free of the Company of Leather-Sellers. He was a confirmed Baptist by 1642.[24] Another of Duppa's congregation, a man named Knight, set out on an evangelical tour of Suffolk. He was arrested by the church authorities, and later escaped from prison, fleeing to the more tolerant atmosphere of Amsterdam.[25]

The members of Duppa's conventicle, then, were a gathering of religious refugees: pamphleteers, evangelists, and at least one proponent of adult baptism. Apart from Eaton, however, who had allowed himself to be baptised in prison, the congregation does not seem to have wholly embraced adult baptism. A notable Baptist, John Spilsbury, later made his own split from the congregation over this issue, and other seceding members formed a Baptist community in Wapping, beyond the city boundaries, in 1633.[26] Kiffin, as has been noted, departed from the congregation in 1638. There are certainly links between Pride and the proponents of adult baptism. Baptist John Mason served as Pride's ensign in the military campaigns of 1643-44, and later as his lieutenant colonel; a Baptist chaplain would serve in the regiment of foot of which Pride was colonel in the 1650s;[27] Pride's granddaughter was recorded at St. Gregory-by-Paul as being born in 1657, yet there is no mention of her being baptised there.[28] How far did Pride's affiliation with baptism extend, and was he a believer himself? The pamphleteer William Prynne appears to name Pride as a Baptist in a publication of 1659, referring to: 'William Kiffin and other Anbaptists in the army, headed by Colonel Pride'.[29] Prynne, however, was a particularly hostile critic, an establishment-man who was only prepared to consider nonconformists' creeds in the broadest terms, and he never forgave Pride for excluding him from Parliament in the Purge of 1648. It is unsurprising, then, that he charged Pride with being a dissenting Baptist while other observers did not. Such a charge would surely have been taken up by other hostile commentators had it been true. There is no mention it made by Royalist satirists who lampooned Pride mercilessly in later years, and who would have surely have used his Baptist faith against him had it existed. There are links to be made, then, between Pride and the Baptists, but no firm evidence that he was a Baptist himself.

Adult baptism was probably a question to which Pride gave much thought. Only one of his children is recorded as being baptised in an Anglican Church, that of a short-lived child, John, born in 1630. As it was, Pride's beliefs may have been enough to dissuade him from committing his other children to infant baptism within the Anglican Church. It may be that his son John appeared on the scene before Duppa's evangelism set Pride's faith alight. Duppa's followers regarded Believers' Baptism as disorderly, the ritual felt to be too ceremonial, an over-elaboration of Christian worship. However, it is likely that there was no strict division between Baptists and non-Baptists among Pride's religious community: when William Kiffin turned to Baptism in the late 1630s he continued to worship alongside the majority of the Henry Jacob church,[30] so it is quite probable that Pride felt free to worship within a mixed group of Baptists and Separatists without fully adhering to Baptist beliefs.

The child John, born to Thomas and Elizabeth in 1630, lived only ten days and was buried at St. Bride's on 22 November.[31] There are other Prides mentioned in the St. Bride's registers: John Pride and his wife, Hester, had a daughter baptised at the church on in July 1628. She also died young, buried at St. Bride's on 7

January 1631.[32] Here is evidence, then, that when Pride was living in London at the beginning of the 1630s other members of his family had joined him, or he them. The surname is surely too rare for the occurrence in the St. Bride's registers to be a coincidence. The young girl's father could well have been the John Pride who emigrated to America in the late 1630s, perhaps following Lathrop after the suppression of 1632. He was to settle in Massachusetts, and owned land in Essex County that is still known as Pride's Crossing.[33]

Coupled to the friction with the ruling powers that Pride and his associates experienced through their religious beliefs was the issue of social status. Until the early modern period English society had been largely polarised, with society divided between the 'noble' or 'better' sort on the one hand and the 'common', 'meaner' and 'vulgar' sorts on the other. By the 1640s, however, a third group had established itself between the two extremes of rich and poor, between the ruling establishment and its subjects – the 'middle sort'. The term seems to have originated in commerce, with goods of the time being divided into three grades of quality: great, middle and small.[34] The term 'middle sort', then, not only describes a particular social group but identifies the background of urban trade from which the group arose. Unlike the gentry who lived off their rents, and the poor who had to labour under their employers, the middle sort aspired to be their own masters. The defining trait of the middle classes is to achieve, to rise above oneself, and the growth of income that men such as Pride were experiencing allowed them a firmer social footing.

The Marxist interpretation of the English Civil War has fallen out of favour in recent years, but its theory of class conflict correspond with the situation experienced by Pride. It can be said that the Civil War divided society 'vertically', with commoners and gentry on both sides, rather than 'horizontally' in a war that pitted the upper classes against the lower, but social status *did* play its part in drawing-up sides. At Bristol in 1643 the Royalist cause was resisted by 'the middle rank, the true and best citizens'. In Gloucestershire, while Charles I had the support of both the rich and the 'needy multitude', Parliament was supported by 'yeomen, farmers, clothiers and the whole of the middle rank of people'; in Nottinghamshire during the Civil War the majority of the gentry were against Parliament, but 'most of the middle sort, the able and substantial freeholders, and the other commons, who had not their dependence upon malignant nobility and the gentry, adhered to the parliament.'[35] The largest cities in England (respectively: London, Norwich and Bristol) were dominated by merchants; each of those cities would side with parliament at the beginning of the Civil War. This is not to say that the 'middle rank' began the war of their own volition. The city of Worcester, for example, was firmly Royalist during the war because its Parliamentarian supporters were 'but of the middle rank of people, and none of any great power and eminence to take their part',[36] and there were no members of the traditional ruling class for the middle sort to unite behind. It is clear, from the above evidence that Parliament drew considerable support from the middle sort, the artisans and tradesmen like Pride.

London's 'middle sort' had a distinct identity, drawn together through shared beliefs that distinguished them from the social groups above and below them. By the end of the 1630s Pride was a part of this new social group that began to question the policing of religion and the control of government. He was one of the urban middle-sort, a prospering brewer. The lack of religious freedom gave Pride a cause to champion; his middle-rank status gave him the power to do so.

3

Service as a junior officer, 1643–44

Civil War

Charles I's personal rule continued through the 1630s. The Jacob Church was again arrested *en masse* for nonconformity in February 1638. It regrouped, only to be broken up again the following May in another flurry of arrests.[1] Charles I's high-handed religiosity not only criminalised Pride's fellow religious independents, by 1639 it had precipitated a war with Presbyterian Scotland. The Haberdasher's company, to which Pride was affiliated, proved a stumbling block to the royal prerogative when it refused the request of a £4,000 loan that Charles needed to equip an army to fight the Scots[2] and the Haberdashers would play an influential role in the city during the coming months.

Although Thomas Pride played no conspicuous part in the political struggles of 1640/41, his life was clearly touched by it. The absence of Pride's name from the historical record would indicate that his own concerns at this time bore little relation to the world of political manoeuvring, as Charles I and Parliament wrestled for authority. He was in his early-thirties by this time, a businessman with a family and comfortably-off. Yet his Separatist views would have meant that he was overshadowed by Charles I's drive for religious conformity, and as the political struggle between Crown and Parliament intensified we can see Pride adopt a more determined and defensive attitude. The first evidence of this is in August 1640, when Pride joined the Honourable Artillery Company in order to be learn the skills of soldiering.[3] There had been ample opportunity for him to have joined the company before this date (membership had been steadily increasing, by Royal command, since 1635),[4] so we may reason that his decision to do so now was precipitated by the political situation that year – principally the onset of approach of another war with Scotland, but perhaps also Charles I's dismissal of the Short Parliament. By the time Pride joined its ranks the Honourable Artillery Company was viewed as a centre of opposition to royal policy, a Royalist pamphleteer later commenting: 'this accursed horrid rebellion is principally to be ascribed to [the] rebellious City':

You may well remember when the puritans here did as much abominate the Military Yard or Artillery Garden as Paris Garden [the location of London's theatres] itself: they would not mingle with the prophane: but, at last, when it was instilled into them that the blessed reformation intended could not be effected but by the sword, these places were instantly filled with few or none but men of that faction.[5]

Thomas Pride should be considered among those men who now saw 'the sword' as the only way to protect their interests, and the timing of his appearance at the Artillery Garden indicates that he and his fellow tradesmen were politically aware. The military training he undertook was limited, if contemporary accounts are accurate. Meetings took place only in the summer months and for just one morning a week, often between 7am and the start of work so as to: 'provide no hindrance to men's more necessary callings, but rather call them earlier to their business affaires'.[6] Narrow though this military experience must have been, it is clear that Pride was attentive to the prevailing political mood in the capital and he had to some degree prepared himself when, eighteen months after he joined the Artillery Company, the political climate became more confrontational.

In January 1642, Charles I attempted to arrest the leaders of his obstreperous parliamentary opposition. Parliament, in return, called for armed guards at Westminster and the London militia was accordingly increased from four regiments to six to counter this apparent threat from the monarch. This expansion of the militia in early 1642 required the appointment of a number of new officers, one of whom was Thomas Pride: April that year saw him rally to the Parliamentarian cause and receive a commission as ensign to Captain Campfield, in the Orange Regiment of the Trained Bands,[7] one month after Charles I had fled the capital and four months before the monarch would declare his intention to fight by raising his standard at Nottingham.

The Orange Regiment was the most junior of the London militia regiments, and one of the smallest.[8] Pride's presence among their ranks re-affirms his association with Farringdon Without, the Orange Regiment's area of recruitment. It also ties-in with his background in the cloth trade. The officers of the London militia were generally 'freeman of the twelve great livery companies, with the Haberdashers predominating'.[9] Campfield himself is described as a salesman of St Sepulchre's parish, and other officers in the regiment were tailors and woollen-drapers by profession, with premises in Holborn, Fleet Street and Snow Hill. The company's muster point, in times of alarm and emergency, was Holborn Conduit, just two hundred yards from Pye Corner.[10]

Thomas Pride does not seem to have been caught-up in the fervour usually attendant on declarations of war. He did not volunteer to serve in any of the London regiments raised in July 1642 to fight under the Earl of Essex. Recent research has revealed that he provided the cost to mount and equip a cavalry trooper, but this would indicate little more than token support for Parliament's cause.[11] Pride, never a political creature, was ready to defend his livelihood but seems less inclined to take the offensive. It is evident that in the summer of 1642 he saw his rightful place not on the march with Essex but in London, ready to guard his home and business if necessary. By early November, however, following the stalemate at the battle of Edgehill, it was clear that the war would be more protracted than many had anticipated. The Royalists' advance on the capital hastened Parliament into raising seven new regiments from around the London area. These were intended to form a new army under the command of the Earl of Warwick, to defend London from a Royalist uprising if the militia was called out to fight the Royalists. The same day that Essex's battered army re-entered London following Edgehill, Pride accepted a captaincy in Harry Barclay's Regiment of Foot, raising and equipping a company from his own pocket.[12]

As with his joining the Honourable Artillery Company, his timing is worth noting. To commit himself at this stage took courage, for by now it must have been clear that there would be no swift victory for either side. Even so, Pride may have got more than he had bargained for: Parliament's losses at Edgehill and Brentford had been so heavy that the idea of a second army to defend London was abandoned and the newly raised units, including Pride and his company, were fed into Essex's army to fill the gaps. Pride would serve with Essex's marching army after all. The Royalists were by this time only thirty miles from the capital, with a substantial garrison at Reading. Londoners began to fortify the capital, surrounding the city with earthworks along its whole perimeter. One observer wrote of 'the daily musters' of the militia and that the city 'hath many courts of guard, with new barricaded posts, and they strongly girded with great chains of iron'.[13] Milton's 'Mansion House of Liberty' had become a fortress.

The commanding officer of the regiment in which Pride was to serve as captain was Colonel Harry Barclay, one of many professional Scottish soldiers who were invited to join Parliament's forces in an attempt to strengthen the officer corps. Barclay had no reservations about fighting Charles I, he was a staunch Presbyterian who had already fought against the Crown in the Bishops' Wars of 1639-40, and he was given command of a brigade of foot under Essex.[14]

A glance at some of the men who served alongside Pride in Barclay's Regiment reveals a common background of London commerce and religious nonconformity. William Goffe, the regimental quarter-master, had first risen to prominence in March 1642 when he was ordered arrested by London's Lord Mayor for his vehement support of the Militia Ordinance,[15] legislation that removed the command of armed forces from Royal authority and placed them under Parliament's control. Goffe's father had been a Church of England rector in Sussex, deprived of his living in 1605 because of his 'Puritan' leanings. The family had subsequently settled in Haverfordwest where William was raised. William seems to have been set apart from the rest of his family: while two of his brothers were Oxford scholars, William was apprenticed to a London grocer; William fought for the Parliament while his eldest brother, Stephen, was a Royalist agent during the war and served as a chaplain to the Queen, Henrietta Maria.[16] Stephen followed the Stuarts into exile after the war and later converted to Catholicism. Both of William's elder brothers in fact were ordained Church of England Ministers, as their father had been; William pursued his own enthusiastic brand of Christian mysticism, averring that 'Christ and his saints had to destroy Antichrist, or the rule of iniquity, during the last days', which he believed to be the upheaval of the Civil War.[17] Described as 'three-quarters a Fifth Monarchist Man', he was affiliated to an extreme sect who believed that the Second-Coming of Christ was at hand.[18] He and Pride would enjoy a long association: they began their military service together in 1642 and would fight alongside each other at Dunbar eight years later. Their names even appear next to one another on Charles I's death warrant. Differing in faith from either of these men was Pride's ensign, John Mason, an apprentice harness-maker and Baptist.[19]

Each of these newly commissioned officers had a background in London trade. Other company commanders in Harry Barclay's Regiment – captains Leete and Cowell – were also wealthy London tradesmen. London wholeheartedly backed its citizen army and kept it well supplied. The Royalist Earl of Clarendon conceded that: 'It is hardly credible what vast quantities… of excellent victual ready dressed were every day sent in waggons and carts from London to the army, upon the voluntary contributions from private families.'[20] At the time Pride enlisted under Barclay, his own Haberdashers' company made a payment of £727 towards the war effort, provided by the sale of the silver plate from Haberdashers' Hall. This was on top of the £7,700 that they had loaned Parliament to fund Essex's Edgehill campaign.[21]

What is interesting, though, is not the similarities between Pride and his fellow officers but the *differences* between them. Each varied in their forms of worship: Pride a Separatist, Mason a Baptist and Goffe a religious mystic. All were at odds with the established Anglican Church and each followed strains of Protestantism that had been prohibited under the auspices of Archbishop Laud. Their enemies might have labelled all of them 'Puritan' – a simplistic term, the reality being far more complex and subtle. The presence of Baptist John Mason, bearing the captain's colour, indicates that Pride's company embodied completely the principles of religious freedom and toleration for which many parliamentarians fought.

Following the fighting in the autumn of 1642 the Royalists had occupied much of the Thames Valley, a major artery of supply and communication between London and central England. The spring of 1643 saw Parliament attempt to regain the initiative.

Royalist forces had established a garrison at Reading, roughly half way between London and Charles I's new capital at Oxford. This outpost would be the Earl of Essex's first objective. During the winter of 1642/43 Parliament tentatively pushed forward from their furthest positions east of London, at Windsor and Maidenhead, to secure the towns east of Reading. Garrisons were established at Marlow and Henley to establish a line of communication and supply that provided

Essex's army with a clear route westwards. April 1643 saw Pride among the 16,000 foot and 3,000 horse of Essex's army as they approached Reading.

The Royalists were ready to meet the attack and the town had been prepared with earth ramparts, bolstered in places with timber palisades and woolsacks. Low-lying meadows surrounding the town had been flooded to provide further defence. On 15 April Essex began to deploy his men to the north and south of the town and by 18 April Reading was surrounded and the bridge across the Thames secured. The same day that the siege was set, Charles I issued a proclamation which all but condemned Pride to his death: Essex and his followers were declared guilty of high treason for waging war against their King (the edict was accompanied with the offer of a free pardon to all who immediately surrendered).

Despite encirclement and sporadic artillery fire, Reading continued to be supplied by Royalist troops from beyond the Parliamentarian perimeter, and although Caversham Bridge and the road to Oxford had been secured much of the river's north bank remained unguarded. On the 22 April a large party of Royalist attempted to break through the Parliamentarian cordon with a supply of forty barrels of gunpowder for the garrison. An outlying troop of Parliamentarian horse were thrown back by the advance 'and so retreated to Colonel *Bartley*'s [sic] Regiment that was drawn over the bridge.' This is likely to have been the moment at which Pride encountered the Civil War at first hand. The action was quick, and Pride could have felt some relief and satisfaction that his men performed efficiently: 'The Enemy charging, the Musketeers gave Fire … so resolutely that they wheeled about and went away'.[22] Sixteen barrels of powder that had been loaded on to a barge were abandoned as the Royalists fell back.

On the rainy afternoon of the following Tuesday a larger Royalist force was spotted on Caversham Hill, to the north. This promised to be a more serious engagement for Pride, not just an attempt to re-supply the besieged town but a full relief force sent down from Oxford: forty troops of horse and nine regiments of foot intent on driving the Parliamentarian army back towards London. Essex had deployed his forces in a thin cordon around Reading, and only the foot regiments of Lord Robartes and Colonel Barclay stood between the town and the Royalist column. Robartes established a line of defence, dividing his regiment into two and bolstering Barclay's ranks with some of his own men. Pride was fortunate that the Royalist attack was badly managed: the April rain made for poor visibility and the Royalist artillery on the hill were unable to range their targets; there was no sally from the town's garrison to reinforce the attack because Reading's Royalist commander was fearful of breaking the ceasefire he had recently brokered with Essex. Two Royalist regiments were sent forward to engage Robartes and Barclay but they were beaten back, Barclay's men pushing up Caversham Hill and forcing the enemy to abandon their position on the high ground. The fight in which Pride found himself was heated (Barclay himself was wounded, though he stubbornly remained in the firing line until the action was over),[23] and again there is the impression of a job smartly done by the Parliamentary foot. Having lost the advantage of Caversham Hill the Royalists abandoned their attempt to relieve Reading. The governor surrendered the town four days later.

The capture of Reading opened up the road to Oxford and the Royalist capital was now threatened by two parliament armies, Essex's from the south and Sir William Waller's army moving up from Gloucester. But in the event, there was to be no opportunity for the two Parliamentarian armies to mount a co-ordinated attack: Waller was occupied in preventing Royalist forces in Cornwall from pushing further east and Essex's own advance was delayed due to sickness that was spreading among his troops, caused by a wet April spent in the fields around Reading. Initial success had given way to a loss of momentum, something which was to become a pattern in Thomas Pride's military career.

It was not until the beginning of June that Pride marched north with Essex's forces, manoeuvring through the Chilterns and carefully by-passing Oxford's outlying garrisons. Essex established his headquarters at Thame, twelve miles east of Oxford. By 12 June his forces had advanced seven miles to Wheately, but an attack made through Islip, to the north of the city, was beaten off. Thereafter Barclay's Regiment remained at Thame, awaiting pay and supplies from London.

On 18 June Rupert's horse raided Essex's outposts at Postcombe and Chinnor but failed to locate the Parliament pay wagons which had been their intended target. On 24 June a similar raid plundered High Wycombe. The ease with which the Royalists had swept around Essex's army caused alarm in London, and in late June the army was ordered to pull back to Slough. Essex's conduct of the campaign was criticised in Parliament. He offered his resignation but it was refused.

Early August saw Barclay's Regiment recuperating south of London, although Pride himself was far from inactive. Army pay records show Barclay's quartered at Kingston in Surrey, where Pride may have been part-owner of at least two breweries in the town by this date.[24] It is probable that was still a London resistant at this time, however, because in April 1643 he was appointed major of the Orange Regiment of 'auxiliaries to the Trained Bands', a new volunteer force raised principally to man London's extensive fortifications, re-affirming Pride's place in the ranks of London's militia. Pride's simultaneous holding of two commissions was not unusual: of the seven Auxiliary colonels appointed, at least five were captains in the trained bands, holding their new colonelcies alongside their existing ranks.[25]

Pride seems to have been unique among the Auxiliary officers in that his captaincy obliged him to serve outside the capital, marching with Essex's army while the other officers that we know of remained in London. It is also apparent that he was especially selected for the job. Nagel (1982) places Pride among the 'Godly' group of militia officers.[26] The militia subcommittee appointed to raise the Auxiliaries were determined that the volunteers should be led by 'known and trusted' officers who were noted for their 'zeale and interests in the cause'.[27] The volunteers of the Auxiliaries were considered to be more committed to the cause than the levied troops of the militia, one Auxiliary company being called upon to disarm supposed 'malignants' discovered among the ranks of London's Trained

Bands. More than social status or military ability, then, it was Pride's dedication to the political cause, and his religious faith, that seems to have distinguished him from his fellow officers and earned him the rank of major in the Auxiliaries.

Parliament's momentum had faltered following the capture of Reading, and the war was beginning to swing the Royalists' way. In July they seized Bristol and their grip tightened as they laid siege to Exeter and Gloucester, Parliament's remaining strongholds in the west. Desperate to keep hold of a western port, Parliament resolved that Gloucester should be relieved. Essex was ordered to march to their aid with his weakened forces strengthened by a brigade drawn from the London militia. The City again provided Essex with the money he required, the Haberdashers loaning Parliament a further £3,850 for the campaign.[28]

24 August saw Essex's troops at Hounslow Heath where the Lord General formally reviewed his regiments. The following day Barclay's regiment was at Windsor, on their way to relieve Gloucester.[29] Of the 900 men who had volunteered for service the previous November only 496 remained with the colours, the regiment having nearly halved through enemy action and the rigours of the campaign[30] For the up-coming campaign Barclay's appear to have been reorganised into a reduced establishment of four companies: those of the colonel, the lieutenant colonel, Major John Innes and that of Pride, evidently now the regiment's senior captain.[31] Pride must have adapted well to soldiering, to judge by the additional role and responsibilities he was given for the forthcoming campaign: the Orange Auxiliaries were to join Essex's forces on the march to Gloucester.

Essex reached Gloucester on 8 September, only to discover that the Royalists had been forewarned of his approach. They had raising their siege and deployed their strength on the hills south of the city, barring Essex's route back to London. Essex would not be drawn into open battle, however, marching north in the direction of Tewkesbury and drawing the Royalists after him. On 15 September Essex suddenly turned about, heading for London and, by forcing the pace, managing to put a day's march between himself and the Royalists. He was making for the safety of Reading and the Thames Valley garrisons, avoiding the Royalist country around Oxford by way of the Wiltshire Downs. But the Royalists took a more direct route through the Chilterns and on 18 September their horse caught up with the Parliamentarians at Aldbourne Chase on the Marlborough Downs. Their attempt to cut off the Parliamentarian artillery train was beaten back, but the action forced Essex to halt his march and allowed the Royalists' main force to push ahead of him. Essex again found his route to London blocked by the Royalist army, at Newbury, and he was forced to fight his way through. It was here, following six months of protracted siege warfare and skirmishes, that Pride would gain his first experience of a set-piece battle.

Pride's company of Barclay's Regiment were deployed among the embanked hedgerows and narrow lanes in a strong defensive position. Essex had chosen his ground well and the patchwork of enclosed fields negated the Royalists' advantage in numbers of horse. The first Royalist attack went in against the Parliamentarian position on Round Hill, but the thick enclosures hampered their advance and, failing to break through, their attack swung south into the area occupied by Barclay's Regiment. The Royalist horse dispersed the Parliamentarian's protecting cavalry but could make no headway against the foot regiments secured among the hedgerows. Barclay's men stood firm against repeated attacks from the Royalist horse and fire from their heavy guns. In spite of eight hours of cannon fire and repeated charges the Royalists ultimately failed to break through Barclay's position and, having spent most of their ammunition, withdrew toward Oxford during the night. With the route to London cleared, Essex resumed his march at noon the following day. Despite being harried by the Royalist horse the Parliamentarian foot made their way to Reading relatively unscathed.[32]

The action at Newbury raised the fighting of the war to a new pitch. Pride's company had been afforded good shelter among the hedges during what is reputed to have been the most concentrated artillery fire of the war. Without this cover their battle would have been more severe. As with the action at Reading earlier in the year, and the badly co-ordinated Royalist attack there, Pride was fortunate to avoid what might otherwise have been a far more deadly outcome. Doubtless his own religious zeal would have persuaded him that the fortunes of both himself and his command were due to Providence. The First Battle of Newbury had bee the bloodiest engagement of the war thus far, with an estimated 3,500 men killed in the field.[33]

Barclay's regiment rested for three days at Reading, where their Sunday morning prayers were given over to thanksgiving for their survival. Believing the town to be now untenable, Essex withdrew from Reading and left it to be re-occupied by Royalists. On 28 September Parliament's army re-entered London and Essex was met at Temple Bar by the mayor and aldermen to receive a hero's welcome. Gloucester had been secured and the campaign viewed as a tremendous victory.

The exertions of one year's fighting had severely reduced Parliament's forces. Reading was swiftly re-taken by the Royalists, negating all the efforts of Pride and others to win the town through the siege that spring. In mid-October a Royalist force occupied Newport Pagnell, threatening to cut lines of communication between London and the Midlands. Although the town was retaken by the end of the month the proximity of the Royalists to London was unnerving. Consequently, Pride's command was sent St. Albans, where they were to be quartered for the following seven months – from November 1643 to May 1644 – in readiness to counter any threat to London from the north. Described as 'resident for want of recruits', they were evidently too weak to leave their garrison town and face a Royalist force in open country.[34] Pride had by now gained valuable experience as soldier, and the aptitude that he must have shown during his regiment's stolid defence among the enclosures at Newbury is shown by his promotion during the winter of 1643/44 to the rank of major in Barclay's Regiment,[35] though by this time their numbers had fallen to a mere 138 men.[36] The regiment remained at St. Albans until campaigning recommenced in spring.[37]

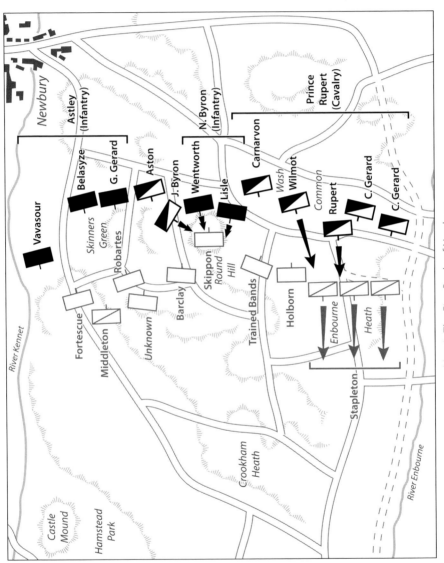

Map 1 The First Battle of Newbury.

Pride's majority was part of a wholesale reorganisation of Essex's army during that winter. By spring they were ready to move out of London and link up with Sir William Waller's forces moving up from Hampshire. The strategy, as in the previous year, was a combined effort against Oxford. The united strengths of Waller and Essex promised to be strong enough to drive the remaining Royalists out of the Thames Valley and end the threat to the capital.

The summer campaign went to plan. By late May Essex's army was approaching Oxford from the east, that of Waller from the south: a two-pronged attack intended to trap the Royalist forces in the city. Charles I ordered Reading to be abandoned and by 21 May Barclay's Regiment had advanced to Henley-on-Thames, their numbers having by now strengthened to 475 men.[38]

On 25 May the Royalists abandoned Abingdon, the southernmost post of Oxford's ring of defences, where they had successfully held off the Parliamentarian advance of the previous summer. Parliamentarian forces entered the town the following day without a fight. With the southern approaches to Oxford now secured, Essex forded the Thames and wheeled north, looking to encircle the city and force Charles I to either giving battle or agreeing to terms. On 5 June Barclay's companies were quartered at Woodstock, having only narrowly missed running into Charles I himself: he had been hunting in the adjacent deer park three days before.[39]

From Woodstock, Barclay would have hoped to have linked-up with Waller's troops approaching from the east, Waller having forced a crossing of the Thames on 2 June. But now the Royalists counter-attacked, wrong-footing Waller by making a southwards feint towards Abingdon. With Essex's main force away to the north of Oxford, Waller felt obligated to retrace his steps and defend Abingdon. As Waller pulled back, Charles I slipped his own army out of Oxford eastwards along the Thames and made towards the temporary safety of Worcester.

Essex and Waller were content that the Royalist army had been decisively forced out of the Thames valley. Consequently, Essex chose a new objective – to relieve the beleaguered Dorset Parliamentarians at Lyme and to reduce the Royalist strength in the south west. Waller was to remain in the Cotswolds to prevent the Royalist's Oxford forces from moving south. Pride and his men found themselves on the march once more as Essex steered his force south west.

Thomas Pride left no personal account of his war experiences, but by plotting his marches the engagements of 1643 and 1644 it is possible to see just how momentous the events must have been for him. He had earned promotion and merit, doubtless for his good conduct but also due to his religious resolve and dedication to the Parliament's cause. He had witnessed considerable hardship, to judge by the depletion of Barclay's numbers during the campaigns, and he had been embroiled in skirmish, siege and a bloody set-piece battle. Pride's experiences in these eighteen months had been considerable, and transformed him from a city businessman to a substantial presence in both London's militia and in Essex's army.

MPs directing the war at Westminster were appalled when they learned of Essex's decision to march into the west and ordered him to send only a small detachment to aid Lyme and to blockade Oxford with his main force. Essex was already in Dorset by the time he received this order and stated in his reply that to divide his force would be foolhardy and accomplish nothing. He argued that a withdrawal at this point would only encourage the Royalists to go on the offensive. Essex refused the order and his army pressed on.

4

Lostwithiel, 1644

'Disaster in the West'

The Royalists abandoned their siege of Lyme at the approach of Essex's army and withdrew towards Exeter. By 25 June Lyme had been relieved and Essex was encouraged enough by this initial success to push further west. He was unconcerned that Royalists under Sir Ralph Hopton were concentrating a force in Somerset, believing that Hopton could be contained by Waller. But Waller was defeated at Cropedy Bridge on 29 June, a reverse serious enough to put Waller's army out of contention for the rest of the campaign. It meant there was now no force to tie down the Royalist Oxford army, or to contain Hopton in Somerset. Charles I, with an army of nearly 8,000, was free to march south in the first week of July in pursuit of Essex's army.

Essex continued to march further west, wrongly supposing that Cornwall would provide him with men and supplies. When it became apparent that there was no support for Parliament in the county, Essex decided to retrace his steps. His army was still marching towards Devon when they discovered that Charles I's army had caught up. Outnumbered, Essex was anxious to avoid battle.

Thomas Pride and his men were by this time 250 miles from their London homes. To them, Cornwall would have appeared much like a foreign country: the buildings fashioned not from the familiar timber-frame and thatch of south England but from clay; Cornish was still widely spoken, and it was believed that towards the county's western extremities no one spoke English at all. This was as far west as Pride was ever to travel.

Barclay's Regiment reached Bodmin on 29 July,[1] making for the Channel coast. Essex refused the surrender terms offered by Charles I and chose instead to establish a defensive line around the town of Lostwithiel, with the river Fowey forming a perimeter along his north and east side. The small port of Fowey, five miles south of this position, would allow Essex to maintain communications with Parliamentary-held Plymouth until such time that a relief came, or the Royalists ran short of supplies and were forced to withdraw. The evening of 4 August saw

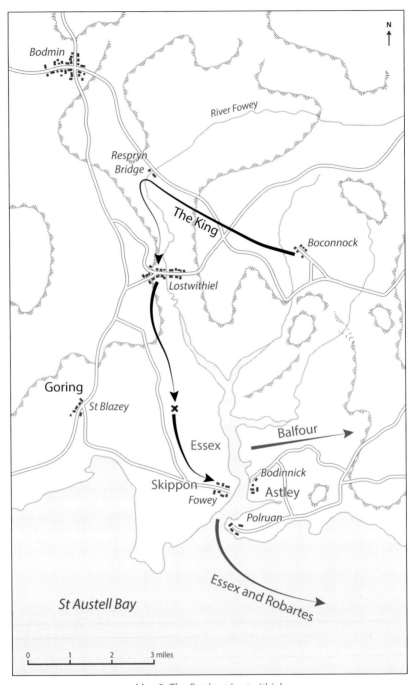

Map 2 The Battle at Lostwithiel.

the first clashes between the two armies and, in a curious turn of events, saw Pride temporarily lose his commanding officer.

Colonel Barclay and other Parliamentarian officers had been dining in some comfort that evening at Boconnoc manor, when the house was set upon by a Royalist raiding party. Led by an Italian mercenary, Royalist soldiers abducted several Parliamentarian officers at gunpoint, including Barclay.[2] Pride may have felt a little nonplussed at being deprived of his colonel just as the fighting around Lostwithiel was about to commence.

There was skirmishing at Braddock Down, north of Lostwithiel, on 8 and 9 August as the Royalists began to close in. However, Pride and his command had yet to see any action: 'for most part of the time the Fight was altogether Horse',[3] Essex recalled. The Royalists suspected that the Parliamentarian force was still strong enough to repel a full assault and chose instead to tighten their hold on the surrounding area, cutting supply routes and hoping to starve Essex's men into submission. Essex himself was conserving his forces, his emphasis still being on manoeuvre. Further efforts made by the Royalists to negotiate surrender were rebuffed, Essex stating that he was unable to come to terms without being ordered to do so by Westminster.[4] On 12 August the Royalists advanced to the lower reaches of the Fowey along the river's east bank, establishing a battery at Polruan opposite Essex's positions and commanding the entrance to Fowey harbour. Royalist troops scattered printed leaflets on Braddock Down, informing their enemy of a general pardon if they surrendered.[5] Still Essex made no attempt to engage the Royalists as they spread their net around his position, and Pride was compelled to play an inactive role during the wet days of August as his foot remained uncommitted.

This waiting game continued until the end of the month, when Charles I's plan of battle changed. The tactic of trying to starve Essex into surrender was beginning to drain on the Royalists' own supplies, and news that a Parliamentarian relief column of 2,000 horse had been scattered by their forces in Somerset gave the Royalists warning that Parliament might soon send a more substantial force into Cornwall to extract Essex. Time was running out.

When the rain eased on the morning of 21 August, Royalist forces advanced on Lostwithiel in an attempt to take the town by force. Essex brought up his foot regiments and established a line of defence to the north and east of Lostwithiel, with Barclay's regiment on the west side of the river, covering the main road south to Fowey.[6] By mid-morning 1,000 Royalist foot had occupied Beacon Hill, half a mile north of Lostwithiel. There they began to raise an earthwork and established a battery. However, this was a cautious advance by Charles I and he made no attempt to engage Essex's defensive line of foot. What fighting there was at Beacon Hill was desultory, a series of sporadic skirmishes rather than a pitched battle. Even so, with the high ground now in Royalist possession and the town in range of their artillery, Parliamentarian's situation was worsening. Although the fighting was not intense it was protracted and Pride would have had little respite during a week of small actions: 'From the 21st until Friday sevennight after,' Essex noted, 'most of the Foot on Bartlet's [sic] side … was in continual fight.'[7] Essex invariably referred to Colonel Barclay as 'Bartlet'.

The protracted nature of the fighting must have been wearing, and it easy to imagine exhaustion setting in among Essex's men. There was now little hope of relief and food was now becoming scarce, the Royalists having driven off the cattle that provided Essex's with fresh meat. Parliament's fleet was unable to assist with supply because of rough seas. On 26 August, Royalist horse under George Goring entered St. Blazy, sealing off Essex's position from the west. Essex decided to abandon his position around Lostwithiel. On the night of 30 August the bulk of the Parliamentarian horse broke through the Royalist lines and made for the garrison at Plymouth; the foot were ordered to withdraw to Fowey, from where they could be evacuated them by sea.

Continual rain on 31 August turned the Parliament line of retreat into a quagmire. Essex was forced to abandon some of his heavy guns in the mud, 'the ways were so extreme foul with excessive Rain, and the Harness for the Draught Horses so rotten'.[8] It was not until first light that the Royalists were aware of the Parliamentarian withdrawal, and at seven in the morning Royalist moved into Lostwithiel. Parliament's main body, meanwhile, were repositioning on high ground to the south, between Tywardreath and Golant. On the right of the Parliamentarian line Essex entrusted his defence to four foot regiments: his own (under the command of Colonel Butler), Weare's Regiment, Lord Robartes' and Barclay's.[9] Butler had been one of the officers taken prisoner at the dinner at Boconnoc along with Barclay. He had returned to the Parliamentarian army the previous day via a formal exchange of prisoners. It is likely that Harry Barclay had also been returned to his regiment through a similar exchange.

It took the whole of the morning for the Royalist army to move south from Beacon Hill. In the early afternoon they began to put in attacks on Essex's left and centre, trying to push the Parliamentarians away from Par and back against the river Fowey. As usual, Essex had chosen good defensive ground. The terrain around Castle Dore restricted the Royalist advantage in horse: 'their foot lay so close under the hedges', noted Royalist trooper, Richard Symmonds, 'which are all cannon proofe and have no avenues wider then one or in some cases 2 horses can approach at a time'.[10]

It can assumed that casualties among the Parliamentarian foot had thus far been low, but late that afternoon Colonel Butler reported to Essex that '[Lord] Roberts's and Bartlet's Men had quitted their Posts, and gone two Fields back'.[11] The result was a gap in Essex's line, allowing the Royalists to work their way behind the Parliamentarian army and cut off Essex's route to Fowey. A third regiment on the right, Weare's, had broken entirely. Butler went on to say that, as he now commanded the only regiment that remained on the right, he felt he had no option but to withdraw. Essex did not bother to conceal his contempt for 'Ware's men (or rather Sheep)',[12] who had also failed to hold a position earlier in the campaign. Essex later confided to Skippon that it was at this point that he realised that the battle was lost: 'after I heard that those Regiments I put most trust in, namely my own, the Lord Robert's and Colonel Bartlet's, had quitted their Posts'.[13]

Pride objected to the implication that he, as major of one of the retreating regiments, was in any way to blame for the Parliamentarian defeat that was slowly beginning to unfold Lostwithiel, or indeed that he had 'quit his post'. Evidence of his feelings can be found in the document, 'An Attestation of the Officers of the Army' (that both Pride and Barclay later signed), in which the Parliamentarian officers concerned set forth their own version of events as they had unfolded that evening in Cornwall.

The officers agreed that the withdrawal south had been conducted in an orderly manner until 'two Regiments of the Army quitted their Post, and thereby gave the Enemy free Passage betwixt us and Foy [Fowey]'.[14] But those two regiments, the officers maintained, had been those under the command of Weare and Butler. The Royalists, too, made much of the farcical conduct displayed by Weare's men, describing them running 'from Field to Field with their Cannon and Colours, only at the appearance of eight of his Majesty's Horse'.[15] It was the conduct of Butler in particular that occasioned the loudest outcry from Pride and the other signatories of the 'Attestation'. Butler's mishandling of the situation was also criticised by Major General Skippon, when he was called before a Parliamentary Committee in the enquiry that was held following 'the late Disaster in the West':[16]

> Butler seemed very unwilling to draw his Men to the Place assigned, which occasioned the Examinate [Skippon] to tell him, that he wondered to see him so unwilling, and again commanded him to the said Place. That afterwards Colonel Weare came to the Examinate, and told him, he could not maintain his post; the Examinate sent him back, and bid him maintain it as long as he could: and afterwards it being dark, Colonel Butler came in like manner, and told him he could not maintain his Post … and that therefore he had drawn off the Regiment.[17]

It was opinion of Essex's officers (Pride included) that Butler had triggered the army's defeat by deliberately withdrawing from the line, and that he had done this because he harboured Royalist sympathies. Essex himself had suspicions about Butler, principally because he had so recently returned to his own side after being held prisoner. Essex believed that the colonel's loyalties had been swayed Royalists during his time as a captive: twice in his account of the battle, Essex stresses that Butler 'was released but the day before'.[18] If this was all merely a ploy by the Parliamentarian command to make Butler a scapegoat, the case against him was certainly built substantially. Barclay also testified at the Parliamentary enquiry, stating that Butler had left the post assigned to him after claiming that there was too much ground for his men to hold.[19] Another of Essex's colonels, Tyrrel, attested that he had been approached by Butler soon after the latter's release, who told him that propositions for a truce had been tendered to him by the Royalists; that

Charles I had considerable support in both Houses at Westminster; that the Scots, who wanted to reform the Church of England on Presbyterian lines, were clearly a much greater threat to liberty than the monarch.[20] Tyrrel had no doubt that Butler's 'defection' had led the Parliamentarian army into a situation where it had no choice but to surrender.[21] The Parliamentary enquiry formally accused Butler of deserting his post and committed him to the Tower where, nine months later, he was still awaiting trial.[22]

Although Pride is unnamed in accounts of the fighting around Lostwithiel, he was far from passive. His signing of the officers 'Attestation' shows him both willing and able to voice his convictions and assert himself against the poor management of those in command of Parliament's army.

Butler's action had lost Essex his right wing, the result being that the Royalists were now able to interpose between the Parliamentarian army and its magazine at Fowey. Now isolated, and with only one day's provision of bread and match available to his men, Essex realised that a negotiated surrender was now the only outcome. Fearing that the Royalists' terms might well include the surrender of his own person, and his execution for high treason, Essex fled. He and his staff boarded a fishing boat and made for the garrison at Plymouth, leaving the army under Skippon's command. Even in this desire situation, Skippon was determined to fight on, briefing his officers that he intended a break-out 'through our Enemies … and account it better to die with Honour and Faithfullness, than to live dishonourable.'[23] But his officers (possibly including Pride) objected, citing the low morale of their men, and preferred instead to come to terms with the enemy and at least have a chance of fighting another day. Faced by this reluctance to continue the fight, Skippon was forced to offer terms.

On 2 September Pride was among the 6,000 Parliamentarian foot that surrendered to Charles I. The Royalists readily accepted the surrender, themselves tired by the protracted fighting and low on supplies. Pride, being an officer, was allowed to retain his sword and horse, and the regiment its colours. Having no resources with which to feed or house their prisoners the Royalists turned them loose and the remains of Essex's foot made their way to safety of the Parliamentarian garrisons further east along the south coast.

Much has been written of the deprivation the Parliamentarians suffered after their surrender. Many commentators draw on the account of the Royalist trooper, Richard Symonds, whose diary notes that there were assaults on the prisoners made by the Royalist rank and file. But Symonds also states that these were isolated incidents: 'our officers with their swords drawn did perpetually beate off our foot, many of them lost their hatts, &c. Yet most of them escaped this danger'.[25] Symonds also recorded that local people 'plundered some of their officers',[26] but his assertion that few of the Parliamentarian soldiers would reach London safely, 'for the country people … will have their pennyworth's out of them',[27] was conjectural, and may not have transpired. The articles of surrender allowed for one hundred Royalist horse to escort Essex's foot as far as Wareham and Poole, and there was also allowance for the defeated and exhausted troops to receive 'all such Monies, Provisions of Victuals, and other Accomodations, as they shall be able to procure'[28] from the Parliamentarian garrison at Plymouth, though admittedly that was nearly forty miles away. Essex's plan to transport his foot from Plymouth to Portsmouth by sea[29] ought not to have been possible, as the surrender terms forbade the defeated troops from entering the garrison – they were compelled to keep on the march. Yet army pay warrants attest that a body of Barclay's men had certainly reached Southampton by the 15 September.[30] From Southampton they then moved to Portsmouth, where Essex had established his headquarters, intent on rebuilding his forces.

Following Lostwithiel, Charles I led his main force back into the Berkshire/Oxfordshire area to relieve his hard-pressed garrisons. Parliament took note, and hurried to assemble a force in the Thames Valley to dissuade Charles I from approaching London and, if possible, to prevent him from reaching Oxford.

The only substantial field army that Parliament had in the south of England was that of the Earl of Manchester, quartered about Reading and fatigued after their summer campaign against the northern Royalists. Manchester marched his forces to Basingstoke, though reluctantly, as his chief concern was with protecting the Eastern Association counties and he was unenthusiastic about moving further west.[31] Barclay's regiment, with the rest of Essex's Foot, had joined Manchester at Basingstoke by the 21 October,[32] together with units from Waller's army and a brigade of foot from the London Trained Bands. Barclay himself estimated that Essex's regiments, having been 6,000 strong when they had surrendered at Lostwithiel, was now only able to muster 1,200 soldiers between them.[33] Aware that the combined Parliamentarians outnumbered them, the Royalists took up a defensive position just north of Newbury.

On 26 October Thomas Pride was with the Parliamentarian force three miles from the Royalists at Thatcham. An attempt to force a way across the river Lambourn was forced back, and Parliamentarian commanders agreed that the best way to assault the Royalist position would be to attack from opposite directions: Manchester would remain on the east side of Newbury and make a second attempt on Royalist positions from across the Lambourn, while Waller would attack simultaneously from the west with the Essex's foot, augmented by Cromwell's horse and with London's Trained Bands under Skippon's command as a reserve. But repositioning the Parliamentarian forces took time, and Waller's insistence on a preliminary artillery bombardment meant that his attack began with only two hours of daylight remaining.[34] Essex's foot nevertheless pushed forward against the rear of the Royalist position among the hedgerows of Speen village. After some resistance the Royalists gave way, abandoning their position and leaving behind them some of the Parliamentarian ordnance that had been captured at Lostwithiel. However, a total victory was not achieved as further advance by the Parliamentarian foot was contained by the Royalist reserve. Deprived of cavalry support, the Trained Band foot were unable to advance further, though Barclay's brigade (his own, Skippon's

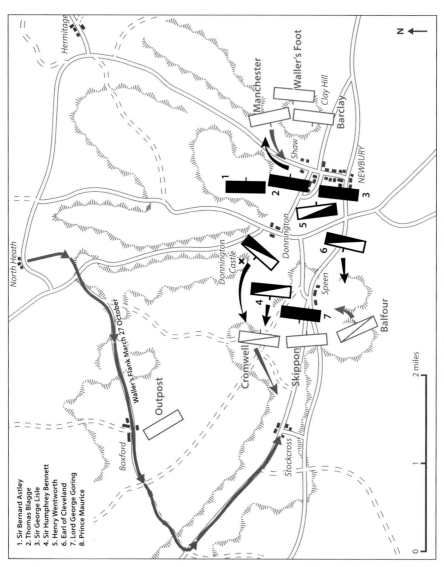

1. Sir Bernard Astley
2. Thomas Blagge
3. Sir George Lisle
4. Sir Humphrey Bennett
5. Henry Wentworth
6. Earl of Cleveland
7. Lord George Goring
8. Prince Maurice

Map 3 The Second Battle of Newbury.

and Lord Robartes' regiments) managed to hold a position on open ground to the east of Newbury until nightfall behind the protection of their pikes. Barclay's 'most resolutely repulsed three violent Charges of the enemies Horse in the plain Field', and the Royalist formations fell into disorder after repeated attacks.[35]

Skippon's calculations of 50 dead and 100 wounded from among Essex's foot place casualties at the Second Battle of Newbury at over 12%, difficult for an already depleted force to sustain.[36] Moreover, Parliament seemed unable to hold what little gains they had made: during the night the Royalists withdrew from the field unopposed, and were even able to return some days later and retrieve their captured cannon. Cromwell's horse had shown particular inertia at Newbury, a point that Wanklyn (2001) argues demonstrated an increasing rift between the religious Independents and Parliament's religiously moderate military command.[37] Fatigue, listlessness and an increasing reluctance to prosecute the war with any vigour were beginning to corrode Parliament's war effort. They were factors which were to become more evident in the coming weeks, and which would ultimately threaten Thomas Pride's rank and position in the Earl of Essex's army.

5

Reading, December 1644–April 1645
According to the new model

Parliament's failure to defeat the Royalists at Newbury was indicative of the malaise from which both sides were suffering. Essex's campaign was by then into its sixth month, and had involved a march from the Thames Valley to Cornwall and back. Parliament's combined strength at Newbury was barely two thirds the size of the army that Essex had fielded at Edgehill,[1] and both sides needed time to rest and recuperate. Following their fight at Newbury, Barclay's regiment retired to winter quarters at Reading which was once again at the forefront of the war, equidistant between London and Oxford, and situated on the territorial boundary between the two warring sides.

The threat to Reading from the local Royalist garrisons compounded a mood of suspicion and discontent that had been growing among Parliamentarian troops since their hollow victory at Newbury. In December, some of Barclay's troops apprehended a Royalist spy who had been attempting to gauge the strength of the garrison. Barclay suspected a conspiracy among Royalists sympathisers living in the town to seize it for Charles I. He ordered the arrest of several townsmen, but the attack that he had expected never came.[2] Meanwhile, the situation for the civilians of Reading deteriorated and Parliamentarian officers began to lose control of their men as troops' morale worsened. Reading's corporation petitioned Parliament 'for the relief of the town, against the insolencies and violences of the Souldyers'.[3] Inhabitants were living in fear of Parliament's troops, who tore down buildings for firewood, robbed from the market and carried out acts of violence on magistrates who attempted to impose some order. Many among the township became refugees, abandoning their homes to what remained of Essex's army, 'who cry out they have no pay, they have no beds, they have no fire'.[4] Losses through action, desertion and illness meant that at the beginning of the new year the combined strength of Essex's foot was only 3,000 men.[5]

Following the armies' poor performance at Newbury, Parliament was compelled to examine and re-organise its southern and eastern forces. It was decided that the three armies of Essex, Waller and Manchester were to be amalgamated into one force. This new army would be centrally commanded by Parliament, who would direct the war from Westminster rather than through the county committees. Importantly, Parliament would appoint new commanders who could be trusted to pursue the war with the more vehemence than the current generals. On 21 January, Sir Thomas Fairfax was voted by the Commons to be the commander-in-chief of the new force.

It was not until 28 February that Fairfax presented a list of proposed company commanders (carefully selected by parliamentary committee), which were duly agreed to by the Commons. Colonel Harry Barclay was to retain his command of a regiment of foot 'to be raised by the new Establishment, according to the new Model',[6] built round the remnants of Barclay's Regiment who had survived the long campaign of 1644. On 18 March the list of commanders was approved by the Lords, who wished it to be made known that 'this House doth agree to pass this List, as it was presented by Sir Thomas Fairefax to the House of Commons… and to let them know, that this House ever was, and will be, willing to concur with them.'[7] While emphasising a fraternal co-operation between the Houses, the statement belied the fact that list of Fairfax's officers had been the subject of much discussion and had been passed by only the narrowest of margins by an upper House dominated by the old generals, Essex and Manchester.

Selecting the new model company commanders had been the remit parliamentary committee chaired by John Lisle (later vice-president of the High Court of Justice that would try Charles I). The officers that they proposed for Barclay's reconstituted regiment make interesting reading, with the new regimental establishment as follows:

> Colonel Barkley
> Lieutenant [Colonel] Emmins
> Major Cowell
> Captain Goffe
> Captain Gregson
> Captain Ramsey
> Captain Sampson
> Captain Leete
> Captain Goddard
> Captain Blagrave[8]

Thomas Pride's name is conspicuously absent. Evidently Lisle's committee had no intention of having Pride serve as an officer in the New Model Army.

The Lords recommended alterations to the officer list that was passed to them for approval. These were rejected by the Commons, but the proposed alterations survive on the original, hand-written list of officers in the House of Lords Record Office. On it, the names of the ten company commanders to serve under Barclay have been bracketed and the word 'que' written beside them, taken to indicate that there was a query with the entire regimental establishment.[9] On the same document, in a second hand, is written: 'Major Pride to be major, and Cowell to be a captain, and Captain Blagrave to be left out.'[10] Though omitted from the Commons committee list, Pride *was* recommended for service by the Lords. Another Commons' committee was convened at this time to find replacement posts for those excluded by the 'new modelling'. Pride of course had his business interests with which to concern himself and may still have held a position in the London Trained Bands, but his situation at this time presents us with two questions: why was he removed from the army, and why would the House of Lords want him reinstated?

Given Pride's promotion to major in May of the previous year it is doubtful that it was a lack of ability that was the reason for Pride's removal by the 'Committee for Sir Thomas Fairefax's Army', or by Fairfax himself. Rather, it would seem that his dismissal was connected to the prevalence of religious radicalism among some of Parliament's soldiers, and the fact that since the 1630s Pride had associations with a gathered church in London.

Religious division was rife in Parliament's army, particularly in Manchester's forces where it was exemplified in the open quarrel between Manchester's Major General of foot, Crawford, and his commander of horse, Cromwell. Crawford's rigid Scottish Presbyterianism brought him into conflict with the independents under his command, notably a lieutenant Packer, whom Crawford placed under arrest for preaching baptism in the ranks. Cromwell found such censure intolerable and spoke up in support of Packer, creating a division between himself and Crawford which threatened the command structure of Manchester's army. This open hostility between Independents and Presbyterians (and, moreover, the urgency of keeping the two factions apart), is further revealed in the case of the religious Independent, Colonel John Pickering. Pickering and his company commanders were to be transferred *en masse* from Manchester's army into the New Model. The House of Lords objected to the entire regimental establishment, but they felt unable to oppose the Commons and were obliged to accept Pickering's regiment as it stood. When the regiment of the Presbyterian Colonel Ayloffe was subsequently amalgamated with that of Pickering, such was the antagonism between the Presbyterian and Independent factions within the reconstituted force that many soldiers deserted.[11]

Religious radicalism was less obtrusive in Essex's army, but friction was still evident: John Lilburne had resigned his commission as an officer in Essex's army, repelled by what he saw as its slavish adherence to the Presbyterian covenant. He subsequently accepted a commission with the Earl of Manchester, among whose ranks he found a greater religious tolerance. It is easy to conjecture a similar division of interests between the Independent Pride and his immediate superiors, Barclay and Emmins, both of whom were Scottish Presbyterians. Even so, Pride had served two years under Barclay without any noticeable religious breech opening between them. He had accepted a majority the previous year, and there had been no sign of him shifting his allegiance to the radicals in Manchester's camp, as Lilburne had done.

Pride's departure from the regiment was certainly not voluntary: a note penned by Skippon, dated 7 April, records that Pride and other officers 'did behave themselves very well upon the Reducement', suggesting that there was a very real possibility that they would not. Seven other officers were dismissed along with Pride: a captain-lieutenant, an ensign, a sergeant, two corporals and two drummers. As the name of John Mason, Pride's own lieutenant, is absent from the list, it would appear the dismissed officers were from different companies.[12]

When Parliament's forces were reconstructed in early 1645 its architects took care to accommodate both Presbyterian and Independent religious views in an effort to avoid a conflict between the two factions. Of the ten colonels commanding regiments in the New Model Army's foot, four were drawn from Essex's army, four from Manchester's and two from the army of William Waller. Denton (2004) argues that this framework was intended to strike a careful balance in the army between opposing religious views.[13] The aim was to contain religious separatism in a number of regiments (those of Manchester's former command) and to allay the concerns of Parliament's Presbyterians, who were worried at the spread of religious extremism in the army; to allow religious Independence representation while simultaneously keeping the Presbyterians on side. Consequently, there was no opportunity for an Independent officer, such as Pride, to retain his position in a regiment intended to be on the Presbyterian side of this balance. It is true that William Goffe was retained on the original list of officers, but Goffe's religious mysticism may have emerged slightly later in his career, first noted in the speeches he delivered at the Putney Debates in 1647. At the time of the New Model Army's formation, Pride's religious Separatism – his involvement in Duppa's congregation and a Baptist, John Mason, serving as his lieutenant – was more obvious. Mason was also to be retained but, following Pride's exit, he would serve under a Presbyterian captain who could be relied upon to keep his Baptist views in check.

As noted above, the Lords had objected to many names on list of nominated officers (being a more conservative body than the Commons) and recommended changes to the proposed establishments. Significantly, however, these changes were not spread evenly throughout the new army establishment. As far as the twelve regiments of foot were concerned, the Lords wished no changes made (or, the case of Barclay's and Rainsborough's regiments, only a single change) to six of the nominated establishments: half of the army's foot. On the other hand, substantial changes were recommended for the remaining six, with those of Montague and Pickering to be entirely replaced.[14] This clearly demonstrates the religious divide of the Parliamentarian army: six Presbyterian regiments, with which the Lords were content; six Independent regiments to which they wished to make wholesale alterations. Yet if the Lords were attempting to create an army that was predominantly Presbyterian, why push to reinstate the Independent Pride?

The officers nominated by the Lords appear to have been endorsed by Essex and Manchester, still active in the Upper House. There is evidence that the Lords attempted to reinstate into Mountagu's Regiment several officers who had previously mutinied against their colonel in support of Manchester, and Essex seems to have been aiming to replace Pickering with his trusted second-in-command, Lord Robartes.[15] As Pride had seen two years campaigning under Essex, we can assume that the general was at least aware of his previous service.

Pride's proposed reinsertion by the Lords should not be construed as favouritism. Temple (1983) is in error when he suggests that Pride was favoured by several peers in the upper house, and his assertion of close ties between Pride and the Earl of Pembroke is surely a misreading of a later Royalist satire.[16] Rather, the recommendation of Pride to serve in the New Model should be seen as part of a move by Essex and Manchester to reassert their influence over the army by endorsing officers whom they saw as favourable to their own position, irrespective of their religious affiliation.

Despite the wish of the Commons' committee to secure the Presbyterian Harry Barclay at the at the head of one of the new foot regiments, however, there were further religious and political complications to upset their plans, and ultimately make Barclay's command untenable. In September 1643 Parliament had accepted the *Solemn League and Covenant*, an agreement between the English and Scottish governments that affirmed the political framework of King, Church and Parliament, an attempt to forge a firmer link between two allied kingdoms. In taking the Covenant both sides had agreed to: 'preserve and defend the King's Majesty's person and authority, in the preservation and defence of the true religion and liberties of the kingdoms...'[17] However, the text of Fairfax's commission as Commander-in-Chief of the New Model, passed by the Commons on 27 March, omitted any reference to the defence of the King's person, an indication that Parliament wished the war to be pursued with more vehemence. Nor was there any reference to the defence of a 'true religion', a term which, though deliberately vague, implied a consensus of worship. Fairfax's commission, then, disregarded the defence of government and a national church, the principles of which many Parliamentarians believed fundamental. Moreover, the wording of his commission was at odds the Scottish *National Covenant* of 1638, agreed upon by the Scots who had taken the field against Charles I in the Bishop's Wars, in which they had sworn to 'maintain the true worship of God, the majesty of our King, and the peace of the kingdom'.[18] Consequently, Colonel Barclay was unable to serve under Fairfax, whose commission specified neither the defence of a specific form of worship, nor respected the majesty of Charles I.

Despite their own objections to its wording, the Lords were again obliged to concede and passed Fairfax's commission on 1 April. Essex laid down his own commission the next day, and Manchester followed. Barclay and Innes declined their New Model commands not long after, perhaps ordered to do so by the Scottish commissioners who sat on the Committee of Both Kingdoms.

The departure of the Presbyterians ultimately tilted the balance of the New Model towards the radicals, with one quarter of the officers in the foot regiments resigning in a similar manner to Barclay and Innes. The cavalry regiments, generally regarded as more radical than the foot, saw only one sixth of their officers depart and there were no changes at all to the establishments of the radical colonels, Montague and Pickering.[19] So easily upset was the equilibrium of the New Model's structure, as a result of Fairfax's commission, that the very idea of maintaining such a balance of religious and political views seems naive and simplistic.

The approval of Fairfax's commission had officially brought the New Model Army into being, but by 3 April the Commons was already having to make changes to the proposed establishment of Barclay's Regiment. Two captains newly appointed to the regiment, John Blagrave and Vincent Goddard, held commissions in the Berkshire militia. The Reading committee was unwilling for their garrison troops to march with the New Model, desiring instead that they remain to defend the town.[20] Blagrave's wealthy and respectable family was prominent among the local gentry and the Reading town corporation, and his command of a company in Barclay's reinforces the idea that the regiment was being intentionally filled with moderates. Blagrave and Goddard continued to serve Parliament in the Reading area: the following August would see them, respectively, at the siege of Basing House and in the garrison at Henley-on-Thames, but they did not serve in the New Model. Their place in Barclay's was filled by captains William Hender and John Ferguson, both of whom had previously served with other regiments of Essex's army.[21]

The case of Hender is interesting because his position in the army during the early months of 1645 was identical to Pride's. Hender had served as captain-lieutenant to Lord Robartes, and he and Pride would have fought in many of the same actions over the previous two years. Like Pride, Hender was omitted from the New Model by the Commons but nominated for service by the Lords.[22] When the Lords finally deferred to the Commons' selection of officers, Hender was sidelined until the withdrawal of the Presbyterians required the Commons to find extra officers to fill their places. Having formerly served under a moderate commander, removed from the army by order of the Commons, and then reinstated only out of necessity – Hender's case proves that Thomas Pride's situation was not unique.

On 12 April – Fairfax travelled to Reading to review Barclay's reconstituted regiment, which mustered at the village of Ockingham and was by this time, according to Fairfax's secretary, Rushworth, 'well nigh recruited'.[23] The regiment was still referred to as Barclay's, though if Barclay were still in command he must have stepped-down not long after.

Fairfax's campaign was to begin at the end of the month, and following Barclay's departure a new colonel for the regiment was quickly found in the form of Edward Harley, a twenty-one year old cavalry officer serving with Massey's army on the Welsh borders. In many ways Harley was Parliament's answer to the dashing cavalier of popular Royalist myth: he was a delicate young man who had been sent down from Magdalen College, Oxford, because of his fragile constitution ('If your tutor does not intend to buy you silk stockings to wear with your silk shirt,' his mother had soothed, 'send me word, and I will, if please God, bestow a pair on you').[24] Yet Harley's apparent delicacy belied a natural aptitude for soldiering, and he had seen a good deal of action despite his youth. Captain of a troop of horse at eighteen, he had fought at Lansdowne, Roundway Down and Cheriton in 1643 under Waller's command. The following year he raised his own regiment of foot. He distinguished himself in action at Redmarley, near Ledbury, in July 1644, when he reputedly routed the enemy's cavalry and captured nearly all the foot, being wounded in the process. The Harleys had been a fixture of Herefordshire gentry since the Middle Ages, and Edward served in and around the county for much of the war. His father, Sir Robert Harley, was MP for Herefordshire and had been Master of the Mint under James I. Edward himself would later represent the county at Westminster and his younger brother was MP for Old Radnor. By the mid-1640s the family ran half the county. It is easy to see why Parliament selected this well-connected young man for a regimental commander: Harley was youthful, courageous, had seen a good deal of action and had a certain amount of dash about him. He was also a Presbyterian, which would maintain the religious balance of the foot regiments. But although Harley accepted the colonelcy he was not fit for the coming summer campaign: in April, Harley was again wounded in action, his injury this time serious enough to require the attention of specialist doctors in London.

Similarly, another of the committee's choice of officers for the regiment was unable to serve: Captain William Leete, who had raised a company for Barclay in the first months of the war, had now become incapacitated through wounds. Leete was still willing to serve and seems to have felt some distress at being forced to give up the fight. Major-General Skippon testified for Leete on his behalf, recounting his faithful service of almost two and half years:

> in which time he hath received severall wounds, & sustained the losse of mutch blood, by reason whereof hee now findeth his body very infirm, & much disenabled to the present service … he hath beheaved himself with much fidelity, diligence & courage in the persuance of the cause.[25]

Barclay and Emmins, as Presbyterian Scots, were unable or unwilling to serve in the New Model; Barclay's replacement was unfit for service; Leete was disabled; Blagrave and Goddard were requested not to leave Reading; yet another captain, Ramsey (possibly another Scot), would not serve with the regiment in the coming campaign: by mid-April the officer corps of Barclay's Regiment, as proposed by the Commons' committee, was in disarray. If the regiment were to march at the end of the month it would need bolstering, and an experienced man found to command them in the field. By the time the New Model took the field at the beginning of May, Thomas Pride had not only been reinstated but promoted to lieutenant colonel. He would command the unit in the forthcoming campaign until Harley was fit for duty. Pride's lieutenant, Mason, would command a company in place of Ramsey.

Two and a half years on from raising a company, and less than two months since his exclusion from the New Model, Pride was now effectively at the head of a regiment. The effect of having a religious Independent in command resulted in an increased mood of religious radicalism, discernible in Barclay's Regiment from this point on and evident in the sequential appointments of its regimental chaplains. Serving Barclay in this capacity at the time of the regiment's transition into the New Model was James Juris, a Presbyterian who had served with the regiment during the previous year's campaign in Cornwall. Tellingly, he seems to have left the regiment at the same time as the Scottish officers.[26] His predecessor had been Jas (or James) Moore, chaplain to the regiment during Essex's push toward Oxford in the summer of 1643. Moore had been orthodox enough to have been appointed the living of St. Thomas the Apostle in London the same year.[27] However, the more conformist faiths of Juris and Moore vanished when the regiment became incorporated into the New Model. The chaplain appointed to serve under the Presbyterian, Harley, was Anthony Wainwright, a man who railed against an organised church – governed either by bishops or presbyters – and was said to have abandoned his own parish, declaring it to be anti-Christian.[28]

When in the fullness of time the over-all command of the regiment passed to Pride, the ideology of its chaplains became increasingly radical, as one would expect under the command of an Independent colonel. The regiment's chaplain in the later 1640s was John Hemmings, who opposed Presbyterianism and refused to administer communion to those who worshipped in Anglican churches, a refusal which corresponded with the view held by Duppa's congregation; that to worship within the Anglican Church tainted the true Christian with High Church popery. By 1660 Hemmings was resident at the vicarage at Lydd in Kent, where the parishioners were to demand his eviction after discovering that he had never been ordained as a minister.[29] The regimental chaplain from 1650, Samuel Oates, was even more wayward. His pedigree was impeccable: hailing from Rutland, he had been an Anglican deacon in the 1630s, with an MA from Corpus Christi, but by the time of the Civil War he had undergone a religious crisis and become an itinerant preacher in Leicestershire, conducting adult baptisms and scraping a living by weaving. He was questioned by the authorities on several occasions, including a court appearance on a charge of adultery, for which he was acquitted. By 1659 his tenure with Pride's Regiment had ended, but he was subsequently expelled as rector of Hastings for 'improper practices'[30] Curious, also, that he was at this time only fifteen miles from the equally objectionable Hemmings at Lydd.

The religious views of these regimental chaplains, then, became manifestly more radical once Pride achieved his colonelcy, a demonstration of how influential the faith of the commanding officer could be on a regiment. Pride's separatist reputation lived on after his death: *The History of King-Killers* (1719) claimed that Pride 'could pray and preach in the blasphemous Strain of those Days as well as any of his Associates'[31] Typically, Pride appears to have left no written record with which might substantiate this claim.

The extent of religious militancy among the rank and file of Barclay's foot is difficult to determine, though it was certainly seems to have been present. The Independents among Pride's men are noticeable by their 'Puritanical' names, recorded in army pay warrants. Independents were notable for their Old Testament forenames, preferable to the names of the evangelists and the saints that were associated with Catholic feast days, and popular in pre-Reformation England. Up to the early 1650s there were, serving among Pride's rank and file, three Moses, two Solomons and five Abrahams; and one each of Ephraim, Zachary, Zechariah, Isaak, Zephaniah and Jonas.[32] Clearly these men were in a minority beside the scores of Johns and Williams that served alongside them, but perhaps a kernel of separatism can be discerned from the names of the regiment's private soldiers.

The resignation of the Scottish Presbyterian officers between March and April 1645 had given religious Independence a much firmer footing in the New Model than it otherwise might have had. The faiths of Moore and Juris were gradually effaced by the more radical faiths of Pride and the Independent chaplains that served under him. This was precisely what the Commons committee had been seeking to avoid when they drew-up the list of officers for the New Model, when they temporarily removed Pride from his command until forced to re-instate him. The promotion of the Baptist lieutenant, John Mason, to captain at this time would surely never had happened in the unit's original conception as a Presbyterian regiment. The fact that Mason's promotion to a company command came just as that Pride was re-instated is surely more than a coincidence. Of the twelve foot regiments raised for service in the New Model, five establishments remained unchanged following the resignation of the Presbyterians; six regiments lost between two and four officers. Barclay's Regiment, however, was exceptional: no fewer than six out of the regiment's ten company commanders had been replaced by early April.[33]

With the new army's structure finally in place, Fairfax concentrated his force at Reading in early May. It was decided that the south west of England, still largely under Royalist control, would be the New Model's immediate area of operations. Taunton, the only inland garrison the Parliament had in the west, was under siege. If Taunton fell, the Royalists would have a base from which to move against the south coast ports, the financial and commercial weight of which could then be absorbed into their war effort.

Harley's foot marched from their quarters at Reading on 30 April heading towards Newbury, the road to which must now have been very familiar to Pride, and by 5 May they were at Salisbury.[34] Fairfax had reached Blandford in Dorset, roughly two-thirds of the way towards his objective of Taunton when further orders from Westminster compelled him to change direction and turn towards Oxford – he was to place the now apparently defenceless Royalist capital under siege. Detaching a brigade to deal with Taunton, Fairfax wheeled his main body northwards.[35]

In spite of Rushworth's remark on the regiment's recruitment, quoted above, Harley's foot was under strength as the summer campaign opened. The average size of the New Model foot regiments at Naseby has been calculated to have been 800 men, only two-thirds of the theoretical establishment strength. Harley's seems to have been weaker than most, and there is evidence that when Blagrave and Goddard failed to march with the New Model, so too did the companies they commanded. The result was that Harley's Regiment needed to be bolstered by at least one company of Ingoldsby's foot to ensure they could at least take the field as an effective body.[36]

Charles I had already marched north by the time Fairfax approached Oxford on the 19 May. As the New Model began preparing siege lines around the city, the Royalists launched a swift campaign against the Parliamentarians in the Midlands in an attempt to draw Fairfax's army northwards, away from his beleaguered capital. The Royalist army stormed Leicester in an assault that resulted in a good deal of fatalities, military and civilian alike. Fairfax's plan of campaign changed once more. On 4 June the New Model lifted its Oxford siege and marched north to engage Charles I's army. The two armies were to meet in Northamptonshire on 14 June.

6

Naseby

A short chapter about a short battle

The name of 'Naseby' is arguably the most resonant of the Civil War battles, and it is also the battle that is most easily recognised: the dispositions of the two armies being formally rendered in Robert Streeter's famous illustration and published in *Anglia Rediviva* (1647), an account of the campaign written by Fairfax's chaplain, Joshua Sprigg. It is not the purpose of this chapter to provide an exhaustive account of the battle of Naseby, however, but to identify Thomas Pride's role in one of the war's key engagements.

The lay of the land is well documented: the Royalist army formed up along Dust Hill on the north side of the battlefield, Fairfax's New Model lined the crest of the slightly higher Red (or Rutpit) Hill to the south; between lay the shallow valley of open land known as Broad Moor. Needless to say, Fairfax had the advantage in numbers. Streeter's plan is invaluable in our understanding of the battle, yet one of the biggest misunderstandings of how Parliament's foot regiments were organised at Naseby is due to this key source.

Streeter depicts two distinct divisions of Parliamentarian foot drawn up along Red Hill. Harley's Regiment was drawn up in the second of these lines along with the regiments of Rainsborough and Hammond.[1] On Streeter's plan this formation is labelled as being that of 'Lieutenant. Coll Pride', with no mention of Harley's name. This labelling seems to have arisen because the plan was not published until two years after the battle, by which time Pride had full command of the regiment. On the day of Naseby the unit's name was properly 'Harley's Regiment', though several contemporary sources relating to the battle still referred to it as 'Barclay's' or 'Bartlett's'.

Unlike many other set-piece battles of the Civil War there is no reference to brigade formations for Parliament's foot in contemporary accounts of Naseby. Streeter depicts two clearly defined divisions of foot: a front line of five regiments supported by a second 'reserve' of three regiments. On this evidence, most histories treat the two lines of Parliament foot as the separate, distinct bodies that they appear to be in Streeter's illustration. However, because it is commonly accepted

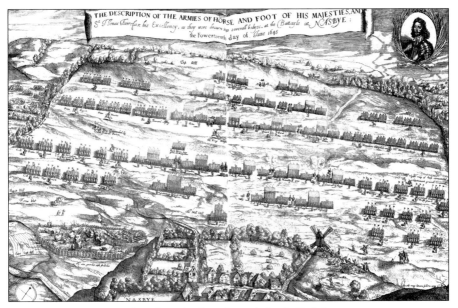

Plan of Naseby, from Sprigg's *Anglia Rediviva*.

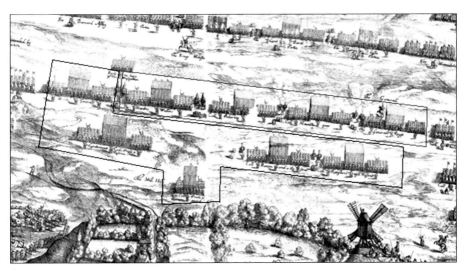

Detail of parliamentarian foot brigade formations: Fairfax (front line) and Skippon
(rear line and left)

that Streeter was not present at the battle we ought to turn to other, eye-witness, accounts to test how reliable the illustrator was.

One such account is that of George Bishop, who described himself as a 'gentleman with the army'. Viewing Fairfax's troops as they moved off on the morning of the battle he described the foot as comprising two 'wings': the regiments of Fairfax, Montague, Pickering and Waller he named as the 'right wing'; those of Skippon, Harley, Rainsborough and Hammond as the 'left wing'.[2] We can assume from this that Bishop watched the battle from Windmill Hill: what he was seeing were the two lines of foot depicted by Streeter, but looking across them *lengthways*, east to west, as they marched on to the field of battle. It is clear from Bishop's account that Skippon's regiment was in the lead of the second wing, and that this was the body of foot that Streeter labelled 'a reserve'. Bishop's account is important because it allows us to see that Parliament's foot at Naseby was formed of two brigades of equal strength, not the unbalanced bodies of forward line and reserve shown by Streeter.

We know that these two 'wings' were units in their own right because the same formations of regiments recur in Fairfax's subsequent 1645 campaign. Rainsborough commanded a brigade at Bristol in September that year that was formed of his own, Skippon's, Hammond's and Pride's regiments. The following month the regiments of Pickering, Waller and Montague were brigaded together at Basing House.[3] The bodies of foot described by Bishop at Naseby can thus be treated as consistent formations – infantry brigades.

We can assume that Parliament's foot marched on to the field at Naseby in the formations described that morning by Bishop. Once in position, Skippon manoeuvred his own regiment further forward to extend Parliament's frontage from four to five regiment's breadth, able to outflank the Royalist foot's shorter line. This deployment, with five regiments in the forward line and three in the rear, meant that the regiments in the rear-most brigade had to be spread wider to cover the spaces between the units in front, in the typical 'chequer board' infantry formation of the period. The result was that Pride's command was split in two divisions, to cover the ground vacated by Skippon.

Streeter's topographical projection of the battlefield (it can hardly be termed a map) shows a smaller body of troops to rear of the Parliamentarian position labelled 'Lt. Coll. Pride a Reare guard'. Foard (2004) suggests that the rearguard numbered about 400, accounting for approximately half of the regiment's strength,[4] although the difference in size between the two formations depicted by Streeter does not indicate a fifty-fifty split. There was some idea at the time that this rearmost division was assigned to protecting the Parliamentarian baggage train. Sprigg explicitly describes the baggage as 'being well defended with the firelocks, and a rearguard left for that purpose', information that he may have taken from a contemporary news book *The Weekly Account,* which stated: 'Collonel Bartlets [Barclay's] regiment and the Firelocks that guarded the Train'[5] The truth of this statement has been questioned, and the modern consensus is that the

Parliamentarian baggage was positioned so far to the rear of Fairfax's position that it would have been impossible for Pride's rear-guard to offer it protection.[6] Fairfax's deployment – two lines of foot, with a single body as a reserve and the baggage to the rear – was almost identical to a formation adopted by the Earl of Ormonde when commanding the English in Ireland in early 1642, where the rear-guard was clearly a part of the main body and not specifically attached to the baggage.[7] However, it should be remembered that troops are able to move around a battlefield, and a minor scattering of lead shot uncovered by archaeologists on the southern slope of Mill Hill, between the Parliamentarian positions and the location of baggage nearer to Naseby village, suggest that at least some of Fairfax's foot were in this area and gave fire to protect the baggage train. The amount of shot recovered here has been considered too small to have been part of the battle between the Royalist and Parliamentarian main bodies,[8] and the archaeological evidence gives some veracity to the *The Weekly Account*'s assertion that the rear-guard came to the baggage train's aid. Although the evidence is far from conclusive, it could be that the lead shot in question may have been fired by troops under Pride's command.

Rupert was encouraged to advance his forces across Broad Moor while the New Model was apparently still manoeuvring into position. Arguments have been made that Rupert was attempting to overwhelm Fairfax's lines at a rush, along their whole frontage. There is no report of preliminary artillery fire: Rupert seems to have attempting to make up for the disparity in numbers by gaining the advantage in surprise. However, in his decision to advance and the urgency of his attack he lost his forces the advantage of the high ground of Dust Hill. Sprigg noted that the Royalists were marching up in 'good order, a swift march',[9] so it is evident that the broken and marshy ground of Broad Moor had not disordered the Royalist lines as Fairfax might have hoped. Edward Walker, Charles I's secretary, provides us with his own account of the Royalist attack:

> [The Royalists] advanced up the hill, the rebels only discharging five [artillery] Pieces at them, but over shot them, and so did their Musquetiers. The Foot on either side hardly saw each other until they were in carbine shot and so only made one Volley; ours, falling in with Sword and butt end of the Musquett, did noticable execution.[10]

Walker's account of both armies being out of sight of each other tallies with what Sprigg tells us about Fairfax deliberately concealing his strength behind the high ground. Walker implies that both sides had reached the brow of the Red Hill simultaneously; because of the rising ground between them neither line of foot saw the other until they were practically on top of one another. The less-experienced recruits of the New Model foot, whose musketry had not taken into account the angle of the slope and consequently fired over the enemies' heads, quickly became disordered under the impact of the Royalist advance and the ferocity of the close-quarter fighting: 'Almost all the rest of the main battle being overpressed, gave ground and went off in some disorder, falling behind the reserves.'[11]

Records of casualties sustained by the New Model foot survive in Treasury accounts. Although they provide only a list the wounded (they do not include those who were killed outright) they nevertheless provide good indication of which regiments bore the brunt of the fighting. Pickering's and Montague's regiments sustained 40 and 33 wounded respectively before they fell back. Waller's foot, which, like Harley's, appear to have been severely under strength at Naseby, suffered only 14 wounded before they were forced to retire.[12] However, the Royalist foot did not succeed in pushing back the whole of Fairfax's line. Fewer numbers of Royalist foot meant that their attack had a considerably shorter frontage than that of Fairfax's first line, and the Royalists seem only to have been able to engage the left and centre of Parliament's position. Fairfax's own regiment seems to have barely troubled at this point in the action and maintained their position: 'the right hand of foot, being the general's regiment, stood, not being much pressed upon'.[13] Skippon's regiment too seems to have held its ground, judging from the number of wounded in their ranks. Skippon's sustained 130 wounded, as many as the other seven regiments of foot put together. Yet in Harley's regiment, positioned to the rear of Skippon, only 3 soldiers are known to have been wounded.[14] How could such a difference in casualties between the two regiments have occurred?

Hammond's and Rainsborough's regiments appear to have been able to move forward into the gap in the line that opened up after the regiments in front of them fell back. It would have been harder for Pride's command to have moved forward with the rest of the second line if, as can be conjectured, Skippon's maintained a position immediately in front. Indeed, as long as Skippon held his ground Harley's regiment did not need to be committed. The very low figure of wounded among Pride's ranks suggests that Skippon had absorbed the shock of the Royalist advance, and that the enemy had already begun to give way when the second line of Parliament moved forward to engage them.

In a scene that would have been horribly reminiscent to Pride of the conduct of Weare's and Butler's men at Castle Dore the previous year, the regiments to the front and right of him were abandoning their position. In spite of their disintegrating front line, however, the New Model still held the advantage in numbers, having begun the fight with upwards of 7,000 foot to the Royalists' 3,500.[15] Pride's military experience would also have prepared him well for this eventuality: he had been in a similar position at First Newbury, where Parliament's foot had been under tremendous pressure for several hours, yet had managed to hold a defensive position under continual bombardment and repeated attacks.

The rapidly deteriorating situation among Parliament's first line was remedied by the second line to their rear. The momentum of the Royalist advance having carried them this far, their attack now stalled. The weight of numbers facing the Royalists was now beginning to tell, and it was at this point that they began to lose the battle. Sprigg's narrative account tells of the New Model 'reserve' advancing up the reverse slope of Red Hill, pushing the enemy back from the crest.

While the fighting was in coming to a conclusion on Red Hill, Rupert's cavalry had broken through the New Model horse on the left wing and, continuing to sweep around Fairfax's position, saw the Parliamentarian baggage as a ripe target. Rupert apparently promised the defenders quarter if they surrendered, but the guard 'fired with admirable courage on the prince's horse, refusing to harken to his offer.'[16] Lists of Parliamentarian wounded contain the names of several individuals whose roles would suggest that were with the baggage during the battle. These included a wagoner, a carpenter, the Master of Miners, and the assistant to the Quartermaster of the Foot, all of whom were wounded. The Quartermaster of the Horse and a parliamentary commissioner were both killed. These casualties, compared to those sustained by some of the foot regiments, suggest that the action around the baggage was quite fierce, but it is hard to determine whether the three casualties from Harley's foot (all from the colonel's own company) suffered their wounds in this area of the battle as part of the rear-guard. The largest company of a foot regiment in this period was that of the senior field officer, the colonel. If Colonel Harley's company had been detached from the main body of the regiment to form the rear-guard, it would mean that the casualties were sustained in this area of the battlefield, possibly while helping to defend the baggage.[17]

In the event, Pride and his men seem to have very seen little of the fighting at Naseby. Rainsborough's regiment only took nine casualties. Hammond's regiment suffered the most among those in the rear of the Parliamentarian foot but, at seventeen men, even these losses could be considered light. From the casualty returns it is clear that it was the front line regiments who bore the brunt of the fighting among the New Model foot. The marginal role of the second brigade (Skippon's excepted) indicates that the Royalist attack had been sufficiently halted before the second line of Parliament foot was committed in the counter attack. The fact that Harley's Regiment was understrength, and that Pride's command had been further weakened by being divided to form the rear-guard, explains why his regiment was not more heavily involved at Naseby. Indeed, so few were the casualties it seems likely that they barely engaged at all. The simplicity and speed of Parliament's victory is underlined by the losses sustained: Naseby was one of the less-bloody battles of the war, with little more than 1,000 casualties.[18]

7

Campaigns in the West, 1645–46

'We dipt our hand in blood'

Tracing the narrative of Fairfax's campaign after Naseby will allow us to follow Thomas Pride through the most sustained period of fighting that he undertook. This is worth examining in detail because it reveals how far-removed Pride's experience of battle differs from the accepted view of the Civil War has emerged through popular history.

It was a caprice of war that led Pride, in early July 1645, through the landscape he had known as a child: Somerset was to be Fairfax's theatre of operations for the coming months. Rupert had established himself here following the defeat at Naseby and was rallying forces at Bristol. The Royalists had an army of 10,000 in Somerset under the command of Lord Goring, and they controlled the countryside through a network of garrisons at Bridgwater, Ilchester and Bath. The only Parliamentarian stronghold in the county was Taunton, which Goring had invested, and this was to be Fairfax's first objective.

Edward Harley had written to Committee of Gloucester six days following Naseby, informing them of 'The good service which hath been done by the regiment of Col. Harley... The state of his regiment you also know, and its present want of recruits, the speedy and effectual supply whereof we recommend unto you'.[1] Although he was not fit to serve in the campaign Harley was evidently busy behind the scenes to ensure that his regiment had the men it needed for the coming campaign. Consequently, nineteen soldiers from the Malmesbury garrison were drafted into Harley's foot, possibly when the regiment passed through the town on 28 June.[2] A further sixty men came to Harley's from Francis Martin's regiment which had formed the garrison at Aylesbury, and which was no longer needed following the victory at Naseby and the decreased Royalist threat. Initially the idea had been to reduce Martin's regiment into that of Fleetwood, but the state of Harley's regiment must have been critical enough to necessitate at least one company of Martin's small command being absorbed into Pride's ranks.[3]

Portrait miniature by Samuel Cooper of Edward Harley, Pride's commanding officer from 1645 to 1647. (Private collection)

Bridgwater: 11-23 July

Bridgwater was a considerable Royalist stronghold in Somerset, well supplied and 'being a magazine for all the petty garrisons thereabouts.'[4] Goring had abandoned his siege of Taunton at the New Model's approach and it was here that he had retreated after being thrown back by Fairfax at Langport on 10 July. Bridgwater had been thoroughly prepared for a siege, the buildings outside the walls demolished and the approaches cleared to deprive any attacker of cover, 'there being not a clod that could afford any advantage against that place.'[5] Eighteen hundred Royalist soldiers garrisoned the town, able to draw on the fire power of about forty pieces of ordnance. The River Parrett divided the town in half, from north to south, which would prove a barrier to any attacker. What had been a Somerset market town now resembled a fortress. Fairfax spent two days observing the town's defences and preparing his own positions. Facing the risk of high losses in attacking such a well-prepared defence, Fairfax hoped that the threat of assault would be enough to persuade the garrison to capitulate. However, the garrison refused all terms and the siege lengthened.

On 15 July Fairfax spent a day sightseeing in Glastonbury.[6] Pedwell was only eight miles from the Parliament siege lines and it is very likely that Pride still had extended family living along the Polden Hills. He maintained a favourable

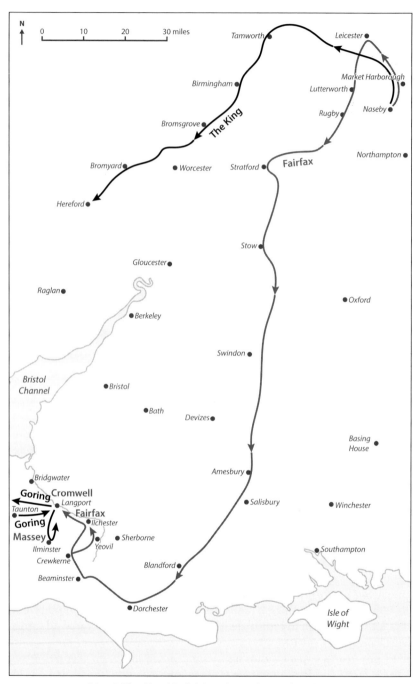

Map 4 The New Model Army's march into the West.

reputation in the area until the end of his life, and it is tempting to think that Pride took advantage of the lull in the fighting to visit his old home.[7]

Good weather could not be expected to last, and time spent waiting in the earthworks around Bridgwater was allowing the Royalists to reinforce their strongholds elsewhere. The decision to attack was made on the 16th, with the assault to take place when the moon was right: Monday 21 July, just before dawn. Lots were drawn to decide which units would storm the defences. On the Sunday, sermons were read to the troops in the morning and afternoon, after which they were marshalled in the nearby fields.

Pride's men were tasked with assaulting Bridgwater on its east side. The assault was led by Pickering's regiment followed by Fairfax's and Skippon's, with Harley's regiment in support. A second brigade was to attack simultaneously from the west, not to storm the defences but to act as a diversion: 'only alarming the enemy, which kept them upon the line, expecting a storm.'[8] The attack began at two in the morning. The leading soldiers were quickly over the walls, breaking through the east gate and occupying the area of the town on the near side of the Parrett. The defenders fell back into the western defences, raising the drawbridge over the river behind them. A forlorn hope of the New Model opened the town gates to allow in the supporting troops, but faced with the impassable obstacle of the river the attack began to falter. Initially in support, Pride's men were now in the thick of the fighting and began to take casualties, including one of the captains, George Sampson. They came under fire from heated shot and grenades, setting the buildings alight and depriving the attacking Parliamentarians of cover. Pride's second-in-command, William Cowell was remarked upon for his firm discipline, keeping his men at their posts and preventing the enemy from sallying out of their defences, despite the buildings on both sides of his position burning fiercely.[9]

By daybreak most of that part of Bridgwater under Parliament's control had largely been destroyed by fire, the western half of the town remaining in Royalist hands. Fairfax summoned the governor, but the terms of surrender offered were refused. The strength of the defences had shown Fairfax that he could not consider a further assault without severe loss, and he chose instead to subject the town to prolonged fire from his heavy guns. The Parliamentarian general advised the town's governor to release the women and children who remained in the town, which was duly done. Soon after, Fairfax's guns began firing heated shot on to what remained of the town.

By the time the garrison surrendered the next morning, Bridgwater had been reduced to a smoking ruin and a large proportion of the population was homeless. The civilians' situation was alleviated to a degree after the garrison's possessions were seized by Fairfax's men and auctioned off to the local populace. The proceeds were then divided equally and distributed through the Parliamentarian ranks as reward for good service.

Bristol: 23 August – 10 September 1645

As the largest port in the country, Bristol provided the Royalists with a substantial magazine as well as a base to bring fresh troops from Ireland and Wales. Rupert had been appointed the city's military governor and there was a good opportunity for him to begin to build a new Royalist army. Fairfax had been reluctant to move against Bristol earlier in the summer because of the presence of plague in the city and surrounding villages, but it was clear that Bristol would have to be taken if the Royalists were to be defeated in the west.

Fairfax's army reached Bristol on 21 August. By 23 August they had the city surrounded and had set their siege lines. Pride's men camped out in a shallow valley on the north east outskirts of the city named Woolcot Park.[10] Repeated sallies by the Royalist garrison allowed Rupert to gauge the besiegers' strength and hinder the Parliamentarian's efforts to entrench. By 1 September these attacks ceased and Rupert had begun to negotiate a surrender, which Fairfax suspected was merely a delaying tactic. He made a show of considering Rupert's terms, even though he had already decided that he would have to storm the city's defences. As at Bridgwater, the decision to assault was forced on Fairfax, who feared that Royalists would be free to operate elsewhere while his own force was tied up in a lengthy siege. Charles I was believed to be preparing to march to Rupert's aid; Goring's horse was rumoured to be moving up from Devon to meet him.

Sprigg reported that 'for the manner of the storm it was referred to a committee of the colonels of the army, to present in writing to the general the next morning, to be debated at a general council of war.'[11] It thus fell to the regimental colonels (and one would assume this included Pride) to decide how best to fight their way into the city.

The Royalist defences were extensive, but lacked strength. Bristol's perimeter of earth banks and ditches was three miles in length, but along the east side of the city the ramparts were reported to be a mere five feet high and three feet thick, and 'all that part of the line much decayed',[12] even though the ditch in front of these defences (six feet across and five deep) effectively made a defence that was ten feet in hight. On the north side of the city the line was especially weak, and where engineers had only been able to dig down a short way before hitting rock the depth of the ditch was as little as four feet. To compensate for the shallowness of the ditch a series of earthwork fortifications had been constructed along the north wall to strengthen it, each fort within firing range of the others to provide mutual support. To the west and south, the city was protected by a further stretch of earth and timber ramparts which augmented the remains of the medieval stone walls and the natural defence of the River Avon.

Fairfax and his officers would have realised that Rupert's strength was not enough to man the whole of Bristol's perimeter. If the Parliamentarians were to assault the defences at several points simultaneously, the Royalists would be severely stretched. To this end, the colonels chose to direct their main attack

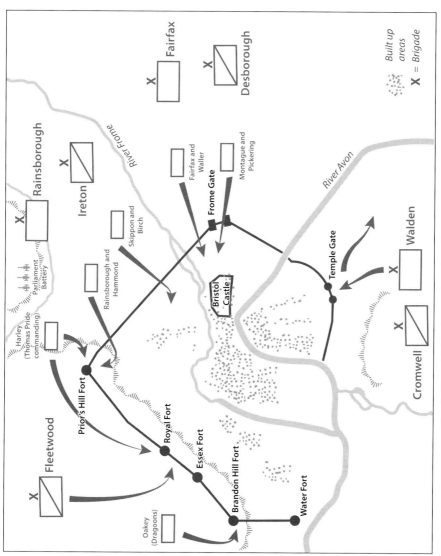

Map 5 Plan of Fairfax's assault on Bristol, 10 September 1645.

against the weaker, eastern line of defence, while at the same time putting in a series of diversionary attacks at key points against the north. Fairfax positioned his heavy guns in a battery on Ashley Hill, the high ground to the north of the city from where he could bring fire down on Prior's Hill Fort. This fort was situated at the corner of the city defences, where the north and east lines met, and was the lynch pin of the Royalist fortifications. If Prior's Hill were taken it would open up both the north and the east lines to Fairfax's soldiers.

The main attack was to go in against the east line and to be undertaken by the brigades of Fairfax and Rainsborough, a total of nine foot regiments. A third brigade of four regiments would make an attack on the south. Each brigade would be supported by a brigade of horse, with a fourth cavalry brigade deployed north of the city to contain Rupert should he attempt to break-out. The enormity of Parliament's assault on Bristol is staggering: under cover of darkness a total of 21 regiments (14 foot, 7 horse) were to advance on a city that was second in size only to London. Fairfax held nothing in reserve, committing his entire command to overwhelming Bristol in one attempt. Further support was to come from a force of sailors, brought ashore and directed against the Water Fort, situated on the Avon. However, when the time for assault came the tide was discovered to be falling and the plan was deemed unworkable. The sailors were instead assigned to bolster Pride's command in the diversionary attack. The storming of Bristol was a far larger engagement than the battle of Naseby and it is regrettable that the action has, to a large extent, been overlooked.

Prior's Hill Fort was not the largest of Bristol's forts, but Rupert was aware of its strategic importance and ensured it was strongly defended. The task of taking the position fell to Rainsborough, commanding a brigade of foot 'consisting of his own, Major Gen. Skipson's [sic], Col. Hammond's, Col. Birch's and Lieutenant Col. Pride's Regiments'.[13] This was in essence the 'left wing' formation of Naseby, now commanded by Rainsborough in Skippon's absence through injury and augmented by Birch's regiment from Edward Massey's Western Brigade.

At midnight on 9 September, Fairfax gave the order to start drawing troops out of the lines to take up their positions. As at Naseby, Pride's command was to be divided into two separate bodies: one part sent in to reinforce the main attack on Prior's Hill alongside Rainsborough's and Hammond's regiments; the remainder to carry out a diversionary attack against Fort Royal on the north wall. Skippon's and Birch's were to breach the walls further down and were not involved in the Prior's Hill attack.

Fort Royal was the largest of the Bristol forts (hence its name) and posed such an obstacle that the Parliamentarians must have ruled out a direct assault. However, it was necessary to make the Royalists believe that an assault would be attempted and a force was assigned, 'to be moving up and down the Closes before the Royal Fort, and ply hard upon it, to alarm it, with a Field-Officer to Command them.'[14] Just how Pride's command was divided is not known. Sprigg simply refers to 'part assigned to the service of Priors-fort' and 'the rest' directed at Fort Royal,[15] with perhaps one force led by Major Cowell and the other commanded by Pride himself. Captains Hender and Lagoe seem to have been the company commanders most prominent in the action.

The defences at Prior's Hill took the form of a sconce: a self-contained, rectangular earthwork defence with a triangular 'bastion' at each corner, raised above ground level and connected to other defences along the line by ditches and earth banks. The walls of the fort were certainly more than twelve feet high and perhaps closer to twenty, their height augmented by the ditch that surrounded the works. Further defences that the attackers met may have included an 'abatis' of tangled hawthorn branches (a 17th century equivalent of barbed wire) and sharpened stakes, or 'storm poles', driven horizontally through the earth walls to impede the scaling of the ramparts by ladder. A Parliamentarian deserter had informed the Royalists that an attack was imminent and 'the enemy stood ready cocked, and the gunners by their guns.'[16] Rupert was later to write that he had 'received intelligence a little before… all were in readiness to receive them.'[17]

Sprigg details the formation of the attacking troops. The unenviable task of leading the assault was undertaken by forty men who formed the ladder party: twenty scaling ladders were to be rushed forward, two men to each. Following close behind were a score of men bearing bundles of sticks which were tossed into the ditches beneath the fort's walls to form makeshift bridges. Once this forlorn hope had the ladders in position the main attack went in: twelve files of men moving forward in two waves: the first of five files, was led by a lieutenant; the larger second wave of seven files followed under the command of the captain. This grouping of files (a platoon, from the French, 'peloton') was common in continental armies and although Sprigg does not use this term in his account, it seems that Fairfax's army was employing a rudimentary platoon formation. A file in this period could number between six and ten men, depending on which tactics were being followed, and the description above would indicate that a single company from each regiment was to spearhead the attacks.[18]

The initial field cry for the coming action was to be 'David', the call shouted back and forth between attacking bodies so as to distinguish friend from foe in the dark. The attackers were inspired by the story of King David, who took the city of Jerusalem from the Philistines by storm, as recounted in the second book of Samuel. Note that the cry was 'David' and not 'King David', the word 'King' presumably omitted for fear that troops might be misheard and taken to be Royalists. The call-sign was to change once the leading troops had crossed Bristol's outer works, with the cry 'God With Us' to be taken up as a general signal that the first lines of defence had been breached.[19]

At two o'clock a great bonfire was lit on the heights at Clifton, visible for miles and signalling to all that the attack was to begin. Simultaneously, the Parliamentarian battery to the north began its fire.

The men of Rainsborough's brigade initially made little progress against Prior's Hill, and the fort's earthen ramparts easily absorbed the impact of the shot from the Parliament battery. Cromwell witnessed the attack from the command post on Ashley Hill and wrote that the attackers: 'fought nearly three hours for it, and indeed there was great dispair in carrying the place, it being exceedingly high, a ladder of thirty rounds scarce reaching the top thereof.'[20] In a classic example of a military blunder the thirty-rung ladders that had been brought up were found to be too short to clear the wall. Those men that tried to climb up were thrown back. The attack ground to a halt against the fort's steep earth walls. There would surely have been some feeling of urgency in the situation as more Parliament troops were waiting to move-up in support of the attacking infantry: pioneers, whose task was to clear the earthworks of any obstacles; a team of gunners from the Parliamentary artillery also accompanied each attacking column, and when the first Royalist guns were seized they were to be turned about and used against the defenders in support of the assault. With the attack at a standstill the only way that Rainsborough's men could reach the enemy was by firing their muskets through the fort's embrasures and loop holes. All this was being done under continual volleys from the fort's cannon: 'The enemy had four pieces of cannon … which they plied with round and case shot upon our men,' Cromwell reported.[21]

While one part of Harley's regiment was attacking Prior's Hill, the other had been employed in creating diversions at Fort Royal and along the north wall. They were joined by the naval detachment, the dragoon regiment and elements of Rainsborough's horse – a motley assortment of whatever remaining troops Fairfax could pull together. Sprigg relates that once this diversion had been played out, and the main attack to the east was under way, Pride's men proceeded to take 'a little fort of Welchmen'.[22] Nichols and Taylor (1882) identify this as a redoubt on the north line of defences, in the Bristol area of Kingsdown Parade.[23] From here, Pride's men pushed on and were able to put themselves in a position to attack Prior's Hill Fort from the city side. Here they were joined by men of Hammond's brigade who had managed to break into the lines by blowing open one of the city gates. Although the main attack on the fort was faltering, Pride's men had successfully breached the weaker, north line, and had shown considerable daring and initiative by developing what had initially been a diversionary attack into a full assault.

At Prior's Hill time was beginning to run out for the attackers – if they failed to take the fort by sunrise then they would be in full view of the heavy Royalist guns at Fort Royal and Bristol Castle. Some of the attackers may have managed to get up on top of the walls by lashing two ladders together.[24] Others attempted to clamber into the fort through the embrasures. There was no such presence of mind elsewhere during the Parliamentarian assault: Walden's brigade, attacking the south walls, faced a similar problem with short ladders against high ramparts. The attack here failed completely and Walden's brigade suffered heavy casualties before withdrawing.

After more than two hours of being pinned down in front of the fort, Prior's Hill was breached by the troops who were attacking from the city side: 'Colonel

Hammond being entered the line … they did storm the Fort on that part which was inward'.[26] Pride's men were also among those who breached the defences forced the Royalist defenders back into the 'inner rooms' of the sconce, the wooden buildings and structures at the centre of the earthwork used for housing ammunition and providing shelter for the garrison and livestock. Captain Hender was wounded; Captain Lagoe was distinguished as 'being the first man that laid hold of the [Royalist] colours'.[26] What followed was grim:

> in the end we forced the enemy within to run below into the inner rooms of their work, hoping to receive quarter; but our soldiers were so little prepared for to show mercy, by the opposition that they had met withal in the storm, and the refusal of quarter when it was offered, that they put to the sword the commander, (one Major Price, a Welshman) and almost all the officers, soldiers and others in the foot, except very few.

The slaughter was justified according to the rules of war as they then stood. An enemy that persisted in holding an untenable position after terms had been offered was deemed to have caused unnecessary bloodshed to the eventual victors, which was considered tantamount to murder. The royalist prisoners were consequently treated as murderers and suffered a death sentence, 'in regard of the great slaughter they within made by their gallant defence'.[27]

The colours laid hold of by Captain Lagoe could may have been those of Colonel Taylor's Bristol regiment, whose standards are recorded as being white fields with red hearts and bearing the motto *Pro Deo et Rege*.[28] In later years Waldive Lagoe, by then elevated to the status of gentleman, would stamp his letters with the seal of a love heart, with flames 'issuant' in the manner of a heraldic grenade or fire bomb, perhaps in commemoration of the colour he claimed in the early hours of that September morning in 1645.[29] Colonel Taylor himself was mortally wounded in the fighting that followed the breach of the northern defences by Pride's soldiers.

Cromwell acknowledged that the taking of Prior's Hill Fort was 'the hardest task of all … without which all the rest of the line to the Froome river would have done us little good.'[30] Yet in his report of the action to the Commons' Speaker Cromwell never mentions Pride, referring only to the full colonels whose troops were involved: 'Colonel Rainsborough's and Colonel Hammond's men entered the Fort, and immediately put almost all the men in it to the sword.'[31] But it was unusual for Cromwell to refer to any officer below the rank of colonel in his reports, unless they were casualties or their actions deserved special mention. By the time *Anglia Rediviva* was published in 1647 Pride was full colonel, which is probably why his name is more prominent in Sprigg's account. Even so, Pride's role in Fairfax's army at this date seems to have been a subordinate one. Both at Naseby, and at Bridgwater, his under-strength command had been placed in the reserve. At Bristol it was still in a supporting role and was divided, as had been the case at Naseby. No other New Model Army regiment appears to have been divided in this way, and it may be indicative of Parliament's reluctance to place a full-strength regiment at the disposal of a man who had never been their choice for a New Model officer. All evidence shows Pride playing a lesser role in the fighting of 1645. He would only be granted a more prominent role as the campaign lengthened and his superiors' faith in him grew.

Berkeley Castle, 23 September 1645

The fall of Bridgwater and Bristol broke the back of the Royalist war effort in the south west. The only substantial Royalist stronghold remaining in Gloucestershire was at Berkeley Castle, whose garrison threatened safe passage between Bristol and Gloucester. Five days after the storming of Bristol, Colonel Rainsborough was dispatched with a brigade of foot (Skippon's and Harley's foot from the New Model, together with Colonel Herbert's regiment of Somerset militia) to reduce it. On 23 September the outer defences were stormed with an efficiency that was becoming a trademark of Fairfax's foot. The castle defenders were thoroughly demoralised by the swiftness of the attack. Rather than suffer artillery fire and further assault, the Royalist governor surrendered. Among the Parliamentarian wounded was one of Pride's captains, George Gregson, though his injury seems to have been minor enough to allow him to continue in service.[32]

Within a month of securing Bristol the Royalist garrisons in Gloucestershire and Somerset had been reduced. Fairfax now prepared to march further into the south-west, to reduce the last Royalist stronghold at Exeter, before moving on to relieve the besieged Parliamentarian town of Plymouth. 600 new recruits were made available to bring Harley's Regiment up top strength, with Pride ordered to travel to Reading at the beginning of October to collect them.[33]

By the end of October, Harley's Regiment had reached the Exeter area. Here, six months into the campaign, Fairfax chose to halt and rest his men. For the first time in his military career Pride would not find himself forced to retire into winter quarters. The Parliamentarians' command of the surrounding country meant that it was now possible for them to remain in the field, and they prepared to winter in surrounding towns and villages in order to keep up pressure on the beleaguered Exeter Royalists. It was a small aspect of the campaign, but it was an indication that the tide of war had turned.

Dartmouth, 19 January 1646

With Exeter securely bottled-up, Fairfax was able to work his way down the coast to relieve Plymouth. Dartmouth was the next stage of this advance. Intelligence had been received that French troops were due to land here to supplement the three foot regiments of French mercenaries that were already had fighting for the Cornish Royalists. Having received a new issue of shoes and stockings,[34] Pride's men crossed the River Exe on 8 January.

The bulk of Fairfax's force halted at Totnes, commanding the road back to Exeter. Four regiments of foot continued the march south to Dartmouth: Lambert's (formerly Montague's) and Hammond's quartering at Stoke Flemming to cover the south-western approaches; Harley's and Fortescue's at Dittisham to the north. Because the heavy guns of the Parliamentarian siege train were unable to negotiate the snowbound roads, and as winter weather was too severe for soldiers to remain in trenches for any length of time, it would again necessary for Pride and his soldiers to seize their objective by direct assault.

Pickets were set up along main roads half a mile from the town. Here, Pride's men were forced to wait at their posts for three days and nights in bitter weather while Fairfax awaited the arrival of Parliament ships to blockade Dartmouth harbour and prevent a Royalist evacuation by sea. Preparations for the assault followed the usual meticulous New Model design: lots were drawn for which units were to lead the attack that night; morning and afternoon were given over to prayer; locals were pressed for information regarding the town's defences, and each attacking regiment was appointed a civilian guide; two hundred sailors from the Parliamentarian squadron offshore supported the attack; ladders for scaling the town walls were collected from nearby farms.

Pride's troops took up their positions on the Sunday evening with the assault to begin at eleven that night. Fairfax's usual time of attack (two in the morning at both Bridgwater and Bristol) was brought forward to take advantage of some milder weather. As was customary, a field sign was to be used to help distinguish friend from foe in the dark. This was usually a scrap of visible, white cloth, worn in the hat or about the body. Accordingly, Pride's men went into the attack with their shirt-tails hanging out of their trousers.[35]

Raised earthworks and a series of small forts around the town's perimeter formed Dartmouth's defence, with the River Dart forming a barrier along the town's eastern side. The Royalists had two small men-of-war anchored on the river, whose guns could be brought to bear on either bank. Pride launched his attack against the northern side of the town, which was defended by the largest of the forts, Mount Boon. The Royalists guns here had been loaded in advance, but Pride's men had the advantage of darkness and came on at a rush. The Royalist guns were able to fire only one salvo before the attackers reached them, Pride's men getting underneath the guns on the earthworks and out of harm's way. The defences were swiftly scaled by ladder, the gunners overwhelmed and their guns immediately turned about and directed against the town. Twenty-two guns of various calibre were captured at Mount Boon, by far the largest haul from any of the Dartmouth forts.

With their first objective taken, the men then pressed on into the town itself. In his subsequent report to Parliament, Fairfax wrote:

> lieutenant colonel Pride attempted the north part of the town, called Harness; where beating off the enemy, he entered and took about eighty

prisoners in it, and possessing all the north part of the town unto the drawbridge, which divided the north part from the rest of the town, where colonel Hammond's and his met.[36]

Dartmouth appears to have marked a significant development in Pride's military career: from commanding a divided and under-strength force the previous year he was now, nine months into the campaign, given the opportunity to lead an attack and earned the general's thanks for his success.

At Dartmouth, Hammond and Pride were continuing the association they had begun when brigaded together in the major battles of Naseby and Bristol. Hammond had attacked through the west gate and had control of the west of the town, Pride's capture of the northern half of Dartmouth brought a temporary halt to the action. The stronger of the Dartmouth forts – Kingsware on the east side of the Dart, Gallant's Bower below the stone walls of the medieval castle, and the castle itself – were not attempted. Once the town had been secured it seems that the Parliamentarians were able to move without hindrance between these fixed positions, content to wait for the isolated forts to surrender. This they did when their hapless situation became clear at first light.

Great Torrington, 16 February 1646

The encirclement of Exeter spurred what remained of the Royalist's western army into action. Ralph Hopton, the Royalist commander in the west, began to concentrate his forces in north Devon and occupied Great Torrington. By nightfall on the 16 February the outer defences of the town were being scouted by Fairfax's dragoons.

Although the foot had by now gained good experience of night assault, Fairfax was anxious not to press home an attack on unfamiliar ground, preferring to wait until he had viewed the town's defences by daylight. However, the Parliamentarian scouts were spotted, and the subsequent skirmish between the dragoons and the town's defenders became a full-scale engagement when Fairfax brought up his reserve brigade: his own, Hammond's and Harley's Regiments. 'The service was very hot,' Fairfax wrote, 'we had many wounded, it was stoutly maintained on both sides for a time.'[37] Repeated pushes eventually cleared the earth barricades to allow the horse to enter and gain the town. Royalist resistance crumbled after their magazine housed in the parish church exploded, taking the church with it. Confusion followed. Hopton fell back through the town and across the River Torridge with little hindrance: Fairfax was reluctant to pursue an enemy across unreconnoitred ground, especially on a night when the new moon meant that his troops would be moving forward with reduced visibility.

Hopton continued to retreat westwards; Fairfax followed him into Cornwall. On 2 March the Parliamentarians had reached Bodmin, eighteen months since Pride had first been there with Essex's army. Hopton retreated ever further west, finally surrendering his forces to Fairfax at Truro on 10 March. Harley's regiment returned to the siege of Exeter, quartered in the village of Silverton.[38] Exeter, now with no hope of relief, surrendered on 13 April. At this point, Colonel Edward Harley himself finally made an appearance in the campaign, negotiating the terms of the city's surrender as a parliamentary commissioner. He was present again in mid-June when Fairfax received the surrender of Oxford.

Most narrative histories end their account of the first Civil War here, with the final defeat of Charles I's western army and the capitulation of the Royalist capital. For Pride and his men, though, the fighting was to continue. Worcester still held out for the Royalist cause and local Parliamentarian forces had thus far failed to make much of an impression on it. Three foot regiments (those of Rainsborough, Hammond, and Harley – brigaded again as they had been at Naseby) were detached from Oxford and sent north to help invest the beleaguered city. Their arrival coincided with the breakdown of a two-day ceasefire, whereupon the New Model's foot lost no time in preparing positions and 'raised works within Pistoll shot of their royal Sconce and the City, the Enemy playing upon them with Case-shot out of Sakers all the time, wherein Lieutenant Colonell *Pride*, and Lieut. Colonell Ewers had a chiefe share.'[39] Again, Pride appears to have been in command of the regiment and Harley absent. Harley was not the only officer whose interests now lay in carving out a political career, but there was an increasing divergence between his own preoccupations and those of the men under his command.

Once Pride had arrived at Worcester there followed three weeks of protracted negotiation and sporadic cannon fire, during which Rainsborough attempted to convince Worcester's Royalist committee that the longer they held out, the less favourable would be the terms of surrender. The last city in Royalist hands finally surrendered on the 23 July.

The actions in which Thomas Pride fought during 1645 and 1646 were not those usually associated with the Civil War period. There were few set-piece battles, with colourful lines of pike and musket and the flamboyant charges of Rupert's horse. What this chapter has shown is that the fighting following Naseby was severe and physically demanding, fought in trenches, over ramparts and across barricades. Pride's experiences in the latter stages of the war were a series of street battles and close-quarter attacks, most of which were carried out under cover of darkness. Contrary to a romantic world of Roundhead and Cavaliers, Pride's war gives us a taste of a very real conflict – swift, harsh and bloody. Gentles (1997) calculates that 17 per cent of New Model Army officers were killed or died in this period of service, between 1645 and the Second Civil War of 1648.[40] It is a figure that is brought into sharp perspective when we consider that 17 per cent was also the casualty rate sustained by the officer corps of the British Army in France between 1914 and 1918.[41] In comparative terms, the fighting that Thomas Pride endured was as severe as that of the Western Front in the First World War.

This overview of the 1645/46 campaign has shown the advance of Fairfax's army to have been seemingly inexorable: every Royalist garrison and stronghold that tried to resist went down in a rapid series of sieges and storms, undertaken with a cool efficiency. The officers and men of Harley's Regiment estimated they had fought an astonishing 114 individual actions in 1645, all of which they claimed as victories.[42] It is little wonder that those veterans, looking back on the conflict in 1660, viewed their successes as acts of God and counted 'his many single providences little less than miracles'.[43] Even as the return of the Monarchy threatened retribution they made no attempt to deny or downplay their part in the war: 'we dipt our hand in blood for that cause, and the blood of many thousands hath been shed by our immediate hands'.[44] The determination with which Pride pursued Parliament's fight against the Crown cannot be stressed enough: before the formation of the New Model he had survived two years of fighting under Essex – wearying and ignominious – without ever seeing a decisive victory. After 1645 he was never to see a defeat.

8

Army Mutiny, 1647

Pride versus Parliament

By the end of 1646 London politics was dominated by Presbyterianism through an alliance of conservative-minded men in the City and at Westminster. Their desire to achieve a lasting political settlement with the defeated Charles I was, they believed, being undermined by the rise in religious Independency, bolstered by a ground swell of support from within the ranks of Parliament's army. Underdown (1971) argues that to view the divisions among the victorious Parliamentarians as a two-way split into mutually exclusive Presbyterian and Independent parties is simplistic; that it was quite possible for a religious Independent to be politically conservative or for a Presbyterian to be politically radical.[1] Though simplistic, such a two-way division is nevertheless convenient when describing the events of 1647, and will be sufficient for our purpose here.

In the Commons, the Presbyterians held a three-fifths majority over the Independents. Local elections of December 1646 returned an even greater Presbyterian majority to the London Common Council,[2] and Presbyterianism was able to flex its political muscle in the capital. In February 1647 the Commons voted that anyone who refused to take the Presbyterian covenant would be barred both from public office and from holding military command.[3] This decision was to have repercussions for the Independent Pride, who consequently faced being forced from his command. After three and a half years of hard fighting to uphold Parliamentary privilege, Pride was now to be ousted – defeated not in the field, but by his political masters at Westminster.

The Presbyterians considered disbanding the army as beneficial in two ways: it would save the cost of maintaining a standing force; it would also rid them of the troublesome minority of religious Independents whom they saw as trying to influence the peace settlement. Disbanding much of the present New Model would diffuse Independent support and deny religious radicalism a political voice.

Accordingly, in early 1647, the Presbyterian group in Parliament voted that the New Model Army regiments were to be broken up. The army was to be halved and religious heterodoxy stamped out by forcing all army officers to take the covenant.[4]

A new army, commanded by carefully chosen Presbyterian officers, would then be formed for service in Ireland and subdue the revolt against English rule there. As Parliament and the army became increasingly estranged, the latter's radical voice would strengthen as it moved to oppose these proposed changes. What was Thomas Pride's role in the radicalism that surfaced in the army at this time?

Pride seems to have seen very little of his colonel in the campaign of 1645 and 46. Edward Harley seems to have made an appearance with Fairfax's army only in the first half of 1646, in negotiating the surrender of the Royalist strongholds of Exeter and Oxford.[5] He had, however, been very active before this in his native Herefordshire (despite the wounds that had prevented him from taking the field at Naseby). In August 1645 he had been made governor of Cannon Frome, and appointed general of horse for the counties of Radnor and Hereford not long after.[6] In September 1646 he was returned as Parliamentary member for Herefordshire, following an electoral campaign in which he spent over £400 on 3,400 invitations to dinners and suppers in order to woo potential voters.[7] By spring 1647, Harley was prominent among the Presbyterians in the Commons and, as with any other member of a political majority, he had a vested interest in the status quo. He felt compelled to defend political and religious conservatism in the face of the rising strength of the army's Independent sects. Harley appears to have been more focused on building his political career, and strengthening his family's influence in his native county, than he was with the concerns of his soldiers.

On 21 March 1647 a party of parliamentary commissioners, including Harley, arrived at army headquarters in Saffron Walden to propose disbanding and to call for volunteers for the Irish expedition. They were met by a disgruntled council of officers that included Pride, William Cowell and Waldive Lagoe. Captain Goffe attended the meeting the following day. They and the other officers assembled presented the commissioners with a list of conditions, only after the implementation of which disbandment and Irish service would be possible. The catalogue of grievances was subscribed by every company commander in Harley's regiment, with the exception of its colonel.[8] There was little sympathy among the Presbyterians in Parliament for any of the soldiers' demands. Harley himself had volunteered for service in Ireland and was anxious to obtain a command in the new army to further his credentials.

On 30 March, Sir Thomas Fairfax received a letter from the Speaker of the Commons informing him that there was mutiny among his troops. The Speaker identified a ring-leader who was collecting signatures for a petition demanding that the soldiers' grievances be met: 'Lieutenant Colonel Pride, Lieutenant Colonel to Colonel Harley, drew his Regiment to a Rendezvous, and that the Petition was read at the Head of them, and signed by above Eleven Hundred of them'.[9] Army officers were drawing on the support of the rank and file to add weight to the army's demands, not just from Harley's Regiment but (as suggested by the figure of over eleven hundred names) from other regiments also. There was some suggestion in the Speaker's letter that soldiers were coerced to obtain support for the petition, and that Pride had declared 'all those Officers and Soldiers that refuse shall be cashiered the Army',[10] but when Fairfax summoned Pride and other officers to his headquarters to call them to account, they were very contrite. 'They did generally express a very deep sense of their unhappiness in being misunderstood in their clear intentions,' Fairfax wrote, insisting that his officers had only meant 'by way of petition to represent unto me those inconveniences which would necessarily befal most of the army after disbanding'.[11] By claiming to have been collecting a list of names to present to Fairfax, Pride and his fellow officers were intimating that their actions were within the army's chain of command, and therefore not to be deemed mutinous. Whether their regret was genuine is difficult to judge. Fairfax supported his officers as far as he felt able to do so, but he felt unable to refuse an order from the Commons that the officers involved should appear before the House to answer for their conduct.

A summary of the demands listed in the petition that Pride appears to have instigated was passed from the Commons to the Lords on 30 March,[12] and Parliament then had a fuller sense of the army's grievances. The soldiers were calling for the right to receive full pay until the question of disbandment was settled, and that the men should receive all arrears owing to them; also that no man should be forced to serve in Ireland against his will; most importantly (and this headed the list) they called for 'an Act of Indemnity passed by the Houses, for any Acts done by them in the Prosecution of this War'.[13] So important to the soldiers was this immunity from prosecution that they even advocated negotiation with Charles I to secure it and that 'the Royal assent be procured thereunto'.[14]

Parliament condemned outright what they described as this 'dangerous Petition … [to] obstruct the reliefe of *Ireland*', with the prominent Presbyterian Denzil Holles declaring its authors enemies of the state.[15] There was little sympathy from high-ranking officers either. Although Fairfax had gone some way to protect Pride and others involved in the petition, Cromwell (who, as an MP, was as committed to the authority of the Parliament as Holles) felt that the soldiers had gone too far in voicing their opinions.[16] For fear that the disquiet stirred by Pride's petition would spread, military units that had already been selected for Ireland were ordered to be separated from those marked for disbandment.[17]

Pride and the other officers involved in the mutiny duly appeared before the bar of the House of Commons on the 1 April. Pride was the first to be summoned into the chamber, which is further evidence that he was considered to be the driving force behind the petition: 'Lieutenant Colonel Pryde [sic] was called in; and Mr. Speaker acquainted him with the peculiar informations this House had received, concerning his promoting a Petition in the Army'.[18] He was charged 'to have read the petition at the head of a regiment', and that he had made 'threats to those that should not subscribe it'.[19] All of this Pride denied:

> [Pride] answered in the Negative to all these particular Informations…
> there was no Petition, either by himself, or by his Appointment, read at

the head of the said Colonel Harley's Regiment, and that there was no
menacing or threatning [sic] words used, and denied the whole Charge[20]

It was a quite different response to that which Fairfax claimed was given to him
at his quarters two days previously. All the officers replied to the charge in the
same way, each denying categorically that any gathering of troops or collecting
of signatures had ever taken place. Pride was clearly lying, of course: Fairfax had
already written to the Speaker, informing him of the officers' remorse for having
drawn up the petition. Nevertheless, the army's Presbyterian opponents could do
nothing without evidence and 'not being able to prove anything, nor the informer
known' they had no option than to dismiss the officers, cautioning them to return
to their respective units and 'keep all Things in the Army quiet.'[21] This amazed
some commentators, who responded to the news of the officers' dismissal without
charge 'not without some wonder, having been so hot in it.'[22]

The unknown informant referred to above was in fact a soldier of Harley's own
regiment. He had written to his colonel on 27 March, telling him of the petition
and convinced that the ringleaders 'do intend to inslave the Kingdom for all that I
can hear by them'.[23] It had been Harley himself who had informed the Commons
of the situation, a move that marked him out as an opponent of his own officers.
Parliament's failure to make an example of his lieutenant colonel must have further
weakened Harley's position in his regiment. Within a few weeks of Pride's appearance before the Commons, Harley's men made their own feelings clear in an open
letter addressed to 'our much honoured commanders Lieut. Coll. Pride, Major
Cowell and the rest of the captaines and commission officers of Collonell Harly
[sic] his regiment', with the hope that the letter would be forwarded to parliamentary commissioners.[24] The content of the letter reiterated the requests for pay
and conditions of service of the March petition, added to which were statements
of support for Pride and the other officers who had done what they could to assist
the men and uphold their grievances. The soldiers deplored the treatment Pride
had received from Parliament: 'our officers are accused and otherwise greivously
molested for noe other cause as we perceive but for appearing and speaking for
us.'[25] They maintained that the officers' actions were not intended to cause a breech
between the army and Westminster, and they were alarmed that their petition had
been not only misunderstood by the Commons but deliberately made out to be an
act of mutiny, 'maliciously endeavoured to breed a misunderstanding betweene
the Parliament and the army'.[26] Moreover, the rank and file believed they knew
exactly who the culprit was: 'one of those incendieries hath soe neere relation to us,
that wee should rather have expected that he should have spoken on our behalfe
then presented false informations against us'.[27] It was a clear indictment of Harley
himself, and it reveals the extent to which he had lost the confidence and support
of the men who served under him.

That Pride maintained close involvement with the petition and its repercussions
is clear. The points set forth in the March petition would soon evolve into the

Vindication of the Officers of the Army, a more public and cohesive statement of the army's grievances that, by May, was in public circulation and which was signed by all of Harley's company commanders. Pride was among the officers who presented the '*Vindication*' to the Commons on the 27 April.[28] But the feeling of mistrust between the army and Parliament was to deepen.

By the end of April the Commons' Presbyterian majority were able to declare that 'some officers of two companies' of Harley's foot and a 'considerable part'[29] of his and other regiments had volunteered for service in Ireland. A handful of officers from only two companies was a modest claim, but the Commons insisted that more than half the total number of troops needed for the Irish expedition had been mobilised, and that the regular force could now be reduced accordingly. None of the army's conditions for disbanding had been addressed.

Most of the New Model regiments were at this time quartered in the old Eastern Association, in a twenty-five mile radius of Cambridge. Harley's Regiment was ordered to disband at Cambridge on 8 June.[30] Only two officers of the regiment, Captain Ferguson and Lieutenant Crocker, were prepared to serve in Ireland (though Ferguson does not appear as a captain in the petitions published that year, and seems to have already left the regiment).[31] The other ranks were ordered to Stanton, thirty miles away in Suffolk, to separate them from any mutinous troops by whom they might be influenced.[32] The order was ignored.

In early June the army published the *Solemn Engagement of the Army*, announcing their intention not to disband until grievances had been met. It then made two moves to strengthen their cause against the Presbyterians at Westminster: firstly, Charles I was removed from confinement at Holdenby House to ensure he would not be pressured into making conciliatory terms with the army's political opponents. Secondly, the army identified eleven leading Presbyterians in the House of Commons whom they accused of plotting to restore Charles I to power and called for their suspension from the House. In mid-June, Pride was prominent among the officers who were present in London to discuss the complexities of impeaching the eleven members. Among the eleven was Pride's commanding officer, Edward Harley. According to *King-Killers* (1719), the officers cautiously discussed the matter at length, 'having had some Conference in *Westminster-hall* with the Speaker, keeping the Doors shut', and it was Pride who was subsequently selected from this group of officers to present the impeachment charge to the Commons on the army's behalf.[33] In 1642, Charles I had attempted to remove obstructive members of the Commons by force. Now the army officers took care to work within the guidelines of Parliamentary privilege.

The Independent members of the Commons felt as threatened by the dominance of the Presbyterians as their fellow Independents in the New Model. Accordingly, an alliance developed between those MPs and the army, with a small group of senior Independent officers (including Cromwell and Ireton) acting as go-betweens. The prominence of Pride at this time, in his involvement with the Army Petition and Harley's impeachment, reveals his place in this

Independent alliance: Cromwell and Ireton were the bridge between Parliament and the army; Pride was a bridge between those Independent officers and the army's rank and file. Further evidence of his role is that on 18 July, Pride was appointed one of six officers to attend Fairfax at his headquarters in Saffron Walden daily to 'advise upon all emergencys and affairs of the army'.[34] He was clearly someone Fairfax would find useful as a gauge of the army's moods, and he was also a link to the impeachment proceedings at Westminster. Pride's position in the army had also been strengthened when, on 5 July, he received promotion to full colonel of the regiment. Charges of impeachment against Harley were delivered to the Commons the following day, after which Harley voluntarily absented himself from the House.[35] Pride's promotion, then, had slightly pre-empted Harley's impeachment.

Pride's new appointment can be read in different ways. On the one hand it suggests he was a reliable spokesman to the senior officer 'grandees' for the disaffected men under his command – an arbiter for the radical camp. On the other, it implies a degree of trust in Pride on the part of senior officers: even if the promotion was a seen as a way of mollifying Pride, he must a man on whom they saw as being able to keep the radicals in his ranks in check. Pride's fellow Independent, Goffe, who had been serving as major from early April, became the regiment's new lieutenant colonel.[36] Harley was simply removed from his regiment, which was now commanded not by a member of the gentry but by London tradesmen.

Following Parliament's acquiescence to the demand to impeach the eleven members, the army further insisted that the London Trained Bands be remodelled and that prominent Presbyterians removed from the Militia Committee. To this end Parliament implemented the Militia Bill on 23 July, which reinstated political Independents to commands within the London militia.[37] Fearing an Independent take-over, members of the London Common Council and Trained Bands officers formed the core of a mob of citizens that converged on the Parliament on 26 July, demanding that the bill be revoked. The mob forced its way to the door of the Commons chamber: 'the House… could not be divided, according to the ordinary and constant Practice of the House in like Cases, by reason of the Multitude and Tumult that was at the Door, that would by no Persuasions withdraw that the outer Room might be cleared.'[38] This deliberate obstruction of Parliamentary procedure, and threat of violence, forced Parliament's hand. The Speakers of both Houses fled London, along with sixty MPs, and sought the protection of the army. Meanwhile, the Commons, now devoid of Independent members, granted the militia the authority to seize all the horses in London: a military force to rival the New Model was beginning to form.[39] Harley and the other impeached members were allowed to retake their seats in the House; there were reports of clashes between the militia and the New Model horse on the approaches to London.

On 29 July Fairfax wrote to the Lord Mayor, informing the City of his (or his army's) disgust at the 'unparalleled Violation acted upon the Parliament'.[40] In a similar letter addressed to the Lords he declared his decision to secure and defend Parliament 'in the Interest of this Nation'.[41] To this end the army marched on London, prepared to forcibly purge the Commons of hostile Presbyterians if necessary. On 4 August a brigade of three foot regiments (including Pride's) and one of horse moved out from their encampment on Hounslow Heath, swept southwards around the city outskirts and entered London through Southwark. South of the river and beyond the City limits, Southwark had long been an area associated with Independency. The army marched through the streets 'without any Opposition, the Soldiers carrying themselves very civilly without doing hurt to any'.[42] However, the gates at the southern end of London Bridge were closed to them: 'finding the City Gate on the Bridge shut, and the Port-cullis let down, as also a Guard within, they planted Two Pieces of Ordnance against the Gate and set a Guard without'.[43] The threat persuaded the London authorities to allow the army to enter.

The confrontation between the Independent-led New Model and the Presbyterian-dominated City never materialised. This was partly due to loss of nerve on the Presbyterian's part, but also due to the moderate nature of the demands now unveiled by the army in *The Heads of Proposals*, which argued for a constitutional monarchy with a strong executive. The army proposed restoring Charles I to power, but with a guarantee of biennial parliaments and securing Parliament's control of the armed forces. Religious toleration was to be upheld by removing power from the bishops and repealing the 1559 Act of Uniformity that compelled people to worship according to the Book of Common Prayer. In addition, an Act of Oblivion would pardon any Parliamentarian's involvement in the war against the monarch.[44] Having been saved from the clutches of the Presbyterian mob, Parliament now began to look more sympathetically towards the army and its proposed political settlement. It accordingly appointed Fairfax Constable of the Tower, strengthening the army's position in the capital.

Fairfax formally took command of the Tower on 9 August, accompanied by his own lifeguard and 'a party of Colonel *Pride's* Regiment of Foot'.[45] On entering the Tower, Fairfax requested to view the copy of Magna Carta that was kept there. When the document had been duly brought before him, Fairfax announced to those assembled that 'this is what we all fight for',[46] a common assertion among those who had fought for Parliament from the beginning of the Civil War. Fairfax exposed a defence of common rights that was more acceptable and popular than that of the political spokesman John Lilburne – who was at that very moment elsewhere in the Tower under lock and key. Lilburne's release, which had been anticipated following the army's arrival in London, never materialised. Fairfax's presence at the Tower at the time of Lilburne's incarceration is an interesting snapshot that reveals how the army's commanders stood in regard to the political radicals.

By the summer of 1647 it seems that Pride matters other than politics to occupy him. His breweries had remained in production during his service with the army, and the result was that he now faced a heavy tax bill. Excise on beer and luxury goods had been introduced in 1643 to pay for Parliament's war effort. It had been a thoroughly unpopular move, in fact such a tax had been expressly denounced by Parliament in its Grand Remonstrance of 1641. Beer was, so the brewers argued, 'the cheapest food, and chiefest nourishment'[47] of the poor and ought to be exempt from tax. Beer was considered a fundamental as bread and the introduction of excise in 1643 had led to riots in London. But now that the war was over, surely there was no need for its continuation? That certainly seems to have been Pride's way of thinking. A petition signed by seventy-six brewers, including Pride, was presented to the House of Lords on the 7 August 1647. It called for the elimination of excise on beer and ale on the grounds that the price of malt had risen to such an extent that brewers faced 'utter ruin'.[48] It may be more than a coincidence that the brewers were prompted to protest against this hated legislation just three days after Pride had arrived in the capital with the army. When we remember that Pride had only recently been demanding that the New Model's soldiers be paid its arrears, this action seems to have placed him in a contrary position: on the one hand he was calling for soldiers to be paid the money owing to them, and on the other he was demanding the abolition of a tax levied to pay for the army. Perhaps Pride had convinced himself that Parliament could afford both, but such a contradictory position would later be viewed as hypocrisy by both his Royalist and his Presbyterian detractors.

The question ought to be asked, who had been running Pride's business affairs while he was on campaign? The obvious answer is his wife, Elizabeth, who would continue to manage the family estates after her husband's death in 1658. His eldest son, Thomas, also appears to have been suitably trained in running a busy brewery as it was to him that Pride would bequeath him the family business in his will.

Although Pride had armed himself with a list of demands during 1647 it is difficult to view him as a politically active man. He attended the Army Council of 16 July but there is no record of his having spoken there. There is no evidence that he attended the later Putney Debates (though his Lieutenant Colonel, Goffe, was conspicuous), nor does his regiment appear to have subscribed to the Leveller constitution, 'An Agreement of the People', in October of that year. A self-made businessman, Pride was certainly not a Leveller. Of thirteen Army Councils held between November 1648 and March 1649, he attended only four. Compare this with a more politicised officer, such as Ireton, who attended eleven, and this was during the time of the Purge, when Pride was arguably at his most prominent.[49] The fact that once he gained his colonelcy he all but disappears from sight as far as army radicalism is concerned leaves Pride open to accusations that he was acting in his own self-interest.

Pride seems to have been driven by a hostility towards the Presbyterians, who were clearly determined to break the army in order to strengthen their hold on the Commons. At the root of Pride's opposition was his religion. In August the previous year, less than one month after the Harley's regiment had been fighting at Worcester, Pride, Goffe and other Independents had presented a petition to the

Commons calling for increased toleration for religious separatism. It attracted the opprobrium of one Church of England divine who decried the petition as 'schismatic' and 'diabolical'. He had labelled Pride 'the Devil's own secretary' and later cited his petition for toleration as the root cause for the publication in England in 1649 of what the Anglican minister termed a volume of 'all the most gross, absurd, ridiculous blasphemies': the first translation into English of the Koran.[50]

Religious toleration was a cause that Pride would champion time and again. A Presbyterian-led government, and the importance it invested in the need for a national church, meant danger for Pride's Independent faith. Thus Pride's political agenda (as far as it existed at all) was a personal one, but it was by no means selfish. The concerns of the petition he championed were his own, but also extended to the welfare of the men under his command. Other higher-ranking, Independent officers did not support their soldiers in this way until it was clear they would not back down, Cromwell for one believing that the army agitators ought to have relied solely on an elected Parliament to implement change.[51] Pride, however, went further than the army 'grandees' in promoting the causes of his men.

9

The Second Civil War, 1648
Pembroke, Preston, Berwick

In March 1648 the Parliamentarian governor of Pembroke Castle mutinied, refusing to hand over his command to a relief force until his soldiers had received their pay. Within a month this mutiny had swelled into a regional uprising, as disaffected Parliamentarians sided with local Royalist gentry and declared for Charles I. On 30 April Cromwell marched from London with a brigade to put down the revolt. He had under his command two regiments of horse and three of foot: those of Ewer and Overton (formerly Hammond's and Ingoldsby's, respectively), together with that of Pride.

By 10 May Cromwell was at Monmouth. Local Parliamentarian forces had already dispersed the rebels' army at St. Fagan's and Cromwell's campaign in South Wales became a mopping-up operation, concentrating on reducing the strongholds that still held out for the Royalist cause. Pride accompanied Cromwell to Royalist-held Chepstow, where they arrived on 11 May. Cromwell immediately ordered Pride's regiment forward to rush the town's defences. The assault was reported as swift and vicious: 'colonel Pride's men fell on so furiously that they gained the town, and beat the soldiers into the castle'.[1] 'Desperate' was how Cromwell described the attack, and his account suggests a heated and audacious assault against solid defences: 'the Walls well lined with Musquetiers; but the soldiers of Colonel Pride's Regiment went on so desperately, that presently the Gate was taken, and so the town and a great number of prisoners.' A substantial and well-provisioned Royalist garrison still held the castle, however, and Cromwell chose to abandon surrender negotiations when one of his drummers, delivering terms to the enemy, was fired upon.[2]

The determination of Pride's attack on Chepstow's gate may have impressed Cromwell because Pride's men were chosen the following night to lead an assault on the castle. But the night was dark, and in heavy rain the attack faltered and was beaten back: 'Major Gregson,' reported Cromwell, 'by a stone received a dangerous wound in the head, and four or five more Common Soldiers were also hurt.' Gregson later died of his injury.[3] No further attempt was made to take Chepstow castle by force, Cromwell was content to contain the besieged Royalists with Ewer's foot while he marched with his main force along the Welsh coast towards the next Royalist stronghold.

Pembroke Castle, May-July 1648

The bulk of Cromwell's brigade reached Pembroke on 21 May and began to establish positions round it. The town was a difficult position to invest, surrounded on three sides by tidal waters and marsh, and protected by a large medieval castle built on a cliff at its western extremity. Local parliamentarians had already warned London that if the castle were well supplied and prepared for a siege 'it will cost about 1,000 lives to regain it'.[4] Cromwell ordered guns to be taken from the *Lion* man-of-war, anchored in the channel, and established a battery on a hill to the north of the town. Lacking siege guns, there was little the Parliamentarian force could do against the castle's stone walls. So instead, Cromwell attempted to reduce the infrastructure that supported the Royalist garrison, directing his hill-top guns against the castle's water conduit and the town's flour mills. The strategy seems to have had little effect on the garrison, however, and Parliament's troops settled down to a long siege and awaited the arrival of heavy guns from England.

The boredom of the siege work was alleviated to a degree with the help of the nearest large town, Haverfordwest, coincidentally the birthplace of Pride's second-in-command, William Goffe. The mayor's account book lists the expenses laid out by the town corporation for a lavish dinner to welcome home their native son: Lieutenant Colonel Goffe was guest of honour and toasted with 'wyne & beare & Syder' for the cost of £1 6s 6d.[5] Despite his superior rank, Pride was afforded no similar luxury when a few days later the corporation paid out a paltry three shillings for Spanish wine or sack for the colonel's refreshment.[6]

Poor weather and rough seas meant that the ships carrying Parliament's siege guns from Gloucester did not reach Pembroke until 4 July. By this stage the besiegers had made one or two incursions into the town, succeeding on one occasion in driving the defenders back to the castle before a counter-attack had forced them to retire with the loss of thirty men (including two of Pride's junior officers). However, with little prospect of being relieved and under threat of heavy artillery fire from siege guns, the Royalist garrison agreed to terms. On 11 July Pembroke castle surrendered to Parliament,[7] by which time the Royalists had succeeded in tying down Cromwell's brigade in South Wales for over a month.

Preston and Winwick, 17-19 August 1648

At the end of October 1647, Charles I escaped from the army's custody at Hampton Court Palace. Failing to find a suitable ship on the south coast he was quickly recaptured and imprisoned at Newport, out of harm's way on the Isle of Wight. He continued to receive official visits, however, and it was at Newport that he began negotiations with the Scots for help against the English Parliamentarians.

In November Charles signed the Scottish 'Engagement', by which he promised to establish a Presbyterian church in England in return for military aid. A Scottish army of 14,000 under the Duke of Hamilton crossed the border into England on the 8 July 1648. Too late to assist the Royalists in South Wales, they were joined in their march south by 4,000 English Royalists from Cumberland and Westmorland under Marmaduke Langdale.

Following the surrender of Pembroke on 11 July, Cromwell lost no time in marching north. He sent his remaining cavalry ahead to join Lambert's northern army (which had fallen back into Yorkshire before the Scots' advance), with instructions to avoid battle until the rest of his force arrived. Pride's men faced a long march, Cromwell taking take them through Gloucester and Warwickshire to en route to join Lambert. It was a weary and depleted force that reached Warwick Castle on 27 July: 'want of shoes and stockings gives discouragement to our soldiers, having received no pay this month to buy them...' wrote Cromwell.[8] The officers and men of Pride's regiment were now owed £1,400 in arrears[9] and their force was now weakened, Pride having lost a lieutenant and an ensign in the desultory fighting before Pembroke Castle, as well as his major at Chepstow, and certainly more from his rank and file.[10]

Cromwell reached Doncaster on 7 August, where his foot rested for three days while they waited for artillery to reach them from the arsenal at Hull. They finally linked up with Lambert's forces at Wetherby on the 12 August. The combined forces of Lambert and Cromwell numbered fewer than 9,000, but it was as large an army as Parliament was going to muster. Cromwell had no precise indication of where Hamilton was but, as he had not appeared on the east side of the Pennines, it was assumed that he was still marching south through Lancashire. Cromwell decided to strike due west across the Pennines towards Preston, hoping to either to strike Hamilton in the flank or emerge some way to the north of him, able to attack his army in the rear and to cut off its route back to Scotland.

Hamilton's Royalist army outnumbered Cromwell's force by nearly 2:1, but by 16 August they were badly extended on their route through Lancashire, the horse having advanced as far as Wigan and the foot trailing some sixteen miles behind at Preston.

Langdale's English troops were marching at the rear of the Royalist army. On the night of 16 August his patrols reported that there was a sizeable Parliamentarian force nearby. Hamilton himself paid little attention to the reports. He naturally expected Cromwell to be approaching from the south, and believed the troops to his rear to be a small force of local Parliamentarians and of little consequence. It never occurred to Hamilton that Cromwell would have marched nearly three hundred miles in thirty days, then proceed to launch an attack against an enemy nearly twice his size. Hamilton did not recall his horse from Wigan, and the following day he resumed his march south.

Only Langdale seems to have been aware of the threat posed by the approaching Parliamentarians. The morning of the 17 August saw his English rear-guard take up a defensive position across the main road at Longridge Chapel, six miles north east of Preston. Langdale held a strong position: the road into Preston was a sunken lane between fields, easily commanded by musket fire. The fields on either side were boggy enough to impede any movement of troops, and their position was enclosed by hedges that would reduce the effectiveness of Cromwell's horse.

Cromwell's force reached Longridge at mid-morning. Cromwell ordered two foot regiments (Fairfax's and Bright's) to the left of the road and another three (Pride's, Deane's and Read's) to the right. The horse regiments were to attack the centre of Langdale's position on the road, the only firm ground in the vicinity that was suitable for cavalry. Pride had held his colonelcy longer than either Deane and Read, and this would have effectively made him commander of Cromwell's right wing. He extended his line of foot to the right in an attempt to out-flank the Royalist muskets and to avoid the marshy ground in front, but in so doing both his regiment and Deane's 'outwinging the enemy, could not come to so much share of the action'.[11] Langdale's 3,000 men held off Cromwell's 9,000 strong attack for two hours, but they received no support from Hamilton's Scottish foot, only six miles away at Preston. Realising that aid was never going to come, Langdale opted for a fighting retreat into Preston itself. However, once he had pulled back from the cover of the enclosures on his flanks, Cromwell's reserve horse were free to manoeuvre into open ground. In Parliament's resurgent attack, Langdale's force was destroyed entirely and most of his foot killed or captured.

The Parliamentarian forces lost only one officer of note in the fighting at Preston: Lieutenant Colonel William Cowell, who died of wounds suffered while commanding Charles Fairfax's foot. He had been, in Cromwell's judgement, 'an honest and worthy man'.[12] Unlike Pride, whose breweries had remained in production throughout the war, Cowell seems to have abandoned his former trade entirely and dedicated himself to soldiering: 'He spent himself in your and the kingdom's service,' wrote Cromwell. 'He being a great trader in London, deserted it to save the kingdom.'[13] In fact the financial cost of military service seems to have left Cowell almost bankrupt, having 'lent much moneys to the state' for the war effort, and his surviving family was 'but meanly provisioned for' as a consequence.[14] Carlyle (1897) appears to have been the first to draw the conclusion that Cowell 'was mortally wounded at Preston Battle' because Cromwell writes of the officer's loss not long after, and Carlyle infers from this that Cowell's demise was pretty swift. Yet there is evidence to suggest that Cowell died not at Preston but sometime later at York. A memorandum in the Court of Probate records a William Cowell of London having died in York at this time, having made his last will and testament in August 1648.[15] The document names his widow as Mary Cowell, and her name appears again in the Commons Journal in reference to army pensions.[16] Cromwell writes of having met Cowell's widow at Northallerton, as the army made its way northwards towards the Scottish border.[17] It seems that Cowell's wounds were not so severe as to prevent him remaining with the army on its march, and that he succumbed perhaps a week or so after the fighting at Preston. The veteran of

Naseby certainly lived long enough to ask Cromwell that his wife and three young children would receive the money they so badly needed. This was duly done and Cowell's widow was granted his arrears of pay by Parliament the following year.[18] To judge from Cromwell's words, Cowell had been well thought of, and the loss of such a well-known veteran – a soldier since 1642, and commended for his service at Bridgwater – would have been a sore loss to those who had served alongside him.

The pursuit of the retreating Scots continued on the 18 August. Hamilton still had the advantage in numbers but he had lost a good deal of his ammunition once Preston had been taken. With the town now held by Cromwell, Hamilton's route home was blocked, the weather was poor and the Scots' moral was low. Hamilton decided to withdraw through Wigan to Warrington, and from there across the Mersey. His objective was to cross into Wales and link up with Royalist forces there. On 19 August a formation of Scots' foot attempted to halt Cromwell's pursuit near Winwick, two miles north of Warrington, at a place called 'red lane' or Red Bank. As at Longridge, the Royalists took up a solid, defensive position: 'in a narrow lane, they made a stand with a Body of Pikes, and lined the Hedges with Muskets'.[19] Cromwell's horse were the first to meet them:

> We held them in some dispute till our Army came up; they maintaining the pass with great resolution for many hours; our and theirs coming to push of pike and very close charges, and forced us to give ground... [20]

Parliament's horse, in fact, were unable to make any headway until Pride's foot arrived on the scene. The Royalists:

> so rudely entertained the pursuing Enemy, that they were compelled to stop (having lost abundance of men, and Col. Thornhill himself) until the coming up of Col. Pride's Regiment of Foot, who after a sharp dispute put those brave Fellows to the run.[21]

Once Cromwell's foot regiments arrived, the Scots were overwhelmed by weight of numbers. A fighting retreat seems to have ensued, with the Scots making a final, fighting stand around the area of Winwick Church, where they incurred many more casualties.[22]

The action at Winwick marked the last resistance of Hamilton's army at the Battle of Preston, an action fought over three days and a distance of some 25 miles. From there, Parliamentarian forces moved north, passing through Yorkshire and Durham, to the Scottish border. Pride was part of the small force that remained at Berwick-upon-Tweed to contain the Scottish garrison there, while the bulk of the Cromwell's army crossed into Scotland. Pride was conspicuous in reports of the subsequent actions to reduce Berwick:

The Lord's Day at Night Colonel Pride possessed himself of Tweed-Mouth, and the Bridge-foot at the English side, and the next Night he blew up the House of Guard which they had built upon the Bridge.[21]

Pride was the only commanding officer to be named in the attacks at Berwick, as had been the case in the attack at Chepstow earlier in the year. The Second Civil War, then, appears to mark an upwards curve in Pride's military career. Now a figure of considerable military experience, the 1648 campaigns see Pride taking a more prominent part in actions: attacking roles that were strategically pivotal and required a good deal of dash and nerve. Cromwell's description of the 'desperate' attack at Chepstow and the night attack at Berwick suggest a bullish character, for which Pride would be remembered after his death. But these actions perhaps reveal another side of Pride. The attacks that faltered in the marshy ground at Preston Moor and in the rain before Chepstow Castle hint at a man whose confidence could only carry him so far. Pride had certainly demonstrated strength of command, but there is slim evidence that tactical ability was his forté. Having examined his military career thus far, it is clear to see that Pride was commonly stalwart in defence, and his determined rushes against enemy positions at Dartmouth, Chepstow and, later, Berwick, demonstrates a man who did not lack courage. But there are several occasions when we can see Pride frustrated by an inability to break through in an attack: Preston was one such example, and Chepstow another. On both occasions, it is possible to see Pride at a loss as to how to remedy the situation when his forward attacks lost momentum. Pride was a man who demonstrated a good deal of courage, but for whom alternative, more subtle, options were sometimes lacking. He had the impetuousness to charge at anything, but when his momentum faltered he seems to have had little other resource to draw on.

10

Pride's Purge
December 1648

Achieving a settlement between monarch and Parliament became more urgent after the fighting of the 1648, but opinion was divided as to how this might be brought about. In September, even as Pride was on active service in the north, the Presbyterian majority in Parliament repealed the parliamentary act that forbade discussing peace terms with Charles I, and both sides agreed to begin a new session of talks. The Independents in the Commons were alarmed that a settlement might be brokered by the Presbyterians, which would compromise their own interests.

Discussions between Parliamentary commissioners and Charles I took place at Newport on the Isle of Wight, where the latter was being held prisoner. Charles I was requested to make certain concessions: Presbyterianism should become the exclusive religion in England for a three year period, during which the authority of the Anglican bishops would be suspended; Parliament would be given control the militia for the next twenty years.[1] But Charles I refused to sign the Presbyterian Covenant himself and the Presbyterians failed to obtain either the permanent religious settlement it wanted (removing the church from the power of the monarch), or the sale of bishops' lands that would pay the cost of arrears due to the army. Nevertheless, they came away from Newport believing that they were now in a good position to negotiate a final settlement. The Independents, who had the support of the majority of the army following the mutinies of the previous year, were not so easily appeased.

Thomas Pride marched south at the beginning of October, following Cromwell's negotiation of a peace with the Scots in Edinburgh. At army headquarters in St. Albans the following month, the army wrote and published its own peace proposals and officially presented them to General Fairfax. *The Remonstrance of the Army*, as this list of demands was entitled, comprised the petitions of the more politicised army regiments, collected and printed in a single volume. It was presented to the Commons on 20 November. The bulk of the text had been penned by the cavalry regiments, notably more radical than the infantry: those of Cromwell,

Ireton, Harrison and Whalley each set forth their demands. Only two regiments of foot were radical enough to publish their opinions: those of Richard Deane and Thomas Pride. By comparing the demands of Pride's regiment with the other contributors to the *Remonstrance,* it is possible to see where Pride stood in relation to the other army radicals at this time.

The main thrust of *The Remonstrance of the Army* was that those responsible for causing the Civil War (and the fighting of 1648 in particular) should be brought to account, and that the financial burden arising from the conflict ought to be addressed. Each of the above regiments approached these issues in slightly different ways. Cromwell's regiment called for those 'principally guilty of all the blood and treasures that have been spent in these Kingdoms' to be rightfully dealt with, and that 'important justice may be dealt upon them'.[2] The wording was judiciously vague, and did not specify any particular culprit. Harrison's regiment took a similar line, but stressed that 'neither birth nor place might exempt and from hands of justice',[3] implying that those higher-up the social scale might face trial for their part in the war. The declaration of Ireton's regiment was bolder and more explicit, demanding that 'justice be done upon THE KING, as if he were the humblest commoner',[4] and that status should be no bar to justice. The petition of Whalley's regiment was more strongly worded: 'THE KING, that capital destroyer of and shedder of the blood of some hundred thousand of his good people in England and Ireland, may be brought to publick justice'.[5]

Of all the petitions included in *The Remonstrance of the Army*, that of Pride's and Deane's regiments was the most vehement in its denouncement of Charles I. They declared that the monarch should assume 'the guilt of blood-shed upon himself; and, accordingly, to proceed against him as an enemy of the Kingdom.'[6] While Ireton was calling for Charles I to face trial, Pride and Deane had already found him guilty. They did not call for justice so much as retribution, announced themselves the instruments of the country's 'deliverance', and demanding that:

> the chief formentors, actors and abetters of the late war, especially those who were the chief encouragers and inviters of the Scotch Army; and that exemplary justice may be accordingly executed, to the terror of evils doers and the rejoicing of all honest men.[7]

Whether Pride's call for justice was influenced by the recent, lingering death of his long-time associate and comrade, William Cowell, is uncertain. But it is certainly possible.

Previously, in 1647, Pride seemed to distance himself from army radicalism once the aims of the army petition had been achieved. However, when it became clear that the Presbyterian 'Peace Party' was pressing ahead for a negotiated settlement with Charles I, he and his regiment were among those most supportive of the army's intervention on behalf of parliament's radical minority, and perhaps the most forceful in their condemnation of Charles I.

The notion that the army should deliberately interpose to stop the peace talks came not from the army but from elements within the Commons. In September 1648, Edmund Ludlow MP had visited Fairfax while he was still besieging the insurgent Royalists at Colchester. Ludlow explained to Fairfax the danger posed by parliamentary moderates agreeing a peace settlement with Charles I. Fairfax acknowledged this and agreed to use the power at his disposal for the good of the people, as he had done the previous summer when the Presbyterian mob had forced its way into the Commons. But Fairfax would not commit himself further. Ludlow then approached Ireton, who was favourable to army intervention but preferred to wait until a treaty between the peace party and Charles I had been concluded until making his move. [8]

Towards the end of November, following the publication of its *Remonstrance*, the army stirred into action. On 30 November Charles I was removed from custody on the Isle of Wight and transferred to the mainland, eventually to be taken under escort to army headquarters at Windsor.[9] The army simultaneously issued a declaration justifying their intended march and stating that their actions would ensure 'a more orderly and equal judicature of men in a just Representative' and to retain as much of 'the present Parliamentary authority … as can be safe, or will be useful'.[10] The statement implied that a limited purge of moderate Commons members had already been decided upon.

On 1 December the Commons was informed that the army was in readiness to march on the capital to demand an answer to the *Remonstrance*[11] However, the Commons had voted the previous day to defer consideration of the *Remonstrance* in favour of the Newport Treaty, and were occupied with preparing a new Militia Ordinance that aimed to return local forces to the direct command of the gentry.[12] This was a clear step towards establishing a power-base to rival Fairfax's army, and doubtless added impetus to the army's drive for London. The Speaker of the Commons wrote to Fairfax, forbidding the army from approaching London. Fairfax replied that the order to march had already been given and that it was too late to countermand.[13] Fairfax had in fact already written to Guildhall informing the City of the army's intention to march and to assure them that the soldiers would not offer violence to the inhabitants, nor would citizens be asked to provide free quarter for the troops. Fairfax made little reference in his letter to the army's constitutional demands, implying that the soldiers were concerned only with their arrears of pay.[14]

On the morning of 3 December the army contingent reached the fringes of Westminster and encamped in Hyde Park. There were seven full regiments, including Pride's, plus an assortment of independent troops and companies from more moderate regiments in which radicalism had surfaced.[15] From Hyde Park they were dispersed around Westminster, to be quartered at St. James' Palace, the Mews and other vacant, grand houses in the area. Fairfax established his head-quarters at Whitehall Palace (as was his right as Commander-in-Chief) and wrote to the Speaker of the Commons, insisting that the actions of his men were 'for the public interest and the safety of the nation'.[16]

The arrival of the army on the outskirts of the city must have alarmed Parliament, but apparently not enough to interrupt the day's business which was a further consideration of the Newport Proposals. No conclusion on the matter was reached and the House was adjourned until Monday 5 December. At Monday's session, however, news arrived of Charles I's removal from the Isle of Wight and Parliament at last began to suspect the army's intentions.[17] The Commons swiftly set up a committee to confer with Fairfax and discuss the army's demands. The House sat until five o'clock the following morning, some indication of the urgency felt by the Peace Party to reach a settlement with Charles I before the army had a chance to exact any influence on him. 340 MPs attended the chamber on Monday evening, a number that had fallen to 214 by first light.[18] The main business of Monday's session, 'That His Majesties Concessions to the Propositions of parliament upon the [Newport] Treaty were sufficient Grounds for settling the Peace of the Kingdom', was put to the vote. The Commons returned a majority of 46 in favour of continuing negotiations with Charles (129 for, 83 against).[19] The result reinforced what the army had feared: a Presbyterian settlement would be achieved between Charles I and the Parliament. They army felt compelled to intervene.

The army strategy to halt the proposed settlement was negotiated with the minority of radical MPs in the Commons. Initially, the army favoured the idea of the radicals removing themselves from the Commons and using the army as their power base, to 'repair to the army, in order to procure their assistance in settling the governance of the nation'[20]. The MPs demurred, as Ludlow explains:

> At a meeting of some members of parliament with the said officers from the army, it was resolved, that though the way proposed by them might be taken, in case all other means failed, yet seeing there was more than a sufficient number of members in the parliament to make a house, who were most affectionate to the publick case, it would be more proper for the army to relieve them from those who rendered them useless to the publick service, thereby preserving the name and place of the parliament, than for the members thereof to quit their stations wherein they were appointed to serve. [21]

To use the army as a basis of authority would lack legitimacy, and radical MPs did not see why they should withdraw from a Commons in which when they rightfully elected members.

On Tuesday 5 December a subcommittee convened in a chamber adjacent to the Long Gallery in the Palace of Whitehall, 'to consider of the best means to attain the ends of our said resolution'.[22] It appears that it was only at this late hour that the decision was taken to purge the House ('that none might be permitted to pass into the House but such as had continued faithful to the publick interest'),[23] rather than dissolve it entirely. This subcommittee consisted of six: three army officers and three civilian Members of Parliament. The identity of the individuals is still open to question. Edmund Ludlow, an anti-Royalist since early 1642, was there by his own admission.[24] Likely candidates for the other two MPs are Lord Grey, who would assist Pride in excluding members the following day, and Cornelius Holland, MP for New Windsor, who was later accused of helping to draw up the list of members to be excluded. For the army officers, Ireton, the army's leading political spokesman, would probably have been in attendance.[25] Underdown (1971) writes that Harrison was also there.[26] The third officer is more difficult to identify. Underdown suggests that it may have been Hardress Waller, who had been acting as a mediator between the army and Parliament and who helped carry out the purge the following day.[27] Greaves and Zaller (1984), however, conclude that 'Pride was probably present when the committee sat to decide which MPs were to be excluded'.[28] If this was indeed was the case, then it was the first time Pride had directly involved himself in politics, the petition of the previous year notwithstanding.

The events of December 1648 would prove a turning point in Pride's career. Prior to this, Pride had demonstrated a good deal of protest in his career – his decision to take up arms being the most obvious – but from this point on Pride would make himself more conspicuous in constitutional and legislative matters, and would maintain an almost continuous presence as a public figure, in one form or another, for the next decade. This period, from December to January, reveals an assertiveness in Pride's actions which argues that he was acting very much of his own volition; that he was not a passive figure who was simply obeying Ireton's orders to carry out a purge, 'the obedient instrument of a policy dictated by others',[29] as he has unjustly been labelled. The Purge marks such a fundamental shift in Pride's outlook that it quite plausible he should have played an active a role in the preparation of the event. Furthermore, Pride had already acted as a mediator between the army and Westminster, presenting to Parliament some eighteen months before the army's demand to impeach the Eleven Members. Their removal at that time can be viewed as a precursor to the more thorough purge of moderate MPs that was about to take place. There is good reason, then, to suppose that Pride was in attendance at that meeting of the subcommittee in Whitehall Palace on 5 December.

There were a handful of reasons why an MP might have found his name on the list of moderate politicians who were to be excluded: he may have voted in favour of the Newport Treaty that morning; or perhaps voted against a motion tabled in August to condemn as traitors those who had assisted the Scottish invasion. The subcommittee of six worked their way through the members' lists to decide which were to be purged.[30]

Contemporary sources seem to agree that Thomas Pride was the officer most prominent in the action of 6 December, and the decision that he should lead the action would surely have been taken at the Whitehall meeting. But why chose Pride? He had, of course, been notable among army radicals through his actions the previous summer, which had shown him at odds with the Presbyterian majority in the Commons. Pride had every reason distrust the Presbyterians, who intended to impose a state religion that was contrary to the way he wished to worship. As a soldier he had no vested interest in parliamentary privilege – the same could not be said of a more moderate figure such as Cromwell, who never associated himself with the army's purge and seems to have deliberately absented himself from London at the time. Pride may even have volunteered to carry out the forthcoming purge: the *Remonstrance* showed his regiment to be one of the most vehement in their call for justice. As the examination of Pride's military service has shown, Pride had an impetuous streak that Ireton may have recognised and believed would be useful for the job at hand.

On the morning of 6 December, Pride and his soldiers would have moved out of their quarters in St. James's before daybreak, to ensure they were in position before the Members arrived at the House, and as the guard there was due to be relieved. It was not a case of the New Model forcibly marching into Houses of Parliament: the army simply replaced the trained bands militia who were customarily stationed at points around Westminster Palace. Rich's regiment of Horse occupied New Palace Yard, while elements of Pride's regiment took up positions at Westminster Hall, the Court of Requests and the stairs and lobby immediately outside the Commons' chamber. Waller's regiment of foot took guard in the public streets beyond the palace.[31]

That morning, the day's session in the Commons began at the usual time of seven o'clock. However, after morning prayers it was reported to the Speaker that several members were unable to attend: instead of being allowed admittance to the chamber they had been escorted outside to the courtyards, Queen's Ward and the Court of Wards. Mystified, the Speaker ordered the Sergeant of the House to 'do to them to require them to attend'.[32] Off the Sergeant went. He duly returned to inform the Speaker that the members 'seemed willing to consent' but that an officer just outside the Chamber had told him 'he could not suffer them to come in til he had received his orders.'[33] When the Sergeant of the House had enquired what those orders were, the officer had replied that they were being sent for.

Pride was almost certainly the officer who was determinedly evading the Sergeant's questions. His men mounted a guard at the Commons door throughout the day, while members who had been singled out as sympathetic to the Royalist cause were refused entry to the House. Most were simply turned away, but those who put up more of a struggle were manhandled into an empty side chamber and locked in. The MP and pamphleteer William Prynne was particularly obstreperous and, after being verbally warned by Pride not to resist ('Mr. Prynne, you must not go into the House, but must go along with me'),[34] had to be virtually wrestled to the ground by Pride and Waller to prevent him forcing his way into the chamber, in Prynne's words: 'forcibly seized upon … [and] haled violently thence into the Queen's Court'. Pride was never forgiven by Prynne for the incident, who would label the Colonel 'the new Faux [Fawkes]' for his violent attack on the Commons.[35] Bulstrode Whitelocke on the other hand, a Chancery Court lawyer and quite unnerved by the morning's events, was surprised to be allowed into the Commons chamber and relieved to be greeted by Pride with 'more than ordinary civility'.[36]

It is clear that Pride was at the centre of the action that morning, and carrying out the arrests personally. The diarist Thomas Burton provides us with another member's account of his own arrest that day:

> 'I found Colonel Pryde at the door, and one by him telling him, "This is the person." I came through the pikes and muskets. I was arrested by that gentleman. He asked my name. I would not tell him. I said I was a member. He said, "You have a mark upon you. You are a noted man." I asked for my charge. When he saw I would not go quietly, two ushered me up into Surrey Court, where I found thirty, and fifteen came after. We were kept in hold that night; then ushered to Whitehall; and kept there till the next day, without food or conveniency. We were carried to the King's Head, and other inns, with great reproach. To prison we had coaches, because it was dirty weather.'[37]

Pride's Purge effectively removed the Presbyterian majority from the Commons. Most sources concur that 140 MPs were turned away from the House that morning.[38] About 40 others were forcibly detained and spent the night in 'Hell', off Old Palace Yard. Among them were Pride's former commanding officer, Edward Harley, and his father, Sir Robert.[39] Most narrative histories refer to 'Hell' as a nearby tavern. More accurately it was a kitchen and dining hall that provided meals for those who worked at Westminster and was 'much frequented by lawyers'.[40] There was a corresponding cook's house, 'Heaven', in New Palace Yard.

Standing at Pride's side throughout the proceedings was the twenty-six year-old Lord Grey, 'and others who knew the members'. Grey was the member for Leicester and had been negotiating for the intervention of the army alongside Ludlow.[41] He had been conspicuous among the anti-Presbyterian group since the previous May, when he had presented Pride's petition to the Commons on the colonel's behalf.[42] From Burton's narrative above it would appear that Grey (the 'one by him') directed Pride throughout, informing him which members were to be barred.

The MPs who had been allowed into the chamber, meanwhile, debated whether or not to suspend the day's session in protest at the army's action. They decided it would be more dignified to continue the day's business, in order to show the army that House's work could not be halted.

Later that day the demands of the army's general council was delivered to the Commons, setting forth the conditions that needed to be met before the excluded members would be allowed to retake their seats: any members that had voted for the Newport Treaty the day before should be suspended; the Eleven Members of 1647, viewed as the core of army's Presbyterian opposition, should be brought to justice; any members who had voted for the Eleven Members' readmission to the House, or who had voted against declaring the supporters of the recent Scottish invasion as traitors, should be permanently excluded; that the Parliament should decide on a date for its own dissolution.[43] This last condition had been at the heart of Ireton's strategy from the beginning, though in the event he had been persuaded to achieve it through a purge rather than wholesale expulsion. These demands amounted to an army agreement to reverse the Purge, provided the Parliament prepare to dissolve itself. The army refused to release any of the Members held in custody until the House responded to their demands.[44]

It should be noted that the army turned away members from the door to the Commons' chamber: there is no report of either Pride or his soldiers entering the chamber itself, as Charles I had done in 1642. In this way, Pride could not be accused of breaching parliamentary privilege. During the riots of the previous summer the Presbyterian mob had forced their way into the Commons chamber to demand legislative change; the actions of Pride's Purge appears quite restrained in comparison.

The army's role in politics at this time has been reviled in popular history ever since. To the modern reader an act such as Pride's Purge is seen as anti-democratic and an act of military repression. But this is surely because the notion of an intervention by the military into politics has been coloured by the dictators of later centuries. It should be remembered that by 1648 the Long Parliament was in its eighth year, during which time the political fabric of the country had been drastically altered, and there were no plans to re-elect the Parliament in order to reflect such change. Given these circumstances, and notwithstanding the bonfires in London some days earlier in celebration of the Newport Treaty, it could be argued that the army radicals – with their mix of Leveller spokesmen, more moderate Grandees, religious separatists, and radical MPs – provided a more effective representation of the public will than the Long Parliament that they purged. It must be remembered also that the idea of military intervention had originated among the radical parliamentary members themselves, who looked to the army for protection as they had done in the summer of 1647.

Nevertheless, the army was conscious of the opprobrium that their actions would attract, and with this in mind the *Moderate Intelligencer* of the following day carried a formal written defence of the purge, penned by the officers and men of Pride's regiment and addressed to their commander-in-chief, Fairfax. Central to their message was the assurance from Pride's soldiers that the Purge was in no way a prelude to wholesale social revolt, and that they were not the political extremists that many suspected them of being: 'we abhoring anarchy, confusion and levelling men's estates, so often charged upon us'.[45] Rather than usurping power for themselves, they saw their role as acting on behalf of others: 'that the contrary minded, false, royal and neutral party may know, that our enemies must not be our rulers'.[46] They were not acting out of self-interest but for 'that good party' within Parliament and for the public will, that 'the people call to us for these things'.[47] Their grounds for a purge were summarised in arguments that had been central to the army's demands for more than a year: the need to bring those responsible for the Civil War to justice and the want of money among the New Model ranks. Pride's regiment itself claimed to have received no pay since May. Having won the war they were now concerned that the Presbyterians in Parliament would lose them the peace: 'the fox stealing that from us by subtilty [sic], which the lyon could not tear by cruelty'.[48]

Most striking about this piece of writing is that the fact that the officers and men of the regiment took full responsibility for the actions of the 8 December, there is no suggestion that they had been duped or coerced into such action by their superiors nor that they had been mere instruments of more politically astute minds, an accusation that has often been levelled at the 'buffoon', Thomas Pride.[49]

Rather than being confined to a single day, as most histories state, the act of purging the House continued for more than a week. On the following morning, 7 December, the regiments of Deane and Hewson relived those of Pride and Waller.[50] Fifty more members were turned away from the House that morning, principally because they had protested against the treatment of the Members arrested the day before. A further three Members were taken into custody and joined the colleagues in 'Hell'.[51]

Those already confined in Hell had spent an uncomfortable night there, having to sleep on wooden benches. Many had preferred to spend the night awake, reading, talking or singing psalms.[52] At eleven o'clock on Thursday morning they were escorted to Whitehall after being informed that the army council wished to discuss their demands. At Whitehall they were kept in 'very cold room without fire' for several hours and provided with brandy and biscuits, the only sustenance they had received in the previous twenty-four hours. It was dark by the time they were told that the army officers would be unable to see them, and they were ordered to return the following day. The members were then escorted on foot to one of two taverns, the Swan at Charing Cross and the King's Head in the Strand, where they remained under guard.[53] On the Friday there was again no opportunity for the members to be seen. Fairfax sent word to Sir Robert Harley that he and several others would be released provided they gave their word not to oppose the army. The MPs refused and remained in custody.[54]

Although the army had rid the Commons of significant numbers of the Peace Party they had not counted on the reaction of other MPs, more than 100 of whom absented themselves from Parliament in protest at the Purge. Within a week of Pride's initial action there were pressing practical reasons for attempting to moderate, or even reverse, the Purge. On 12 December several of the MPs were freed, but nine further members were excluded by soldiers at Westminster; two more were excluded the next day.[55] That some of these members had formerly backed the army reveals how far the army's actions had gone in alienating some of their supporters. On 14 December attendance in the House dropped below forty, the minimum required to form a quorum. The Speaker had to request that half a dozen suspected moderates, detained that morning by soldiers in the lobby, be admitted to the chamber so that the Commons could legitimately sit.[56]

Edward and Robert Harley were not released until Christmas Day. They were then placed under house arrest, which continued until 12 February. Sixteen members remained in custody until well after 25 December.[57]

The MPs that were allowed to remain sitting in the Commons – known popularly as the Rump Parliament – eventually turned their attention to matters that the army considered to be of the highest importance. Discussion of the *Remonstrance of the Army* began on 12 December; the vote of the previous summer that had allowed the re-admittance of Edward Harley and other prominent Presbyterians was repealed, and the Vote of No Addresses was reinstated. On 15 December the vote to accept the Newport Proposals, which had sparked the Purge, was also repealed.[58] The moderate view, that had so recently enjoyed a majority in the Commons, was now anathema.

On 28 December the parliamentary committee appointed to consider Charles I's future brought its bill to the Commons for its first reading. The ordinance accused Charles of subverting the ancient liberties of his people and waging war against the parliament and kingdom. The clerk of the Commons immediately resigned, refusing to play any part in the bill's progress.[59] The bill named 3 judges and 150 commissioners appointed to try the monarch, among whom was Thomas Pride. The bill went through its second and third readings and was then sent up to the Lords on 1 January, where it met comprehensive opposition from the fifteen peers present. The Lord Chief Justice, and two Lords Justice appointed as judges for the coming trial, declared the motion illegal and refused to have any involvement in it.[60] The Lords rejected the bill and then promptly adjourned themselves, believing that the Commons could proceed no further without them.

In response, the Commons removed the names of the six Lords from the list of commissioners, replaced them with six others and nominated John Bradshaw, a sergeant-at-law, to preside over the trial in place of the Lords Justice. They then proceeded to enact the ordinance themselves without recourse to the Lords, arguing that since cross-House committees were able to function irrespective of whether or not any Lords were in attendance, then the Commons should be within its rights to pass legislation without the House of Lords' consent.[61] It was the thinnest of legal precedents, but the Commons declared itself the Supreme Authority of the nation and passed the 'Act Errecting a High Court of Justice for the King's Trial' on 6 January.[62]

11

London, 1649-50

'Wound for wound, stripe for stripe'

Popular history is quick to condemn the trial of Charles I as a sham, and the event has done much to garner sympathy for the Royalist cause and to cast the monarch as a victim of injustice. But though the trial may have been a formality, it provided the veneer of legality necessary to distinguish a capital punishment from a murder.

Charles I's adversaries need never have resorted to trial at all. English kings had been deposed before: William Rufus had been assassinated in the New Forest; Edward II, Henry VI and Edward V had all been murdered in their prison cells, and Richard II starved during his confinement in Pontefract Castle, all on the order of their political rivals among the aristocracy. The difference in the case of Charles I is that he was removed by the representatives of the common people. It says much for both the army and the Rump that they chose to remove Charles I through a formal trial and in full view of the public; much easier to have dispatched him in a prison cell in the dead of night. It would have been a simple matter for the army to have done away with Charles I while he had been in their custody and replace him with a more pliant monarch – two of his sons, James and Henry, were both considered suitable candidates by some. But the Rump needed to prove itself a legitimate government, and its members seemed to have felt the need to depose the monarch with a sense of propriety and in a business-like manner.

On 15 January, Pride was appointed to a committee that was to arrange the accommodation of Charles during the trial. Suitable lodgings had to be found, the prisoner's route to and from the court meticulously planned and arrangements made for the deployment of troops as security.[1] Pride was suitably dressed in a high-crowned, broad-brimmed hat when, on 20 January, he took his place alongside the sixty-seven other commissioners in Westminster Hall on the first day of the trial: the advice of the College of Heralds had been sought as to the dress and ceremony appropriate for such a solemn state occasion.[2] Most of Westminster Hall was taken up by members of the public. A wooden rail ran the width of the hall, separating the court from the general populace who were enclosed in two large pens with a central aisle running between. The perimeters of the public area were lined with soldiers of Hewson's Regiment, armed with pole-axes. Charles I was led in, seated with his back to the public and the charge was read. He was accused of formulating a 'wicked design to erect and uphold in himself an unlimited and tyrannical power to rule according to his will, and to overthrow the rights and liberties of the people'; that he was the 'occasioner, author, and continuer' of 'unnatural, cruel and bloody wars' and was therefore 'guilty of all the treasons, murders, rapines, burnings, spoils, desolations, damages and mischiefs to this nation, acted and committed in the said wars, or occasioned thereby.'[3] Charles I refused to answer the charges. The formalities of the trial lasted six days, during which time selected witnesses were called who could testify to having seen Charles I leading troops into battle – proof of his having waged war on his own subjects.

Sentence was passed on the 27 January declaring that 'the said Charles Stuart, as a tyrant, traitor, murderer, and public enemy to the good people of this nation, shall be put to death by the severing of his head from his body.'[4] Charles I was not allowed to speak following the passing of the sentence and he was escorted from the hall. He made two requests, to see his children before he died and to be attended in his last hours by an Anglican bishop. Both of these requests were granted.[5]

Of the 135 commissioners named as having attended Charles I's trial, only fifty-nine went on to sign the warrant for his execution. Fifty of those commissioners present when the warrant was signed refused to add their names, objecting to the sentence passed by the court.[6] It was generally the men of rank that flinched from the act of sending Charles to the scaffold: of eleven baronets that had been named as commissioners only four signed the death warrant; the only member of the nobility to sign was Lord Grey of Groby.[7] Fairfax had attended just one of the court's sessions before he vanished from the scene, wanting nothing to do with the affair.[8] Pride, however, attended all but one of the court sittings.[9]

Underdown (1971), in his view of the Civil War as a social conflict, remarks: 'although the court as originally nominated was indeed representatively respectable, the court which actually tried and sentenced Charles I was drawn, proportionately, from less impressive social groups.'[10] Of those Regicides whose educational background can be identified with certainty, 48% had attended university (including Cromwell, who famously left Cambridge without a degree). More than half the Regicides whose education is known had not attended university.[11] 26% had entered the Inns of Court after leaving school and the same percentage had, like Pride, a background in apprenticeship. Contrary to Underdown's statement, then, the proportion of Regicides from less-auspicious social groups would seem to be more-or-less equal to those from university backgrounds. Nevertheless, Pride's signing of the death warrant was a move that would help shift himself, and others of his middling-sort social rank, closer to the centre of English political life.

Pride's less-than-impressive social group was certainly the target of William Winstanley, whose *The Loyal Martyrology* of 1663 labelled Pride as an 'Ignorant, Illiterate Fellow',[12] and certainly Pride's handwriting as it appears on Charles I's death warrant seems to bear this out. The letters of his name seem to have been penned with frenetic energy rather than ease, a series of compressed and tightly-angled oblique strokes: 'his name is so strangely written, that it is scarce legible',[13] commented eighteenth century historian, Mark Noble. This is not to say that Pride was illiterate, but it is not an educated hand by any means, neither fluid nor elegant. He scrawled with confidence though, making his presence known with one of the most expansive signatures on the document. Other examples of Pride's signature are extant, and provide a useful comparison. So different is the signature that appears on army pay warrants, one can easily conjecture that Pride deferred from signing these documents at all and had his name penned by an amanuensis. In another example, from a reference of 1652, his writing is even more wayward.[14] Compared to the latter, the signature that appears on Charles I's death warrant appears to have been scrawled more diligently, less crooked and attempting to be more cursive: this is clearly what Pride considered his formal, best hand writing. Even so, it is one of the more ungainly signatures on the document.

Pride's expressive scrawl is accompanied on the death warrant by a wax seal bearing a heraldic device: a chevron between three lions' heads. What could be the origin of this? His apprenticeship indenture attests that Pride was the son of yeoman,[195]so he would hardly have been entitled to bear a coat of arms. Neither does his father's use of yeoman as a title argue for a gentrified family fallen on hard times. Cockayne's *Complete Peerage* (1916) maintains that Pride took the arms from another man entirely, named Kettleby (or Ketelby). Kettleby bore the Pride arms quartered with others on his escutcheon in right of one of his ancestors, Pryde of Shropshire, and line which went back to the early 1300s. Cockayne concluded that Thomas Pride 'probably had no right to these arms'. Certainly there is no direct link between the Shropshire Prides and those of Somerset, although a connection cannot be ruled out.[16] However, there is reference to another army officer, Colonel Isaac Ewer, who received a grant of arms to suit his military rank in January 1648, and it is possible that Pride was granted a similar honour at the same time, and for the same reason.[17]

Cockayne describes the arms Pride's arms as 'gules a chevron between three lions' heads [e]rased argent'.[18] An additional detail, barely discernible on the Death Warrant's wax seal, is what are variously described as two serpents or eels on the chevron. In fact they are a representation of two lampreys, 'chevronwise respecting each other'. This is an example of 'canting', a heraldic pun on the name of the bearer. In Pride's West County dialect a 'pride' is the colloquial name of the mud lamprey. The tinctures described by Cockayne reveal Pride's arms to be very close to those of General Monck (which are identical, minus the lampreys), but this can only be coincidence, as the Monk and Pride family were not yet connected in marriage when Pride signed the death warrant (see chapter fourteen).

The only other extant depiction of the Pride arms is found on the grave of the Norfolk gentleman, John Gibbs, in the parish church of Attleborough.[19] Gibbs

Facsimile of Charles I's death warrant, bearing Pride's signature and seal (third column, fifth down).

married Pride's granddaughter Elizabeth and, as a family heiress, her arms were impaled with Gibbs's own into a single device. The Pride arms, then, were not merely acquired for the occasion of sealed Charles I's death warrant, but were retained within the family and used by Pride's heirs.

On the morning of 30 January, Charles I walked under escort from St. James' Palace to Whitehall. There he was taken to the first floor of the Banqueting House, led through the main hall and out through one of the first floor windows (of what was effectively his own dining room) on to the scaffold that had been erected against the west side of the building. He was to be executed literally in the street. A rectangular area in front of the Banqueting House had been railed off, keeping the public at some distance[20] so that as Charles I stood and gave his final speech it is quite probable that not one word would have been heard by the assembled crowd.

The identity of the man who was to wield his axe is unknown, and has naturally been the subject of much speculation. It was commonly believed, so Charles II reputedly told his mistress, the Duchess of Portsmouth, that the executioner was Pride himself.[21] Needless to say, there is not a shred of evidence to substantiate this claim.

Following the execution, Charles I's body and head were placed inside a waiting pine coffin and removed to Whitehall Palace to await the arrival of the Army's Surgeon-General, Dr. Trappam, who had been directed to embalm the corpse and to reattach the severed head so that the body would be intact for the Day of Judgement:[22] though he had been publicly executed, Charles I was not dealt with as a common criminal but was treated with due deference. The body was taken to Windsor Castle for burial. There, the military governor refused permission for a service to be read from the Anglican *Book of Common Prayer*. The Bishop of London, who was to conduct the rites, was told that he could use any other words he wished. The Bishop, knowing Charles I's dedication to the Church of England service, declined the offer and chose instead to say nothing. Charles I was buried in complete silence at Windsor on 28 February.[23]

Moves followed to disassemble the old form of government, although it took time. The purged House elected a Council of State almost entirely out of its own membership to act as the executive power and, over the following four months, a rudimentary republican government took shape. The 'Office of King' was abolished on the 17 March and the House of Lords, termed 'useless and dangerous to the people of England',[24] was scrapped two days after. On 19 May England was officially declared a Commonwealth and Free State.[25]

Due to his role in Charles I's execution, Pride's name had become widely recognised. His purge had made him a public figure, but it also made him a focus for animosity. A pamphlet published that February labelled him a 'Jew', for having condemned his sovereign to death as the Jews had handed Christ over to the Romans.[26] A married couple in Hammersmith, Paul and Mary Williams, were fined for publicly calling Fairfax, Cromwell and Pride 'sons of whores'.[27] Pride could at least take satisfaction that his name was now uttered in the same breath as the two highest-ranking officers in army. Moreover, Pride's prominence in enforcing the Commonwealth's rule put him close to the centre of government: two days on from Charles I's execution saw Pride sitting on a committee investigating accusations of members of the public whose words and actions were critical of, and inciting violence toward, the High Court of Justice that had tried the monarch.[28]

During the period immediately following the Regicide, Pride's regiment of foot was quartered in St. James's. Then on the fringe of the countryside, Westminster's outermost suburb was the first call of anyone travelling to the capital from the west. Pride's regiment was on hand to ensure that security here was at its tightest.

Pride's duties in London in the following months were the mundane tasks of an army in peace time: the requisition of horses from London's inns for use by the army's Irish expedition;[29] one hundred deer to be driven from Marylebone Park to St. James's to provide soldiers with a supply of fresh meat.[30] His soldiers were called on to maintain a guard at the Tower, to escort the Duke of Hamilton to the scaffold when the Scottish general was executed for his role in the Second Civil War,[33] and required to guard the body of the English envoy to Holland as it lay in state following his assassination by Royalist agents.[32] By far the most important duty allotted Pride at this time was the task of raising troops for expedition to Ireland, and in autumn of 1649 he was commissioned as commander-in-chief of 5,000 new army recruits and granted the authority to convene and preside over courts martial to keep them in order.[33]Conveying them to the waterside took Pride to Liverpool in January 1650.[34]

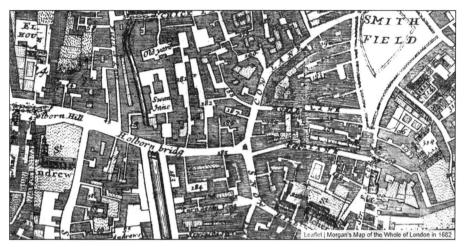

Detail of Morgan's 1682 map of London showing Holborn, including Ely House hospital (top left) and Pye Corner (bottom right).

Taken together, Pride's duties in London appear to have been quite diverse. The thread that ties them is that they are primarily concerned with the movement of men and supplies. It is easy to conceive that the onerous task of 'raising, conducting, and landing' troops in Ireland was taken in his stride by a man with a lifetime in business and experience of managing men and materials. Even here, though, was the whiff of fraudulence that seems to have followed Pride wherever he went. He petitioned the Council of State for £1,400 in February 1650 for the cost of having raised 2,000 troops for Ireland. The Council of State withheld payment, however, when they discovered that only 1,056 troops had been dispatched and they ordered Pride to make up the shortfall in men.[35]

From the summer of 1649 and during the time he was in charge for recruitment, Pride had his headquarters at St. James's Palace. Former Royal possessions were removed to allow room for billeting soldiers and money was provided (stipulated not to exceed £150) to convert the riding house there into a barracks.[36] Soldiers were also quartered in the tennis court and timber was supplied to build shelters in the adjacent Park.[37] No evidence has yet come to light that the regiment was quartered there at the time of Charles I's execution, which would effectively have placed Pride in charge of the guard on the monarch's last night alive. Curiously, Moore (1918) states that Pride was resident at Saint Bartholomew's Hospital in 1648, although his prominence in the Second Civil War and after does not suggested he was wounded or suffering any illness at this time.[38]

St. James's at this time was also being used as a military prison. Supervisory duties fell to Pride, who may have found it expedient for his recruiting role: at least some of those held at St. James's were offered early release providing that they agreed to serve in the army in Ireland.[39] Pride's own men were not beyond

Engraving of Westminster, after Hollar. On the right is St. James' Palace, where Pride's regiment was quartered in 1649/1650.

criminality, one attempting to steal a deer from St. James's Park with a soldier of Fairfax's as his accomplice. The perpetrators suffered a painful and humiliating punishment:

> stripped naked from the waist upward and a lane to be made by half of the Lord General's regiment of foot and half of Colonel Pride's regiment, with every soldier a cudgel in his hand, and they to run through them in this posture, every soldier having a stroke at the naked breasts, arms, or where it shall light; and after they have run the gantelop in this manner they are to be cashiered the regiment.[40]

Pride had jurisdiction over the immediate vicinity of St James's, and his soldiers were acknowledged the 'principle guards about this town'.[41] For the safety of the Commons and the Council of State sitting at Westminster, Pride was ordered to take into his possession the keys of all the gates leading into St. James's Park, including the house keys of any dwellings that backed on to park, and to nail shut any gates and back doors,thus securing the eastern approach to Whitehall.[42] As part of these duties it fell to Pride to secure the area known as 'Spring Gardens', roughly the area occupied today by Admiralty Arch and the offices to the south of it. Pride was ordered by the Council of State to 'give notice to the inhabitants of Spring Garden to move out', and ten days later he was further ordered 'To see that all doors leading to Spring Gardens are fastened up'.[43] These were popular pleasure gardens, an extension of the larger St. James's park and often frequented by royalty. Features included archery butts and a bathing pond; in 1629 a bowling green and garden house were added. By 1634 there was a hostelry there, with 'continual bibbing and drinking wine under the trees',[44] and by the end of the 1630s the reputation of the pleasure gardens had taken a nose-dive. Charles I had ordered the bowling green closed because public behaviour had 'grown scandalous and insufferable'.[45] There were also said to be three active brothels in vicinity of St. James' Palace and Spring Gardens, described as 'Three *Nurceries* of *Sodomy*, *Lust* and *Uncleanness*' named 'The Whipping School', 'The Mopping School' and 'The Nunnery'.[46] It was supposed by critics at the time that Pride had forcibly closed the gardens because he had seen it as his moral duty to do so. But the order to close Spring Gardens was given on grounds of public safety, rather than morality and, given Charles I's edict concerning the area, a disdainful opinion of this part of Westminster cannot be claimed to be solely the view of Puritans.

Such was Pride's conspicuousness in and around the capital in 1649, the Royalist news book *Mercurius Elencticus* felt obliged to provide its readers more information on the man and offered a résumé of Pride's life to date:

> Collonel John [sic] Pride, a Beggar borne in a Village called Ashcot, three miles from Glasterbury, in the Countie of Somerset; hee kept for divers yeares together a heard of Swine for one Trye in that Parish; his Dame is yet living and her name is Philippa Trye; who when her servant Pride left her service and would goe to London caused a purse to be made for him in the Parish, whereby she got for him between 40 and 50 shillings with which hee came up to London and served a Brewer in carrying of Firkins, running of Errands and the like.[47]

That the authors made a mistake with Pride's first name reveals this to be a rather feeble piece propaganda. The name Trye is also an oddity, though curiously the name Fry occurs in some transcripts of early Ashcott parish records (spelt variously Fry, Frie and Frye); a Philippa Frye was born in Ashcott in 1641, so perhaps there are some dregs of truth in the account.[48] Royalist writers felt obliged to point out the apparent discrepancy between Pride's origins as a brewer's dogsbody and the influence he had now achieved. *Elencticus* continued:

> Yet this swine heard was one of the prime Judges who sat on the Bench at the Tryall of the murdered King and who now possesseth his stately house at St. James's ordinarily calling it his house where he is guarded by day and night with a hundred foot at least.[49]

Of course he was not so much guarded as in command of them. To the Commonwealth's opponents, however, it seemed clear that Pride had not only stage-managed the death of Charles I but was now living in luxury of the former Royal palace. The notion that Pride was now sleeping in the old King's bed and swaggering about London with his new found authority seems to be substantiated to a degree. Pride can be observed following a personal agenda in his public duties, spurred by his religious beliefs. In August 1649 Pride and Goffe presented a petition to Parliament that called for the repealing of all statutes and Ordinances 'whereby many conscientious people are molested, and the propagation of the gospel hindered.'[50] It was demanded that religious practice be un-impinged by the law, that political prisoners be released, and also demanded the suppression of 'open acts of prophaneness, as drunkeness, swearing, and uncleanesss,'[51] which correspond with the attitude towards Spring Gardens. Pride undertook a similar piece of religious pamphleteering some months following this, when he helped circulate the writings of his fellow parishioner Samuel Chidley among the General Council of the Army. Chidley had penned a tract – *A Cry Against Crying Sin* – in which he called for an end to capital punishment for theft. He quoted Exodus in arguing that it was wrong to take someone's life unless they had killed. 'It is not life for eye, but eye for eye', he wrote,

> To take away the life of any man only for theft … is not good, because it is not of God; it is not correspondent with his will, it hath no agreement with his righteous law.… . [judges] have broken the statute-laws of god, by killing of man merely for theft.[52]

In place of the death penalty Chidley favoured a more practical and meaningful punishment for theft:

> [thieves] might work in mines, heave coals and earn three or four shillings a day … or they may be transported to some of our own plantations, where some … . have soon become honest [53]

Repentance for sin is Chidley's theme. Pride never penned any of his own views on religion (nor any subject), but he endorsed the writing of Chidley and so we should assume that these views tally with those of Pride himself. It may explain why the punishment of the deer thieves, noted earlier, was as lenient as it was: theft was a capital crime and the two soldiers might easily have hanged for it. Cromwell himself dclared that the punishment for plunder when the English army had entered Scotland in 1648 to be 'Death'.[54] Pride was prepared to send a monarch to the scaffold but appears to have been less-willing to deal a similar punishment to his own soldiers. The discrepancy Chidley found between his own morality and that of England's new government is discernible in his quoting from Hosea, chapter 8, verse 12: 'I have written to him the great things of my law, *but* they were counted as a strange thing'.[55] If the rulers of the new Commonwealth baulked at Chidley's views, it must have signalled to both he and Pride that, despite the end of Monarchy, there was still much to do to make the country, and the 'sinful City of London'[56] a godly place.

Pride's involvement in attempting to further his own brand of Protestantism reveals a rather distasteful side of his character, that of someone who would not hesitate from imposing his own moral views on others for what he believed to be the common good, or the well-being of the people (the root of the word 'Commonwealth'). His exuberance could easily tip into overconfidence: an attempt to further his business interests at this time suffered a reverse when he failed to be nominated to a committee of the Honourable Company of Brewers.[57] Pride's often bullish way of exercising his new-found influence naturally exposed him to ridicule by his Presbyterian and Royalist opponents. This was the case in his apparently failed attempt to curb prostitution Spring Gardens, where the brothels were reputed to have remained open 'under *Pride's* very nose, yet un-controul'd, so that *Pride* and Lust liveth together'.[58] Here, as in the account of his life by *Elencticus* above, Pride seems to have been a figure who was easy to caricature.

Pride had certainly attained an authority through his influence in the army, and these powers evolved as Pride began to exercise a civil authority as well as military one. His election to the London Common Council in December 1649 gained Pride a legitimate foothold in local government, and increased the Independents' influence in what had been a Presbyterian-dominated body.[59] Given Pride's visibility in 1649 – his role in Charles I's death, enforcing Commonwealth law, attempts to influence religious polity – it is perhaps not surprising that the Royalists should have seen him as seizing power for his own ends.

12

War with Scotland, 1650–51
'A very considerable fight'

Dunbar, 1650

The execution of Charles I united Presbyterian and Royalist factions in the Scottish Parliament. Charles II accepted Scottish support to regain the English throne, promising to enforce the Presbyterian Covenant in England in return for military aid. A Scottish invasion of England, supported by English Presbyterians, seemed imminent. The Commonwealth resolved to attack Scotland first, intending to engage the Scots before their forces had been fully mustered and save the north of England being laid waste by an invading army.

Accounts of the actions at Preston and at Berwick, in which Pride had been involved two years before, has shown us that he had by this time been granted more independence of command. His military role further expanded as the Commonwealth prepared for war with Scotland. With nearly eight years service to his credit, Pride was now one of the more experienced colonels among the English foot. We can assume that it was for this reason that he was given command of a brigade of foot for the forthcoming campaign. This was to be the senior of the three infantry brigades assembled for the campaign, comprising the foot regiments of Lambert (General of horse) and of Cromwell (Commander-in-Chief), as well as Pride's own. This indicates that Pride's was now considered the third most senior regiment of foot in the army, behind those of the two highest-ranking general officers. Pride's seniority among the other colonels of foot is clear: he was the only Parliamentarian officer to command a regiment of foot at both Naseby and Dunbar. Another veteran officer of Barclay's, William Goffe, was to lead Cromwell's regiment of foot in the field.

Pride was prominent enough to have received a name-check when Cromwell arrived at Durham on 14 July, accompanied by 'Colonel Pride and other officers' and 'sumptuously entertained' by the town's governor, Arthur Heslerigg. Just how sumptuous this entertainment was is a matter for conjecture, as: 'there was a fast kept, to implore God's blessing upon the army's undertaking'.[1]

At the time they had been ordered north, Pride's regiment had been quartered for some weeks at Coventry. Their conduct had been less than exemplary, with one soldier being punished for theft: 'tied neck and heels together, and to be set where the whole regiment should march by him … for stealing a hen, and putting it under his coat in his march: which justice pleased the country'.[2]

This sentence should be considered lenient: Royalist trooper Richard Symonds noted three occasions in his service when soldiers in Charles I's army were sentenced to be hanged for looting.[3] The 'strappado' punishment metered out to the soldier in the above account can be taken as another example Pride's endorsement of Chidley's views on theft, detailed in the previous chapter. In a situation similar to the soldier charged with killing a deer in Hyde Park the year before, there is good reason to suppose that Pride considered the death penalty too severe a punishment for merely stealing a hen. The incident in fact seems to have been out of character for the regiment because in June 1650 the Coventry corporation wrote to Parliament, commending Pride's men for behaving 'very civilly and orderly' during their residence.[4]

When on 22 July Cromwell crossed the border into Scotland, Pride's Regiment had the honour of being the first regiment to cross the Tweed.[5] Reliant on being supplied by sea, the English were from the start restricted to the roads along the east coast. They reached Dunbar in four days, but it seems it was only then that the army commanders discovered the enormity of what faced them.

The Scottish' general, David Leslie, had chosen to retire before the English advance and had taken up position behind a series of fortified lines along the Firth of Forth. The Scots had stripped the countryside south of Edinburgh of forage, and their defensive tactics frustrated the English and denied them the decisive, pitched battle they wanted.

By 29 July the English foot had advanced as far as Musselburgh, six miles from Edinburgh. English war ships bombarded Leith, but could make no impression on

'The Strappado', by Jacques Callot, a punishment for theft metered out to Pride's soldiers.

the Scots' fortifications. Leslie was not tempted out of his lines and they were too strong to storm. The English army spent the night in the rain before Leith and then withdrew the next morning, harried by the Scots' horse, Pride's foot 'being on the rearguard, behaved themselves daringly'.[6]

By the end of August the English army had been severely reduced through sickness. Cromwell was facing supply problems, with rough seas resulting in fewer ships arriving at Dunbar from Newcastle. Having shadowed the English army from Mussleburgh, the Scots occupied the high ground above the town of Dunbar on 1 September, blocking the road to Berwick and barring Cromwell's escape to England. Cromwell formed his own forces in line on the lower slopes, facing the Scots behind the slight natural defences of a burn and, further to the west, a steep ravine.

Bad weather on the 2 September, prompted the Scots to leave their positions on top of Doon Hill and redeploy further down the slopes nearer the town. The English suspected that Leslie was readying for a fight. Indeed, at about four o'clock that afternoon the Scots made some probing attacks on the English outposts.

Pride had secured his position in the English centre by placing guards at shallowest points of the burn where it was easiest to cross. On the evening of the 1 September he sent thirty men of his own regiment forward, accompanied by six mounted pickets, to occupy a lone cottage at a ford across the burn in what can be described as the no-man's-land between the armies. Their position was exposed, and there seems to have been some error made (possibly made by Pride himself) in reinforcing them as they were 'not seconded by those appointed to bring them off'.[7] Late on the afternoon of the 2 September the position was attacked by two troops of Scottish lancers. The cavalrymen killed three of Pride's men and took another three prisoner for questioning – one of whom only had one arm, his other being fashioned from wood with an iron hook for a hand; he nevertheless got off three shots from his musket before being overpowered. Other soldiers from Pride's detachment received harsh treatment by the Scottish cavalry, who 'wounded all the rest after quarter given', and were driven back to the English lines.[8]

Thomas Pride was now embroiled in something approaching a military disaster. The English had been frustrated and outmanoeuvred by Leslie at every stage of the campaign. The weather was bad and likely to worsen; perhaps a third of Cromwell's force had already been lost to sickness and fever; the English were in hostile country with their route southwards blocked. To Pride, the scenario would have been horribly reminiscent of that of Cornwall, six years before: in enemy country, unable to be supplied and trapped with his back against the sea.

The force of Oliver Cromwell's personality is encapsulated in his decision – outnumbered by 2:1 and with the Scots commanding the high ground – to attack. Believing that could at least seize initiative, he was not prepared to simply wait helplessly for the Scots to advance.

Throughout the evening of 2 September the English had watched the Scots move down the slopes, closer to the English lines, as they prepared their attack. It slowly

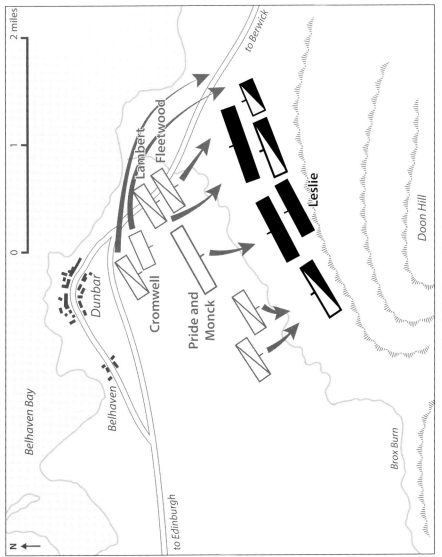

Map 6 The Battle of Dunbar.

became clear to the English that the redeployed Scots' centre would now find it difficult to manoeuvre, hemmed in as they were by the natural obstacles of the burn and the ravine. Their left wing was now positioned directly behind behind the ravine, which made any advance from that quarter impossible. Their right wing, adjacent to the sea, was now exposed on lower-lying terrain. The English commanders understood that an assault could be made on the Scots' right and centre, while their left would not be able to be brought into the attack: the bulk of Scottish foot would be snared in a pocket of ground, trapped between the ravine in front and the high ground behind.

The English plan of attack was workably simple but it required a major reordering of their line during the night to concentrate their forces at the point where the attack was to be made. At day break, Pride drew his three regiments out of the line and moved them to the centre of the English position, doubling the number of foot regiments there in preparation for a strong frontal assault. The initial attack was to be undertaken by the three regiments of Monck's brigade, backed up by those of Pride.

The movement of English troops in the dawn did not go unnoticed by the Scots. Sentries raised an alarm but, as no attack came, their soldiers returned to their shelters.

The English attack began at first light, Lambert's brigade of horse seizing the ford where the Berwick road crossed the burn, then pushing on to engage the main body of Scot's horse. Monck's brigade of foot began to advanced up the slopes to engage the Scots' centre. They needed to contain the Scots here until Cromwell could bring his reserve into action against the right of the Scots' centre. This reserve consisted of Cromwell's own regiment of horse and Pride's brigade.

Pride's three foot regiments were duly formed-up into a line of battle, and advanced against Campbell of Lawer's brigade. Although the Scottish commander swung his formations around to meet the attack, the English foot came on too quickly: 'The Lord General's [Cromwell's] regiment of foot charged the enemy with much resolution and were seconded by Colonel Pride's.'[9] Despite being caught off-guard Lawer's brigade held its ground and the Scots and English were soon fighting hand-to-hand: 'at push of pike and butt end of musket,' recorded John Hodgson, a captain in Lambert's foot regiment, 'until a troop of our horse charged from one end to another of them, and so left them at the mercy of our foot.'[10] Hodgson noted the brutality metered out to the Scots: 'Colonel Pride's men … were even with some of them for their cruel usage to their fellow-soldiers the day before',[11] Pride's men being implicated, not for the first time, in a vengeful attack on an enemy.

Support came from Cromwell's regiment of horse, which swung into the Scots' flank, and Lawer's brigade was completely destroyed. 'I never beheld a more terrible charge of foot than was given by our army,' Cromwell informed the House of Commons, 'our foot alone making the Scots foot give ground for three-quarters of the mile together.'[12] Hodgson describes how Cromwell ordered the foot to press on, 'to incline to the left; that was, to take more ground, to be clear of all bodies; and we did so, and horse and foot were engaged all over the field'.[13] In the confusion the Scottish army began to withdraw in the hope of being able to re-order themselves.

Dunbar was a startling victory for the English, but it by no means concluded the campaign. Cromwell may have avoided a catastrophe but he had achieved little else. Leslie still had a substantial army at his command, and three out of his five brigades of foot had escaped intact. A truce with the English was not even contemplated. Leslie may have lost up to 3,000 men at Dunbar, however,[14] and he now considered the fortified lines between Leith and Edinburgh untenable, choosing to fall back on the defences of Stirling. As before, Leslie was not to be tempted out of his lines into open battle. Rather than face a bloody assault, Edinburgh's gates were opened to the English army, although the castle continued to hold out. Cromwell therefore waited at Edinburgh for siege guns to be brought up from England. Monck and the foot regiments were occupied in reducing the garrisons south of Edinburgh. But while his regiment were still consolidating their position in the lowlands, Colonel Pride headed back to England. His brigade command in 1650 was to be the summit of his military career. He would never again hold such a high command, nor would he see further military campaigning.

Less than a month after the victory at Dunbar, Pride was back in London. Appointed head of army recruitment, the Council of State consulted him as to how many men needed to be raised to replace the losses of the summer campaign, and he also dealt with arrears of pay owed to the soldiers.[15] At the end of October Pride appears to have been the highest ranking officer and representative of the regular army at a military display at Hyde Park to celebrate the recent victory: 'Colonel Pride and many eminent commanders and souldiers of the trained bands of the City, and other gents and clerks (in honor of the Company) trailed pikes this day'.[16]

Pride's work in recruitment extended to the care for the sick and wounded that the newly enlisted men were to replace. While he was still in London following Dunbar he was appointed a governor to St. Bartholomew's Hospital. A man of straightforward and uncomplicated thinking, Pride was apparently forced on the hospital board by the London Common Council, without the consent of other governors, in order to implement needed reforms. Among the new rules laid down by Pride was the proviso that no woman could be appointed as a sister on the wards unless she had had previous experience as a nurse. It might seem an obvious condition but it was something that had either been overlooked by those in charge of the hospital, or merely dismissed as unimportant. His other duties were largely administrative, including the examination of 'persons employed therein and their allowances, the number and qualities of the sick and maimed men, and pensioners maintained from thence, and the allowance made for relief of those sent there for care'.[17] Even as his regiment continued to campaign in Scotland, then, Pride had returned to the kind of logistical work that had fallen to him while he had been in London in 1649.

Perhaps overseeing the movement of men and supplies better suited Pride's temperament as businessman than the rigours of campaign and the demands of a command in the field. It may have been with such thoughts in mind that, in November 1650, encouraged Pride to enter into a business venture, along with several others, for victualling the navy.

Oppenheim (1896) notes that the 'honesty of the victualling agents both steadily deteriorated during the Commonwealth. Complaints began to be frequent about 1650'.[18] Complaints included embezzlement of charitable monies set aside for wounded soldiers, and in May 1650 a clerk at the victualling office at East Smithfield was found to have taken £117 from the funds. The clerk was not dismissed but merely suspended from his post, an indication that such conduct was regarded as endemic and inevitable. It is a testament to Pride's reputation, then, faced with deep-rooted corruption and negligence, that it was to he that the Admiralty turned to rectify the situation.

One striking aspect of the administration of navy supply in this period is the attention that was given to the well-being of seamen. There is ample evidence of 'a conscientious recognition of justice due to the sailors, and of responsibility for their welfare … more clearly marked among captains, admirals and commissioners than among the ruling politicians'.[19] With his connections to brewing and London business Pride was an ideal choice for the responsibility of navy supply, yet the indications are that Pride's involvement in navy victualling had as much to do with this concern for the health and comfort of soldiers and sailors as it did with the self-interest of furthering his own business. Indeed, the near future would see Pride in close association with the London hospitals at Ely Place and the old Savoy Palace that were responsible for the treatment of wounded servicemen, and whose funds had been open to fraud.

The Navy Commission was asked to prepare a contract and it was signed at the end of November 1650 by all parties involved,[20] all of whom were London citizens: Pride, Nathaniel Andrews, William Beale, Thomas Alderne, John Upton, Slingsby Bethel, Henry Brandreth, Nathaniel Lacey and Richard Price. It is worth exploring the background of the other signatories to understand a little more about Pride's associates, and what connects them.

Both Nathaniel Andrewes and William Beale served with the London militia.[21] Andrewes was a religious nonconformist and in 1652 he was included on the government committee appointed to discuss the 'propagating of the Gospel',[22] and a justly promotion of the word of God among the people. Slingsby Bethel was a London cloth merchant with ties to European markets. Although his uncle had been a Royalist (and executed for his part in a Royalist plot), Bethel was a noted republican who had voiced his approval 'of the late king's death in very indecent terms'.[23] His success in the cloth trade brought him considerable power and influence. He joined Pride on the London Common Council in 1651, represented Knaresborough in the Parliament of 1659 and, in the fullness of time, would become sheriff of London and Middlesex. Late in life it was remarked that he had 'never before received the sacrament in the Church'.[24] Of the other signatories of the victualling contract, Alderne, Price and Brandreth would all be elected to the Committee for the London Militia in August 1651.[25] Brandreth would also be appointed commissioner for the peace in London in 1656 along with Pride and William Kiffin, Pride's associate from the Jacob Church.[26]

None of the signatories were directly responsible the production of beer and other victuals. Indeed, only Pride and Bethel seemed to be connected directly to trade. They should instead be regarded as the men responsible for overseeing supply from butchers, brewers, etc. to the fleet, through the victualling offices at East Smithfield and at Chatham.[27] Some were closely associated with naval supply for many years: Beale and Andrewes had overseen the supply of wheat and biscuit to the army at Dunbar,[28] and Alderne would be appointed victualling officer after the end of Pride's tenure. Another associate, Dennis Gauden, who dealt in corn and cheese, would be granted the contract for navy victualling under Charles II.[29]

The link between each of the signatories of the navy contract was religious non-conformity and London business. Four of these men served on the militia committee, and Pride and Bethel were on the London Common Council, proof that the Independents now controlled the public bodies that a few years before had been dominated by the Presbyterians. The military roots of government ran deep: William Goffe sat on the religious/moralising committees with Andrewes.[30] Pride was clearly working within a network of associates, many of whom shared common interests in politics and religion.

Pride was by this time in his mid-40s, which may have had some influence on the fact that he seems, as domestic conflict drew to a close, to have distanced himself from an active military career. Pride was a businessman by profession, a soldier only through necessity. What then of his regiment, still campaigning with the English army in Scotland?

Worcester, 1651

Paradoxically, the defeat of the Scots at Dunbar managed to reinvigorate the Royalist cause north of the border. The Presbyterian party was now out of favour following the defeat and, as a consequence, many Scots were more accepting of Charles II's leadership. A new Scots army was built around the remains of Leslie's force at Stirling during the winter of 1651.

The new year brought inactivity. The English were in Edinburgh but could advance no further. English soldiers were reportedly pilloried and flogged for looting and drunkenness. One of Pride's drummers was said to have received a death sentence for killing another soldier and was shot against the market cross in Leith.[31]

In Pride's absence his regiment was commanded by Lieutenant Colonel John Mason, and it was he who led an unsuccessful attempt to take Burntisland in a water-borne attack across the Forth in January, an action that was frustrated by bad weather.[32] Leslie was still not to be drawn out of his defences. Cromwell was seriously ill, suffering from malaria and dysentery, and his army was inert until he recovered in June. At the end of July Cromwell finally chose to go on to the offensive and the English crossed the Forth *en masse* and invested St. Johnstown (the common name for Perth in this period). Pride's was one of three foot regiments tasked with taking the town in August, but just as the moats and defensive ditches were being drained of water to prepare their attack the town governor agreed to terms. Pride's major, Thomas Parsons, was handed over to the Scots in a mutual exchange of hostages to ensure both sides stuck to the ceasefire.[33]

By concentrating his forces at Perth, and occupying the English army in a siege north of Edinburgh, Cromwell (deliberately or otherwise) tempted the Scottish commanders with an open road into England. Leslie was lured out of Stirling, bypassed the English army, and began to march south with the aim of restoring Charles II to the English throne. Cromwell responded by disengaging from Perth and pursuing the Scottish army into England.

The English horse shadowed the Scots for the entire length of their march, shepherding them along the west roads through Carlisle and Lancashire. The English foot took a parallel route south, on easier roads through Durham and Yorkshire. By the time the Royalist army had reached Lichfield, Cromwell's foot were south of them and had successfully barred Charles' route to London. Failing to have encouraged a widespread Royalist uprising by his march into England, Charles II barricaded himself inside Worcester, hoping to use the city a base from which to recruit from Wales.

With the scene set for the last set-piece battle of the Civil Wars the question has to be asked, where was Thomas Pride? Mason had led the attack across the Forth in January we must presume that Pride was still in London at that time, immersed in his logistical work. It is possible that he returned to Scotland with the reinforcements he had been assigned to raise before the Scottish campaign re-opened in late June, but there appears to be no evidence to support this. There is only one contemporary report to suggest that Pride was even present at the Battle of Worcester: a letter written by George Downing, Cromwell's scoutmaster, provides an account of the fighting to the north east of Worcester that day, as the Royalists attempted to break out of their encirclement. The action there was reported by Cromwell himself as 'a very considerable fight … for three hours' space'.[34] Nowhere does Cromwell connect Pride with the action. Downing, however, provides a little more detail: 'there was a very desperate charge on that [north east] side also, between them and ours, both horse and foot, where Colonel Pride was'.[35] A man central to army intelligence, we would do well to trust Downing's account. Even so, there is some doubt as to whether Downing is referring to Pride himself or merely to his regiment. Other sources credit Lambert with the command of the brigade (including Pride's foot) on the eastern side of the city that contained the Royalist thrust, which provides us with further difficulty. If Pride *was* at Worcester, and in command of a single body of foot under Lambert, it would have meant an effective demotion for him, having commanded a brigade at Dunbar twelve months before. Does this mean his role in the earlier battle had been so uninspired that he was not be trusted with a large, tactical command? The likelihood is that since Pride's absence in London, command of his brigade had passed to Lambert, who would have understood its capabilities better. To have returned the brigade to Pride at this juncture would have confused the chain of command and proved a disadvantage in battle. Until more evidence comes to light we should satisfy ourselves with the knowledge that these eighteen months of war in 1650/51 marked the point at which Thomas Pride removed himself from an active military career and prepared for peace.

13

The Dutch War, 1652–54

Trouble Brewing

The tasks that occupied Thomas Pride after the first Civil War (raising recruits, policing St. James's) had been largely logistical and administrative, duties for which his background in trade had equipped him well. The early 1650s saw a resumption of such tasks as Pride began to distance himself from active military service. We have already identified Pride as one of the burgeoning 'Middle Sort', a proto-middle class with a preoccupation of attaining money, status and respectability. In 1650 he attained the apogee of middle-class aspiration and purchased a house in the country.

When Parliament had taken control of Crown lands following the abolition of monarchy, one of the properties confiscated was Nonsuch Palace, a sumptuous former royal residence in Surrey and a masterpiece of Henrician Renaissance architecture. The palace and the large estate in which it stood were leased separately, the building and its immediate grounds known as 'Nonsuch Little Park' and the larger estate – 1,000 acres of parkland that lay to the north – referred to as 'Nonsuch Great Park'. It was this latter property that Pride purchased, securing the lease against the arrears of pay due to his regiment and paying off the money owed to his men through the profit earned from the estate. The similarity of the two parks' names led to confusion over which property he acquired, perhaps muddled with the memory of Pride being quartered in a Royal palace (St. James's) during his stay in London in 1649. The idea that he had taken up residence in a former royal residence seems to have begun with a satire penned in 1680, just as Pride's life was passing out of living memory and myth started to occlude fact: "I die here in my own house at Non-such. It was the king's house, and Queen Elizabeth love this above all her houses".[1] A Regicide who had grown wealthy enough to live like royalty was too obvious a target for the satirists to miss. Pride was not living like a king in Tudor splendour, however, and far from palatial, his new home was quite modest in comparison.

The Great Park was commonly known as Worcester Park, named for the Earl of Worcester who had been the keeper there during the reign of James I. The Surrey suburb that was later built over it retains the same name to this day. The Earl had a lodge built for himself on the estate – Worcester House – a modern and expensively built residence (entirely of brick and with a tile roof) but quite modest in size: three storeys and a cellar, with five bedrooms. This was to be the Pride family home for much of the 1650s. The estate – including house, outbuildings and deer park – was valued at just over £4,200.[2]

The park keeper, Charles Kirke, received compensation for the loss of his job when Pride took over the running of the estate. Kirke was granted a portion of the land, Great Park Meadow, worth £110 a year (although Pride reserved the right to any wood growing there). Kirke, whose father had been Gentleman of the Robe to Charles I and a staunch Royalist, was to receive no such compensation at the Restoration when, after a brief return to his keepership, the park passed again into private hands and Kirke once more lost his position.[3]

Worcester Park was conveniently close to Pride's Surrey breweries, six miles away at Kingston-upon-Thames. Aside from the obvious business opportunities in Kingston, the Prides may have been attracted to the area because of its reputation for religious separatism, the town described at this time as having long been a 'hotbed of radical agitation'. When the Quaker preacher Edward Burroughs was tried for libel at Kingston in 1658, he announced to the court that he wished Pride could have been in attendance as the Colonel was a sober man who would have favoured his cause.[4]

Although Worcester House was by no means palatial, its purchase by Pride was a sure sign of his success. He appears to have used the house as a show-piece for his new-won status, emulating the country squire. Visitors would be greeted by mementoes of Pride's military career – in the main hall of the house were hung a musket, a half-pike and a brace of pistols, as well as an antique two-handed sword.[5] But as well as reminding guests of his military past, Pride could also show that he had a cultured side. Other accoutrements were more genteel: a painted virginals in the downstairs dining room; the striking clock in the hall; stylish bedrooms, each of which was carefully and distinctly furnished as the red, yellow and blue chambers. It is telling, given the lingering rumours of Pride's illiteracy, that there was not a single book listed among the house's contents when he died.

Pride, expedient man that he was, found a much better use for the park than a mere status symbol, and its purchase at times appears to have been little more than a calculated business investment. A survey carried out in 1650 numbered 6,000 trees in the park, two-thirds of which were to be felled and sold to the navy for ship building.[6] Over the next few years Pride would systematically strip Worcester Park of its assets, felling trees for timber and ploughing land for agricultural use. His business acumen and a drive for profit led to Worcester Park becoming a working farm as much as a comfortable country estate. Not everything was sacrificed to the axe or plough, though: when, in 1851, the Pre-Raphaelite artists Holman Hunt and John Everett Millais rented the dilapidated buildings of Worcester House for use as a studio, Hunt noted a "glorious avenue of elms" along the drive leading to the farm house. These had been retained by Pride, who rightly saw them as an ornament to his new home, and are visible on the earliest Ordinance Survey maps. Hunt and Millais produced several of their best-known works at Worcester House. In Millais' painting *The Huguenot*, the red brick that forms a backdrop to the two lovers was once Thomas Pride's garden wall.[7]

On top of this healthy dose of self-aggrandisement, the early 1650s saw Pride increase his involvement with local government in London. His place on the London Common Council at the beginning of the Commonwealth allowed him scope to promote his own religious and moral views in a way that would have been impossible before the war. In 1651 the General Baptist preacher Edward Barber had praised the army officers for releasing the English people from the bondage of the established church, but demanded further reform from them, including the abolition of tithes. The tract in which he set forth his arguments was addressed to Cromwell, Fleetwood, and to Colonel Pride: Pride could now count himself as one of the foremost army grandees in pursuit of religious reform – at least, that seemed to be the view of Barber, one of London's leading General Baptists.[8]

In 1652 Pride put his name to a pamphlet entitled *The Beacon Quenched*, an appeal to the Commonwealth's parliament to restrain the censorious Presbyterian press. The pamphlet was an answer to an earlier tract entitled *The Beacon on Fire*, in which certain London book sellers had condemned recent publications for heresy. The authors of *The Beacon Quenched* argued that they were not 'Popish' publications, as the censors alleged, but the sermons and addresses of London separatist churches, whose religious views the London publishers could not tolerate. The book sellers were named and condemned for wishing to 'lash their neighbours with *Presbyterian whips*'. By appending his name to *The Beacon Quenched*, Pride reaffirmed his hostility to the '*Episcopal Bondage* and *Presbyterian Slavery*'[9] that had previously brought him into conflict with Edward Harley, and which may well have led to his brief exclusion from the army in early 1645.

The argument of *The Beacon Quenched* is that the threat from pro-Catholic writings was not so great as the risk of losing the freedom of the press or freedom of speech, the 'dear-bought precious Freedomes' secured by Parliament's victory over Royalism. The authors argued for a greater freedom of the press, to promote understanding and toleration of others' religious views, rather than an outright ban of publications considered heretical. It was nothing less than call to allow Catholics freedom of the press: 'We desire nothing more than that they [Papists] and all dissenters should propound their doubts in a Christian way, either by Word or Epistle, and meet in the love of Christ for better instruction'[10]

Pride's subscription of *The Beacon Quenched* reveals him, again, closely allied to the Baptists, who were doubtless eager to recruit a prominent servant of the Commonwealth such as Pride to their cause. But, significantly, Pride's associates were *Particular* Baptists – those who believed in the 'puritan', Calvinist principle of predestination. There is no evidence that Pride responded to the 1651 petition of the General Baptist, Edward Barber. Other subscribers to the *Beacon Quenched* included Pride's long-time associate and Particular Baptist, William Kiffin, and the leader of one of the London Particular Baptist churches, Samuel Richardson. Pride also obtained the support of his lieutenant colonel, William Goffe, indicating some solidarity from within the ranks of his own regiment.

Pride's growing influence in 1652 was not limited to London. That year he was appointed one of the commissioners of the peace in Somerset, maintaining a link with his childhood home and the extended family he may well have had there,[11] and he had ties to the Somerset County Committee. Other ventures of a political nature were less successful: in May 1652 he failed to be appointed as a commissioner in a Parliamentary bill to block the sale of former Royalists' lands. The commission was to be made up entirely of army officers and their supporters – no MPs were to be included. The army were concerned that the confiscation and sale of former Royalists' estates would breech the terms on which the owners had surrendered or been paroled, which might lead to tension and, possibly, renewed fighting. The Rump wished to sell the lands to raise some much-needed revenue, and the officers' attempt to amend the bill to prevent the sale demonstrates the rift that was now developing between the Commonwealth's army and its Parliament.[12]

Pride's interests in Commonwealth government concerned subjects with which he had a genuinely personal concern, including religious worship and the welfare of soldiers. In the spring of 1653 he was appointed inspector of two London hospitals, the Savoy and Ely House, both of which had military connections.[13] The Savoy Hospital on the Strand was the remnant of a medieval royal palace largely destroyed during the Peasants Revolt. Bequeathed to the nation as a hospital by Henry VII, it had formerly served as a military hospital in the 1620s and in 1642 a parliamentary committee had ordered the wards cleared to make way for its wounded soldiers. With a permanent and salaried nursing staff, the Savoy might be considered the first modern hospital in London. Its amenities included a 'hot room', as sweating was considered a vital treatment for many ailments, and the hospital's position on the Thames waterside allowed for the smooth and swift arrival of casualties by boat.[14] The smaller of the London hospitals, Ely House, formerly the London residence of the Bishop of Ely, had been requisitioned by Parliament at the beginning of the Civil War to house Royalist prisoners and had been converted into a hospital during the Second Civil War of 1648. By 1653 both these establishments were receiving wounded from the war at sea against the Dutch. Their supervision was deputised to one of Pride's officers, Captain Richard Mosse.[15] In May of 1653 Pride's officers supervised the conduct of 220 sick from London to Bath, where they could take the waters and convalesce, much to the disgust of the town's corporation. The most prevalent ailment seems to have been the scurvy that had developed while serving at sea, and for which fresh water and exercise were believed to be the cure.[16]

Not all ailments were physical, however: among the accounts of the Savoy hospital is a record of three staff being paid for attending and assisting 'ye distracted man',[17] evidence that some patients had psychiatric disorders. How such a condition was

Engraving of Ely House, a Civil War hospital presided over by Pride.

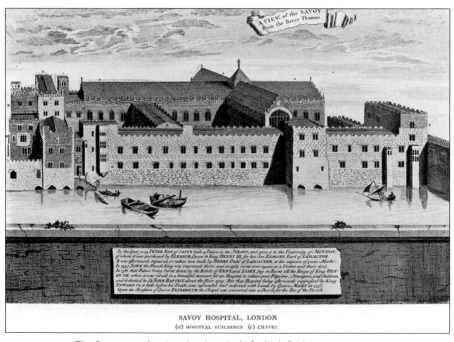

The Savoy, another London hospital of which Pride was governor.

treated is uncertain, although it is very clear that the patient was provided with care and supervision. A nurse was paid to sit with the patient for several nights, with the attendant men perhaps being on hand to restrain the patient if necessary. The need for such close observation suggests that the 'distracted' patient was suffering from some violent form of night terror. Another patient, John Elmes, also received nightly supervision before being discharged, in spite of the fact that he was recorded as being 'a fitt man'.[18] Reference to these men in the Savoy's accounts is evidence that some Commonwealth soldiers experienced post-traumatic stress following combat, and that this was not only recognised as a sickness but those suffering from it were able to receive some form of hospital treatment.

As an extension of his administrative role at St. Bart's, Pride was also one of four men appointed from October 1652 to supervise the services conducted at the church of St. Bartholomew-the-Less,[19] overseeing those who led the worship and to ensure that there were no readings from the much loathed Anglican *Book of Common Prayer*. The following summer he headed a Parliamentary committee to examine the state of two of London's most notorious debtors prisons, the Fleet and the King's Bench (known as the 'Upper Bench' during the Commonwealth and Protectorate). The committee's investigation led to the detention of the Upper Bench's warden over suspected fraud and the deaths of several prisoners in his custody, and resulted in a fairer treatment for debtors with the passing of the 'Act for the Relief of Creditors and Poor Prisoners' in October 1653.[20]

From the early months of 1652 increasing political friction with the Dutch over trading rights brought threats of raids on the English coast. War with the United Provinces finally came in June 1652 and, as fighting escalated in the early months of the following year, Pride's regiment was deployed in a scattering of garrisons along the Devon-Dorset coast, over a distance of some one hundred miles. Pride's soldiers provided garrisons at Exeter Castle and a file of men at Brownsea Castle in Poole harbour.[21] The detachments appear to have been under the overall command of Pride's Lieutenant Colonel, Waldive Lagoe, himself based at Weymouth.[22] Captain Mosse was placed in charge of Dutch prisoners of war at Southampton[23] and Major Thomas Parsons performed similar duties at Greenwich, and also seems to have taken charge of the regiment's detachments that were to serve at sea with the English fleet.[24] All of which indicates the extent to which the Commonwealth forces were stretched.

At the end of March 1653 Pride himself was in Portsmouth, overseeing preparations for the fleet.[25] He was to provide a 'sea-bed' (hammock) and blanket for each of his men, the cost of which came out of the colonel's own pocket and was to be reimbursed later by the Navy Commission. Not all commanding officers were as diligent as Pride in equipping their men. Another of the regiments to be deployed at sea, Ingoldsby's, lacked an issue of shirts and were noted to be 'new raised men and not so well provided as Colonel Pride's old soldiers'.[26] By May 1653 Pride had made ready 280 of his regiment for the manning of war ships, and by August the regiment was recruiting specifically for the war at sea.[27] 300 new recruits were

An engagement in the First Dutch War. Pride was responsible for supplying the
English navy during the conflict

enlisted and issued with firelock muskets,[28] a much more practical weapon than
the matchlock for fighting at sea, given the amount of room that would be needed
for slow match on a cramped man-of-war.

As overseer of victualling, Pride had tremendous difficulty in readying a fleet for
what was to be the largest naval operation since the Spanish Armada. The problem
was scale. The Admiralty Committee was demanding over 3,400 tonnes of bread
and the same weight of preserved meat; 10,000 butts of beer were to be provided,
together with a ready supply of cheese, butter and salt fish to eke out the meagre
diet on board ship.[29]

Pride's contract was fraught with problems from the start. Money to purchase
the grain needed for brewing had not been forthcoming from the Admiralty,
and as a result the supplies of beer had dwindled. Pride censured the Whitehall
bureaucrats for withholding payment and accusing them of jeopardising the 'care
and well-being of the Commonwealth'.[30] His solution was simple: the prize money
raised from the sale of 'fine wine' seized from captured enemy vessels should be
channelled into beer production.[31] But lack of money continued to dog the victuallers' efforts and criticism began to build against Pride and his associates, beer

being the most frequent cause of complaint. One brewer, further down the supply chain from Pride, 'laid the blame on the prices paid by the Admiralty Committee and said he could provide nothing better for the money',[32] which equated to 9 pence for each man in the fleet. In July 1653, even as Pride's soldiers were fighting the Dutch at sea, the Council of State was informed that 'There is a great complaint of victuals, especially beer and water. Col. Pride promises a better supply.'[33] Pride had in fact personally condemned the beer on two ships two days previously and he later claimed that £1,600 had been lost on beer that had been delivered to ships but found to be undrinkable.[34] This was likely to have been due to a deficiency in the barrels, the wood insufficiently seasoned because of the need to ready the fleet quickly. Provisions that were not fit for consumption were licensed to be exported free of customs duty, in the hope of finding a suitably desperate buyer and recouping some of the loss.[35] 4 July saw Pride at Harwich inspecting provisions; two days later he was aboard the flagship *Resolution*, anchored off Southwold, to discuss the problems directly with generals Monck and Blake.[36]

Pride now faced the predicament of how to replace the beer that had been lost. The 'sea-beer' that he had been providing was intentionally low in alcohol, a weak, small beer that ensured the English sailors and soldiers would remain refreshed without allowing them to become drunk. The victualling offices at East Smithfield reported that following the loss of beer at the beginning of July there was very little, if any, sea-beer available for the fleet. They did, however, come up with expedient solution: there were 600 tuns of strong beer in stock, and for every three barrels of beer that had been lost they could supply two barrels of this best beer (reported to be of 'extraordinary strength', possibly in the region of 10-11% alcohol),[37] together with one barrel of water with which to dilute it. Colonel Pride was confident that 600 tuns of strong beer, calculated to be worth approximately £6,300, was enough to supply the whole fleet for three weeks, after which time further supplies of sea-beer would be available.[38]

In January 1654, as the war with the Dutch was winding-down, and as soon as the rate of work at East Smithfield's Victualling Office could be allowed to slacken, Pride and his associates gave notice to end their contract, although supplies would not terminate until the following October.[39] The efforts required, and problems encountered, in victualling the English fleet seems to have left Pride content to step back from naval supply.

Following Pride's departure, the Admiralty reached the conclusion that victualling should be centralised under the direct control of the Navy Commission, and not civilian contractors, in an attempt to make the system more efficient and better able to cope with supplying a large fleet. In the event, very little changed. Supervision of victualling passed to Thomas Alderne, already central to the task of navy supply during Pride's tenure, and the business continued to be fraught with error and mismanagement. In 1655 brewers and bakers complained to the Admiralty of non-payment of supplies for Blake's expedition to the Mediterranean, while Blake himself complained bitterly about the quality of beer and biscuit

Detail from Morgan's 1682 map, showing the navy victualling office and yards in East Smithfield. Tower of London, bottom left.

provided for his fleet. The continued short-comings allow us to see how little real chance Pride had of succeeding in his role, dogged as it was by financial difficulties and a supply chain overburdened by demand. Naval supply was found wanting throughout the period,[40] and no blame appears to have been levelled personally at Pride for the shortfall during his tenure. Indeed, he should be credited with being able to continue to provision a fleet at all, irrespective of the quality of the goods.

As an aside, it is worth examining just why the navy victuallers were able to obtain a ready supply of 'extraordinary strength' beer at the time of the supply crisis. From 1643, when excise was first imposed on beer, the authorities recognised only two strengths of beer for tax purposes: 'small', which included the weak beverage known as 'sea-beer', and 'strong'. But there was a loop-hole in the excise rate, in that extra-strong beer was only liable for tax at the same rate as 'ordinary' or 'common' strong beer. It was quite legal for a brewer or retailer to take one barrel of extraordinary-strength beer and mix the contents with two barrels of small beer. The result would be three barrels of a beverage with a strength equal to that of common, strong beer, but for which the higher rate of excise had only been paid on one barrel. The drink was known as 'Two Threads' or 'Three Threads', depending on the number of brews or different strengths involved in the mix. This was the reason why, in the summer of 1653, there was a ready supply of extra-strong beer in stock: it was an easy way for brewers to reduce the amount of excise payable on their product.[41] We have already seen evidence of Pride attempting to avoid paying excise on the beer he produced (see chapter 8), but if he and his associate brewers had not been so unprincipled in paying their taxes the English fleet might never have been able to put to sea against the Dutch.

In May 1653 a detachment of Pride's foot had been appointed to the forty-six gun frigate *Sussex* as soldiers at sea (the term 'marine' in this period was not designate).[42] The English victory at the two-day battle of The Gabbard, off the Sussex coast, allowed the Commonwealth to secure the Channel and extend their control into the North Sea. The Dutch were driven back into their home ports and the United Provinces were thereafter subjected to an English naval blockade. On the 18 June *Sussex* put into Harwich laden with the fleet's sick and wounded, many suffering from fever and the onset of scurvy. So virulent and widespread was this sickness that rumour abounded of plague sweeping the English fleet. General Blake was reported to be so ill that a replacement was sought: 'we fear for his life; some report him dead, and that Col. Pride must be his successor'.[43]

Just how the rumour began that Pride was to take command of the fleet is unclear, though he was by this time quite a feature of the navy establishment. As well as the responsibility for victualling Pride was a burgess of the Portsmouth corporation, a post he had held since the previous year, when navy supply was under way and a close working-relationship with the town was needed. The office frequently included those with connections to the navy: other burgesses included George Monck and, in later years, Samuel Pepys and Admiral Byng. Pride himself was to be elected burgess twice more, in 1656 and 1658.[44] The fact that over 4,200 trees on Pride's Surrey estate were marked for use by the navy, 70% of the trees in the entire park,[45] further indicates that Pride was a figure with close navy associations during the early 1650s. It is interesting to conjecture whether, if Blake and Monck had both been killed, Pride would have taken command of the English fleet (and what the result might have been).

By August, the privations caused by the English blockade had forced the Dutch navy to attempt a break-out. The result was the largest engagement of the war thus far, a three-day running battle off the Dutch coast at Scheveningen, fought from the 8 to 10 August. The losses sustained by the English in terms of ships and men were serious enough to force them to break-off their blockade; likewise, high numbers of casualties among the Dutch sapped any remaining enthusiasm they may have had for continuing the war. Both sides were now willing to seek a political solution to the conflict. The extent to which Pride's foot soldiers were involved in the fighting with the Dutch is revealed in state papers, and a petition to the Admiralty made by a private soldier, Joshua Stevens, who was persuaded to seek compensation after losing his left hand, and a finger from his right, while serving at Scheveningen aboard *Sussex*.[46]

During October 1653 Pride's Regiment were guarding Dutch prisoners of war at Greenwich.[47] In February 1654 a further 100 soldiers were drawn out of the regiment for naval service, because although fighting had ceased a peace settlement would not be signed until the coming April.[48] Even as the Dutch War was drawing to a close, however, conflict had broken-out elsewhere: on 13 April the regiment was recruiting again, this time for a campaign to suppress a Royalist uprising in Scotland.

The recruiting drives of Pride's regiment at this time provide an insight into the organisation of the Commonwealth army: in August 1653 and April 1654 Pride's found it necessary to raise men for active service and on both occasions they recruited exactly 300 hundred men.[49] They were speedily equipped: 300 new firelock muskets were ordered for fighting at sea; and when recruitment began for Scotland a further 200 muskets and bandoliers, as well as 100 pikes, were requested on the same day.[50] 300 seems to have been a set figure, a precise number of men to be raised and equipped accordingly on more than one occasion. It is reasonable to suppose, then, that the regiment was reduced in peacetime to a two-thirds strength. This significantly lowered the cost of maintaining a full establishment and left a cadre that could be suitably expanded when necessary, thus retaining a core of experienced veterans who were able to train the new recruits. Recruits had been raised for the Dutch War on a short-term basis of three months, which was then extended as the war continued.[51] Those raised for Scotland were to serve on a month-by-month basis, their service extended as necessary. Presumably, their numbers would have been reduced when hostilities ceased, leaving the core of the regiment intact.

In 1653 a Royalist uprising in Scotland began under the leadership of the disaffected Earl of Glencairne. Exiled Royalists did all they could to encourage the rebels, realising how stretched Protectorate forces were with fighting the Dutch. 'let the King's whole work be to supply Scotland'[52] was the strategy, and they fed what resources they could to encourage an uprising against the English Commonwealth (very soon to be reconstituted as the Protectorate, under Cromwell's direct rule). The English Lord Middleton was despatched by Charles II to supervise the rising, seeking to expand the Highland insurgency into a full military campaign. By February 1654 Middleton had 5-6,000 men under his command,[53] engaged in what can be termed a guerilla war – disruptive attacks on English forces undertaken by small groups, who would then retreat to their crofts and seemingly vanish. By mid-1654 it was understood by Royalist intelligence that Glencairne's uprising had forced the Protectorate to deploy more than two-thirds of its military forces north of the border, including the bulk of Pride's regiment. There were said to be only four foot regiments and little more than 1,800 horse of the regular army remaining in England, and these mostly in the vicinity of London. It was an ideal opportunity for English Royalists to strike against the Protectorate.[54]

14

An Instrument of Government, 1654–56

Rebellion, plots and bear-baiting

As with the preparations for the war against the Dutch, Pride took a close interest in the well-being of his foot soldiers before they departed for Scotland. He wrote to the Council of State requesting that they not only consider how to pay his men the £800 owed to them in arrears but also to advance them a month's wage, presumably to pay for food and quarter.[1] Pride was willing to pay for 1,000 snapsacks and 200 tents out of his own pocket (provided he received a guarantee from the Council of State that he would be reimbursed).[2]

Pride's second-in-command, Lieutenant Colonel Lagoe, arrived in Scotland with the regiment in April 1654 as part of the English military build-up. Monck, however, did not begin his campaign until June, allowing time for sufficient grass to grow to provide adequate forage for his horses. Monck made thoughtful use of the units at his disposal, carefully conserving his fighting strength and planning a highly mobile strategy. He divided his forces into two independent columns: one, led by himself, to advance against Glencairne from English headquarters at Dalkeith; a second, led by Major-General Morgan, and including Lagoe's men, was to advance from Aberdeen. From these positions the English could simultaneously close in on Glencairne's bases in the Grampian Mountains from the south and east.[3] But while his regiment was campaigning in the Scottish the Highlands, where was the absent Colonel Pride?

In June 1654 an intercepted Royalist letter reported that Pride had been 'commanded home from Scotland' shortly after he and his regiment had been ordered north.[4] A similar letter was received by Edward Hyde, advisor to the exiled Royal court in France, which seemingly corroborated the report that Pride had been recalled from his command (though it is of course possible that this was a subsequent report of the same information).[5] Questions seem to have arisen regarding the loyalty of Pride's foot to the newly established Protectorate. Before starting for Scotland the regiment had apparently refused to swear an oath of loyalty to Cromwell, which may have stirred rumours of republican sympathies among Pride's rank and file.[6]

Pride himself was not cowed by Cromwell's leadership, as will be seen in the following chapter. He may already have blotted his reputation through an incident that had come to light in autumn of 1653: believing that Cromwell might misuse his new-found power as Protector, the governor of Portland, Colonel Joyce, had quipped that it would have been better if the army had shot Cromwell when they had ousted the 'grandees' like Harley in 1647. For this remark the governor was gaoled. When Pride offered to stand bail to have Joyce released he was roundly admonished, the offer being interpreted as a wry show of contempt for the Protector.[7] There appears, then, to have been rumours current at the time of Pride and his men showing a lack of regard to England's newly reconfigured government. Royalists believed that Pride had been ordered to remain in England where the authorities, aware of his inflammatory nature, could keep him under close observation. Doubts over his regiment's loyalty increased when details of a military plot to overthrow the Protectorate and restore the Commonwealth implicated certain officers and men in Pride's regiment.

Under Lagoe's command Pride's foot spent five weeks manoeuvring through the Highland passes and glens as they closed-down the Royalist forces. Middleton had difficulty in mustering more than a few hundred men at any one time. Any large body he managed to assemble was quickly dispersed as he was forced to move continuously from area to area to avoid the English columns, nor did his men relish marching far from their homes.

Monck's progress through the Highlands cut Middleton's strength considerably: 'having marched them from 3000 to 1200 … We have burnt such parts of the Highlands where they were utterly engaged against us …'.[8] Despite their foot-slogging through the hard country of the Highlands, Pride's men were ultimately denied the satisfaction of facing their enemy in battle. What remained of Middleton's army was driven back to the banks of Loch Garry, where they were finally dispersed by a regiment of Monck's horse that blundered into them at dusk while both sides were scouring the area for billets for the night. In the ensuing twilight skirmish Middleton's 1,200 foot were scattered. Middleton himself was wounded and was among the 300 Royalists taken prisoner. The remaining Scots sought the safety of their homes and thereafter the Royalist threat in the Highlands dissolved.

The English campaign did not finish here. Monck wanted to ensure that the Royalists were unable to mount a subsequent rebellion, and he wrote on 5 August that he had ordered Pride's foot to destroy 'some parte of the country neere Loughlomond'.[9] His methods of driving the Royalist sympathisers from the land were brutal, and there are clear parallels to be drawn with the Clearances ninety years later: crops were burned, cattle killed, and fines imposed on families whose members were involved in the uprisings. Scottish Royalists, in retaliation, threatened to burn the lands of any Scot who remained neutral. The Marquis of Argyll believed 'that the whole of the Highlands will, in all probability, be laid waste'.[10] Those rebels who had been captured were offered the choice of military service in

Ireland or deportation to the West Indies. Most of those that opted for the latter did not survive the voyage.

Middleton had been defeated in just five weeks, but Pride's men were to march hundreds of miles between June and September policing the Highlands. It was during their time in Aberdeen that radicalism resurfaced in the ranks of Pride's foot. At the root of this was the regimental chaplain, Samuel Oates. Oates was a Baptist minister with a chequered history, including a court appearance on a charge of rape and an accusation of drowning one of his own congregation while baptising them. His position as regimental chaplain is a further sign of Thomas Pride associating with Baptists.

Whilst in Aberdeen, Oates was summoned before a court martial for circulating a letter that had called for representatives from each of the English regiments in Scotland to convene in Edinburgh to demand political change. Disaffected republicans in the army were bitter over the dismissal of the Rump parliament and wary of the monarchical nature of the Cromwellian government that replaced it, having themselves fought so long against such tyranny. Oates himself wrote:

> Wee have made the hearts of the rightous sade [sad]… for wee have promised to make them a free people, and that they should have free and successive parlements, but performe neither… . Sure its a sad thing that wee should build agayne the things wee have destroyed.[11]

The meeting at Edinburgh was an attempt to gather republican support from the army, and Oates' involvement was to have serious repercussions for his regiment, and its colonel.

In December 1654 a plot was uncovered to have Monck arrested and for Colonel Overton, Governor of Newcastle, to take command of the forces in Scotland forces in support of the Commonwealth. Monck himself reported that Oates was 'a very greate contriver and formentour'[12] of this plot, which naturally threw suspicion on others around him. An unknown informant reported to Monck that Pride and his former subordinate, John Mason, were also involved.[13] The so-called 'Overton Plot' was linked to a more widespread design, formulated by the Leveller pamphleteer John Wildman, to encourage a nation-wide, pro-Commonwealth uprising and demand 'a full and free Parliament'.[14] Here again Pride was implicated, albeit indirectly: his associate, Pyne, with whom he was connected through the Somerset Committee, was supposed to have been tasked with overseeing a potential rising in the West Country; Pride's soldiers were said to have been among 'the regiments that they relyed on' to give the rebellion the necessary military impetus.[15]

In actuality, Monck have seems to have placed little trust in the information given him. His order to have Overton arrested was put into effect by lieutenant colonel Lagoe, which indicates that Monck, for one, was prepared to trust some of Pride's officers. There *were* suspected republicans among them, though, for when Overton's secretary was placed under arrest for his involvement in the plot a letter was found in his possession from one of Pride's captains, Richard Mosse. Mosse had paid compliment to Overton and wrote at length of his despair for 'this poore languishinge commonwealth ... so many men's lives lost for'. The London newspaper *Mercurius Politicus* announced that Mosse had been taken into custody along with Oates.[16] But although Mosse displayed feelings of war-weariness, there was no evidence of any direct support on his part for Overton's plot, and no further steps were taken against him. Indeed, he would later receive promotion to major and, later, lieutenant colonel under Pride. His republican politics, however, and his die-hard support for the Commonwealth, was to resurface following Pride's death.

Further evidence of sedition among Pride's men can been seen in the previous conduct of John Mason, although Mason had by this time left the regiment and was serving as lieutenant colonel to Charles Fairfax. In March 1652 the clergymen of Newcastle complained of the Mason's conduct after he nearly started a riot in the town: Fairfax's regiment formed the town's garrison and Mason had summoned a crowd to hear a 'heretical' sermon delivered by a lay preacher. This display of religious nonconformity caused alarm amongst the town authorities and it was decided that Mason should henceforth be confined to a backwater where his antics would prove less troublesome. He was subsequently appointed governor of Caernarfon.[17] As for Oates, he remained in custody until he had convinced the military authorities of his future peaceable behaviour.

Pride's regiment remained in Scotland until September 1655.[18] Thereafter the regiment was quartered in Kent with their headquarters at Canterbury,[19] in warmer and altogether more comfortable country than the Scottish Highlands. Having surveyed the documentary evidence it seems doubtful that Pride played any role in the republican plots of 1654/55, although the report of his recall from campaign might suggest it. Other colonels, named along with Pride in Royalist letters, were rapidly dealt with for their involvement: Colonels Alured, Okey and Saunders were brought before a court martial for signing Wildman's petition, although they were subsequently cleared of treason. No similar action was taken against Pride. As for the supposition that the Protectorate wanted to keep him at close had and under observation, there were good reasons for Pride to have remained in England at this time. He and his associates would not cease their work with naval supply until October, so there was still unfinished business to oversee. Pride had other important duties to attend to in London at this time, having been appointed to the Common Council there in May 1653. Cromwell desired that any army officer selected to serve on the council decline the invitation to do so, because 'those are that are soe chosen are to lay downe their commands in the army'.[20] It would seem, then, that Pride was unable to join the Scottish campaign in 1654 because his civilian duties in London took precedence. There were also soldiers to command in England, because not all of Pride's men had gone north. Royalist intelligence recorded that his regiment numbered 600 when it was sent to Scotland,[21] implying that some companies remained behind.

There is further reference to Pride's men being selected for duty on men-of-war in February 1656, although the main body of men remained in Scotland until that September: 'Out of that part of Pride's regiment (come lately from Scotland)', wrote a Royalist informant, 'they take 20 out of each company. It is thought they will quarrell againe with Holland.[22] Pride's men were therefore divided into more than one body at this time. Pride's eldest son, Thomas, was reported to have been still serving with the fleet until at least October 1654, when he attended a Council of War aboard the *Swiftsure* and added his name to a petition which demanded an end to pressing sailors for naval service.[23] It is possible that Pride was to supervise those of his regiment that were quartered in England for the manning of war ships, while his lieutenant colonel commanded the division sent to Scotland. Moreover, Pride *did* journey to Scotland in May 1655, when he witnessed the signing of the peace accord with the Scottish lords and the clan chief Ewan Cameron of Lochiel, that officially ended Glencairne's rebellion and the fighting in the Highlands.[24] The responsibility granted to Pride for accepting the Scots' surrender gives lie to the idea that Cromwell deliberately kept him in England for fear that he would formulate rebellion elsewhere. Offering to bail the apparently menacing governor of Portland may not have endeared Pride to the authorities, but he was no traitor and he did nothing to actively advance the cause of republicanism against the Protectorate.

The contract for victualling the navy netted Pride and his associates £284,000 in three years.[25] How much of this sum was pocketed by Pride personally is hard to determine, but what is certain is that Pride's business ventures had attracted the attention of the excise men. While Pride had been serving with Parliament's army in the 1640s his breweries had continued to run successfully without him. However, no excise had been paid for beer produced by Pride's breweries during the war and the excise commission were now investigating as to why. We have already seen the strength of Pride's opposition to the taxation of beer, and his signing of the 1643 petition against it. In his defence, Pride claimed that it had been the fault of his clerks at the brew house, who had not made provision for the tax in their accounts and that, due to his own absence with the army, they had been unable to seek his advice on payments.[26] In any case, Pride argued, the precise amount of excise to be levied had never been decided on by Parliament. Neither did he consider himself obliged to pay the arrears for 1643-45 (a total of £682) as they were pardoned by the Act of Oblivion, which had rendered all legal matters during the Civil War null and void.[27] The excise commission pointed out that Pride had already paid £124 on goods produced before the Act of Oblivion had come into effect, and they took this as his acknowledgement that the excise ought to be paid, the more so because he had promised to pay them the balance at a later date. The excise commission highlighted the danger of precedent: if they agreed to let Pride off his payments they stood to lose £20,000 in similar cases.[28] They kept up their pressure and Pride was requested to pay the outstanding £558 3s 6d.[29]

Pride was an obdurate man when it came to business. When purchasing equipment for his regiment before their Highland campaign he sought £50 reimbursement from the Council of State for the cost of 1,000 snapsacks, as well as £268 for 230 tents.[30] Two months later he was still awaiting full payment, though the amount owing for the tents had dropped to £218 4s 6d.[31]

By the mid-1650s Thomas Pride was at the height of his power – successful in business, a noted establishment figure and owner of a substantial country estate. It is at this time that we find fewer references to Pride and Farringdon Without and more connections to the Aldgate area, closer to the Tower. In later years the treasury, bent on reclaiming Royal property confiscated during the Commonwealth, made reference to 'a small discovery of traitor's estate, being a purchase by Thomas Pride ... in East Smithfield, over against the said Pride's brewhouse'.[32] This could be a reference to the Navy Victualling Yard, situated off the East Smithfield road near Tower Hill, although beer had not been brewed on site since the time of Elizabeth I. Alternatively, it may refer to the Hartshorne brew house, which provided beer for the navy and in which Pride owned a share (see chapter 18). There are further ties between Pride and the Aldgate area, namely references to his elder children in the parish registers of St. Botolph without Aldgate. The parish has been described as 'a very large, poverty-stricken out-parish',[33] though in general rich and poor lived in close proximity and London had not in this period separated into well-defined 'high class' and 'low class' districts. During the 1650s, Pride made moves to consolidate his new-won status, and he achieved by making connections with established gentry. He legitimised his rising fortunes by forging a link between his own family and those of two men who the history books would account the most noteworthy men of the Interregnum: George Monck and Oliver Cromwell.

Elizabeth Monck was 26 when, in 1654, she married Pride's eldest son, Thomas. She was the daughter of George Monck's elder brother, Thomas, a Royalist officer who had been killed at the siege of Exeter in 1644: returning to quarters one evening, Thomas had failed to remember the password and was promptly killed by one of his own sentries.[34] A thousand pounds had been bequeathed to Elizabeth in her father's will, as well as land worth £350 a year. She would thus have been considered a good match for Pride's son: twenty six years was the average age for marriage of spinsters in this period.[35] As she had only been sixteen when her father had been killed her money had been kept in trust by her mother until she was of age. However, soon after Thomas' and Elizabeth's betrothal in April 1654, the couple made a complaint to the Court of Chancery that money owing to Elizabeth was being withheld by her mother's family, the Goulds. The identities of the two young people betrothed has always proven a stumbling block for historians as there are so many Elizabeths and Thomases in the family tree, but the marriage register of St. Botolph's Aldgate makes it clear in the following entry: 'Thomas Pride Esquire, son to Collonell Pride, [and] Elizabeth Monck the daughter of Mrs Mary Monck'.[36] Chancery papers record that Colonel Pride made a statement to the court declaring, 'what a great liking he and his sonne had unto the said Elizabeth and desired the said sonne to enter marriage with her, if he might obtayne her consent.'[37] But consent was not forthcoming from Elizabeth's mother, Mary, who seems to have suspected Pride of having arranged the marriage solely to gain access to Elizabeth's wealth. Mary was willing for Elizabeth to receive her inheritance but demanded that a marriage settlement be drawn up that would offer her daughter a degree of financial security before marrying into a family of Parliamentarians (it was her opinion that the Pride family 'doe intend to avoid the said marriage agreement').[38] Given what we know about Pride's business, his wrangling and avoidance of excise payments, Mary Monck's suspicions are perhaps not unreasonable. A marriage jointure was eventually signed by the two parties, stipulating that Colonel Pride should provide half the cost of buying the newly-weds a house and demonstrating a willingness to part with some of his own money before his son could obtain that of Elizabeth.[39] Thomas and Elizabeth were eventually married at St. Botolph's church, Aldgate, on 28 August 1654.[40]

The second of the familial ties came the following year when Cromwell's nephew Robert Walton wedded Pride's daughter, Elizabeth. The marriage took place at St. Katharine's parish church, just to the south of the navy victualling office in East Smithfield (the banns had been read at St. Botolph's). Walton was an officer in the London militia,[41] and a draper and tailor by profession. His marriage to Elizabeth appears to have been a good way of expanding business interests: Pride entered into a contract to supply coats and shoes to English soldiers fighting on the continent in 1658, possibly with Walton as a partner.[42] A marriage indenture secured the Walton family estate of 1,000 acres at Great Staughton, Huntingdonshire, for Elizabeth and her children in the event of her husband's death, and also makes reference to a £3,000 dowry bestowed on Elizabeth by her father.[43]

Colonel Pride and his wife had six children in all, if we include the child, John, who died in infancy and was buried at St. Bride's church in London. There were five surviving children referred to in Pride's will.[44] Thomas was the eldest son. Next came William who, like his elder brother, served in his father's regiment. As Thomas and William were the eldest sons they consequently bear 'family names', named for their father and grandfather respectively. Likewise Elizabeth, Pride's only daughter, was named for her mother. There were also two younger sons, Samuel and Joseph, whose names underscore the family's religious faith and, perhaps, its political affiliations. Samuel was the judge of Israel who renounced his King for one who was more godly: 'thou hast rejected the word of the Lord,' Samuel told King Saul was told, 'and the Lord hath rejected thee from being king over Israel' (1 Samuel, 15:26). Joseph was Pride's youngest son, yet to come of age when his father died. His namesake would have been the Joseph of Genesis, the last and favourite of Jacob's sons, and whose father was an old man by the time of his birth.

The cost of fighting a war on two fronts, against the Dutch and against Scottish Royalists, was a crippling financial burden for the Protectorate. To lessen expenditure it was decided, from 1655, to reduce the size of the standing army by half, making up the loss in manpower by placing the county horse militia on a semi-permanent footing. Unlike regular soldiers, whose food and accommodation had to be paid, the militia covered their own costs, living under their own roofs and being in paid work. The changes would allow the government to cut direct tax by a third.[45] To ensure the militia would provide an effective military force they were to be called out on exercise every three months. Unlike the New Model, which had been centrally funded and controlled from London, the militia was raised and commanded at county level. In order to command these forces in their localities English counties were parcelled into ten (later eleven) districts, each governed by a major-general who were given extensive powers over local (often non-military) matters. Pride had by this time returned to his duties in London. His own authority was to be extended at this time, although it was not a promotion to major-general: in May 1656 he was created High Sheriff of Surrey, a similar office to that of commissioner for the peace in London, to which he had also been appointed two months earlier.[46] This meant that he was able to wield authority in both Surrey and Middlesex, on both sides of the Thames. They were positions that (one would like to think) required some measure of responsibility, but – perhaps tellingly – they were not military posts. It is possible that Pride's dealings with London hospitals and his own business interests meant that he did not wish to be removed from the capital and relocated to a major-generalship in the counties; but the fact that there were noted republicans in the ranks of his regiment, and his own outspoken nature with regard to case of the Governor of Portland, means that a question mark still hangs over whether the Protectorate trusted Pride with any increased, and independent, military powers that a Major-Generalship would have provided.

It is through Pride's responsibility of overseeing law and order that we come to the episode that was to shape his future reputation more than any other single event, and which was given an inordinate amount of attention in the years after his death, immortalised by anti-Protectorate satirists: namely, the banning of blood sports in the London borough of Southwark.

London's foremost bear pit was the Hope Theatre on Maiden Lane, situated the Thames' south bank. Built originally as a playhouse, plays had not been staged there since 1616 and by the 1650s it was used exclusively for blood sports. Nineteenth century historian Thomas Macaulay wrote that 'The Puritans hated bear-bating, not because it gave pain to the bear, but because it gave pleasure to the spectators'.[47] As a picturesque narrator of Britain's history Macaulay has few rivals, but this is a typically Victorian view of joyless, Cromwellian England. It is also patently untrue. Despite the closure of playhouses and other places of entertainment during the civil war, bear-baiting was allowed to continue more or less without interruption throughout the Commonwealth/Protectorate period.[48] An order had been passed by the Commons to prohibit bear-baiting during the Civil

A Victorian depiction of 17th Century bear-baiting. Pride closed the bear pit on Southwark's Bankside during his tenure as high sheriff of Surrey.

War, but it was so poorly enforced that unemployed actors, out of work since the playhouses closed, complained of discrimination. The Council of State had sanctioned Pride and others to suppress blood sports and 'playing for prizes by fencers' in Southwark nearly three years before but, as bear-baiting continued with impunity, the Council's order does not seem to have been carried out with any urgency.[49]

In fact, the suppression of bear-baiting at the Hope had nothing to do with a puritanical ban on popular sports. The contemporary diarist, Henry Townsend, gives his version of the incident at the Hope, which took place on the 6 February, 1656:

> Col. Pride, now Sir Thomas Pride, by reasons of some difference between him and the Keeper Godfrey of the Bears in the Bear Garden in Southwark, as a justice of the Peace there caused all bears to be fast tied up by the noeses and then brought some files of musketeers, drew up and gave fire and killed six or more bears in the place (leaving only one white innocent cub), and also all the courts [cocks] of the game.[50]

The Bear Garden was an older name for the Hope. From the above account it can be inferred that blood sports were brought to an end because of personal a disagreement between Pride and the keeper, and nothing to do with the repressive nature of Puritan killjoys. Rather, there seems to have been concern over Godfrey's mismanagement of the Hope, which resulted in a child being killed by a bear the previous September. The child's mother never received the compensation she was promised for her loss.[51] Godfrey had been in trouble with authorities before, having spent time in Newgate in 1642 for threatening behaviour.[52] Hotson (1925) asserts that the Hope had also been forcibly closed for a period in 1654 following a death there,[53] and Royalist news letters from the time concluded that the Hope was closed 'to prevent any great meeting of the people'.[54] Public safety, then, is the most likely factor that prompted Pride and others to have the Hope closed, the idea of a Puritanical drive against entertainment seems to have been only an idea thought up by later historians.

For satirists, however, the killing of the bears was analogous to the harsh rule of Cromwell and his major generals. The incident was seized upon and put to scurrilous use. Pride was portrayed, as many so-called Puritans were, as a ridiculous figure because of his hostility to popular entertainment: 'The crime of the *Bears*, was, that they were *Cavaliers*, And had formerly fought for the *King*' mocked a song of 1660, which dedicated a quarter of its twenty-two verses on Pride's life to his suppression of bear-baiting, and even renames his wife as a she-bear, 'Ursula'.[55] William Winstanley references the incident in his 1665 *Loyal Martyrology*, allowing it as much room and consideration as Pride's role in the Purge and Regicide, surely far more significant events in his career, and in history.[56]

Little more than a month after the Hope's closure its buildings were converted into tenements.[57] Bear-baiting would not return to Bankside until 1663, when it was held at new premises. Pride's expedient of killing the animals was a particularly heavy-handed way of closing the venue, and not untypical of his overbearing manner. However, not all the bears appear to have been killed. Townsend places the number at six or more; another source references 'Seven of Mr. Godfries Beares' (which implies there were more), and the news received by the exiled Royal Court in France was that only 'some' bears and game-cocks' had been killed.[58] The idea that blood sports were eradicated in Cromwellian London is a myth: another venue for bear-baiting near Islington remained active throughout the Protectorate.[59] The popular imagination recognised a parallel between the closure of the bear pit and the authoritarian rule of Cromwell, which is why the event was so readily retold by contemporary satirists and by the historians of later years: the closure of the bear pit was an obvious and convenient metaphor for Cromwellian England, and became perpetuated as such, with the finer details of the episode fading through time.

15

London, 1656–57
King Cromwell, Lord Pride

In September 1656 Cromwell was obliged to call a new Parliament to vote him extra revenue for a war with Spain. The newly returned members, determined to hold on to their seats, called for a more permanent and controlled form of government than that offered by the major generals. Within a month of the new Parliament's opening it was mooted that the office of Protector should be made hereditary, rather than an elected position, a move intended to provide the Protectorate with a permanent and more stable political settlement. Momentum gathered for this kind of conservative thinking: proposals were put forward to re-establish a second chamber in Parliament, akin to the old House of Lords, and at the end of March 1657 Cromwell was formally offered the Crown by the Speaker of the House. Opposition to Cromwell's kingship was notable among some of the army officers closest to the Protector, among whom was his brother-in-law, Major General John Desborough. Edmund Ludlow recalled that Pride was also prominent in the army's opposition to constitutional change.

On 10 April 1657, there was a low-key meeting between Cromwell and Desborough in St. James' Park, during which the latter made it clear that he would not support Cromwell's acceptance of the Crown in any way. Desborough made his way home where he found Pride waiting for him:

> Having imparted to him Cromwell's desire to accept the Crown, Pride answered, 'He shall not.' 'Why,' said the Colonel [Desborough], 'how wilt thou hinder it?' To which Pride replied, 'Get me a petition drawn and I will prevent it.'[1]

Ludlow claimed that the incident was recounted to him by Desborough himself. It displays Pride's determined, no-nonsense manner, and a typically blunt response to this particular political crisis. And there is, again, a hint of his reputed illiteracy in Pride's request that the petition be penned by a third party.

The author of the petition was Dr. John Owen, a prominent theologian and Independent minister. Owen had served as chaplain to the army during the Dunbar campaign and shared the views of the army officers. Importantly for Pride he was also sympathetic to Independent polity, ministering to conventicles that were convened in worshippers homes and believing it was necessary for Christians to separate themselves from unwarranted ceremony and church worship in order to avoid being tainted by the sins of others.[2]

That Desborough had found an ally in Pride is understandable because there was a similarity in their characters. Both men had a reputation for being outspoken in their views. Desborough, like Pride, was mocked by his opponents for his rustic manners: he managed a Cambridgeshire estate, which allowed his opponents to write him off as a yokel with no understanding of government (while conveniently ignoring the fact that he was a qualified attorney). Furthermore, Pride and Desborough had marital ties to Cromwell's extended family, a closely-knit oligarchy that had positioned itself at the centre of English government. In January 1656 a further link to Cromwell's establishment had been forged when Pride had allowed himself to be knighted by the Protector at Whitehall Palace. This was grist to the mill for those who felt that Pride was bent on self-aggrandisement, one former army officer declaring that he 'was real before, but now he was knighted he was grown as bad as the rest'.[3] Understanding Pride's role in persuading Cromwell to reject the crown is important if we are to appreciate his particular strain of republicanism.

Ludlow's assertion that Pride was the driving force behind the army's statement of opposition is borne-out by the fact that it was Pride's erstwhile comrade, John Mason, who gathered signatures for the officers' petition and then led a delegation to Westminster to obtain more. On 8 May, the morning that Cromwell was to address the Commons and give his answer to the question of Kingship:

> some 26 or 27 officers came with a petition to the parliament, to desire them not to presse H. H. [His Highness – Cromwell] any further about kingship. The petition was brought to the barr by lieutenant colonel Mason, who was the cheife man, who promoted it, and went up and downe from man to man to get hands thereunto.[4]

Pride's animosity towards Cromwell's decision went even further, if Arthur Onslow, a future Speaker of the Commons, is to be believed. Onslow relates that Pride confronted Cromwell personally, threatening that if the latter accepted the crown 'he would (if nobody else would) shoot him through the head, the first opportunity he had for it'.[5] As Onslow was not born until 1691 this anecdote is second-hand at best, but it found its place among the myths that surrounded Pride because to voice such a threat did not seem out of character. The early 18th century text *The History of King-Killers* puts Pride's objections to kingship down to his 'hauty Temper'.[6] What Cromwell's reaction was to Pride's attitude is not recorded but he seems to have been quite familiar with the colonel's forthright manner. 'I think wee must labour to have Collonel Pride's Common Councill again',[7] was Cromwell's wry comment when he was considering dissolving the First Protectorate Parliament, 'Pride's Council' being shorthand for a blunt response to complicated political difficulties.

Pride's name had become a byword for candid, no-nonsense problem-solving. His objection to Cromwell's acceptance of the crown, however, was not merely a knee-jerk reaction to all things regal. A closer understanding of his thoughts can be gleaned from the wording of the petition that John Mason presented to Parliament. This declared the army officers' belief that they had:

> hazarded their lives against monarchy, and were still ready so to do, in defence of the liberties of the nation: that having observed in some men great endeavours to bring the nation again under their old servitude, by pressing their General to take upon him the title and government of a King, in order to destroy him, and weaken the hands of those who were faithful to the publick; ... for the preservation of which [the officers] for their parts were most ready to lay down their lives.[8]

The tone is unmistakably belligerent, and clearly the belief was that it was pro-Royalists who wished Cromwell to accept the crown in order to stir rebellion. A hereditary head of state had already crept back into English government. Placing the crown on Cromwell's head would have affirmed the idea of monarchy even more strongly, serving only to bolster the Royalist cause and bring the restoration of the 'old servitude' one step closer. The wording of the petition revealed the determination of Pride (and others) to avoid such an action, using force if necessary, and to 'discountenance all such persons and endeavours, and continue steadfast to the old cause'.[9] Intended to be read before the House, the petition in fact never made it that far. Firth wrote in 1894 that the petition 'was printed, but does not seem to be in existence now; great care was taken to suppress it.' General Monck was ordered to seize any copy of it that found its way to Scotland.[10] Cromwell urged its reading before the House be postponed and there are indications that, following his meeting with Desborough, he had already decided to refuse the title of King.[11]

Given Pride's role in organising a resistance to the monarchists, it can be no coincidence that this period of the Protectorate was the only time in Pride's life that he played an active role in central government. In December 1656 Pride stood for election at Reigate in Surrey.[12] The second Protectorate parliament had been called the previous September, but now was the time that the question of Cromwell's constitutional role was being discussed. It is possible that Pride, who already had some influence at a local level in Surrey, saw the need to secure himself a place in Parliament in order to influence the direction that the government was taking.

As with nearly everything in which Pride involved himself, his election as member for Reigate was not without controversy. As the winning candidate in the election, Pride was to be formally returned by the Sheriff of the county, which happened to be himself. So embarrassed does he appear to have been by the predicament of returning himself as the election's victor that he did not return himself at all. The parliamentary diarist, Thomas Burton, intimates that Pride was in a quandary concerning the legality of being able to return himself as member for Reigate, as well as issues of propriety: 'some call it Sir Thomas Pryde's modesty, that will not return himself; but Mr. Highland said, Sir Thomas Pryde would fain be returned, but he ought not.'[13] How the situation was resolved is unclear, although Burton notes that by April 1657 Pride had taken his seat as Reigate's MP.[14]

His presence in the Commons during the time the petition was being circulated was predictably stormy. Some members had taken offence at being coerced by the army into signing against Cromwell's kingship, 'and some moved that the house would take [it] into their consideration as a breach of privilege'. One MP named Goodwin labelled the petition's authors (i.e. Pride and Desborough) 'evill councellors who advised his Highness without doores not to hearken to the advice of his Parliement.' Goodwin further declared that it had been similar 'evill' councillors who had persuaded Charles I to take up arms in 1642. Pride, who was in the members' lobby at the time, did not take kindly to the comparison, demanding that Goodwin be called to the bar for insulting a fellow member. Once Pride's 'hauty temper' had subsided however, the matter seems to have been forgotten.[15]

Between April 1657 and the end of June, Pride is recorded as having sat on twelve government committees, including bodies appointed to discuss Cromwell's position within England's newly-drawn constitution, *The Humble Petition and Advice*, and how Cromwell's executive role was to be 'bounded, limited and circumstantiated'.[16] Desborough and Goffe, as well as Pride, were in attendance at these sessions. Despite Pride's presence at the heart of government, however, it seems that his real political interests lay not in the new constitution but elsewhere. Of those committees on which Pride sat, four concerned Cromwell and the kingship; the rest dealt with more routine governmental matters. There were committees to discuss a bill to curb vagrancy (5 May, three days before Cromwell formerly rejected the crown), discussion of a bill to restrict the building of houses in London suburbs (9 May), a treasury committee (30 May), and Pride flexed his moralistic muscle when attending a reading of the 'Immoderate Living Bill' (17 June), which was intended to punish those who lived beyond their means and whose expensive lifestyles led to them becoming indebted.[17] All of these committees were concerned with day-to-day life in London. On 22 June Pride was present in the Commons as a teller when the House voted on a subject that was of especial interest to him: not (as we might expect in the political tumult of 1657) a constitutional matter, but the passing of a Parliamentary bill to reduce the excise on beer.[18]

Irrespective of any personal interests, however, Pride kept himself at the centre of constitutional developments. Towards the end of June 1657 he oversaw the investiture of Cromwell as he accepted the Lord Protectorship under a new constitution. Pride's was the most prominent name among four persons nominated by the Commons to oversee preparations for staging the Protector's investiture. Westminster Hall was to be 'prepared suitable to such solemnity' and Pride was required to obtain 'a Chair of State, a Canopy, Tabl, &c.' for the ceremony.[19] The ample provision of luxurious drapes (pink Genoese, velvet edged with gold fringe) would have been easily procured through Pride's connections among the London haberdashers, or perhaps his draper son-in-law, Walton, who would provide the black mourning cloth for Cromwell's funeral ceremony fifteen months later.[20]

During the early summer of 1657 Pride was instrumental in focusing opposition to those who were calling for a return to Monarchy. His presence at Westminster at this pivotal time would have served as continual reminder of the force of opposition that was weighted against them. Pride's petition had not only the support of the army but was visibly endorsed by the religious Independents through its authorship by John Owen.

The second clause of *The Humble Petition and Advice* stipulated that Parliament was to consist of two chambers: since the abolition of the Lords in 1649 the House of Commons had been in session alone. This new 'other house', as it was now euphemistically referred, was to be of between forty and sixty member, nominated by Cromwell. Eighteen of these new lords were related to the Protector, either directly or through marriage, and Pride accepted a place among the mix of army officers, government officials and suitable members of the old peerage in the reconstituted House of Lords: from 1657, Pride would style himself *Thomas, Lord Pride of Worcester Park*.[21] Any political influence he might have wielded as a consequence of this appointment was minimal, however, as Cromwell chose to dissolve his second Parliament in February the following year.

As with many of his associates, Pride had achieved status with astonishing speed. Having held considerable military power since the late 1640s, he had gained civic influence and local government positions by the mid-1650s; had been knighted by Cromwell in January 1656; elected MP for Reigate in December the same year, and now in 1657 he had been created a Lord and appointed to the upper house. Such swift progression would argue a deliberate strategy to gain political power, but Pride's own political outlook appears rather more equivocal. Active in local government in Surrey, as County Sheriff and a Justice of the Peace, he might well be viewed as part of the apparatus of the Protectorate. But his open opposition to Cromwell when the latter was offered the crown challenges this view, with his consolidating the officer's hostility through the army petition. Finally, Pride accepted Cromwell's decision, and later took a seat in the second house.

In 1657 Pride can be seen steering a course between the two factions in the constitutional debate, instinctively opposing Cromwell's acceptance of kingship while continuing to uphold the establishment in the Protectorate parliament. It is not dissimilar to the position he adopted during the army mutinies of 1647, when he had asserted the rights of his men against the Presbyterian officers but appears to have paid no heed to the radical, 'Leveller' politics. Both situations reveal a man who was outspoken in his views and ready to use coercion as a political expedient, and the evidence argues a purposeful move on Pride's part to place himself at the centre of political debate when it best suited him. His reputation as a maverick went before him, shown in Cromwell's aphorism on 'Colonel Pride's common council', proof that Pride was recognised as a radical and not simple a factotum of an increasingly conservative regime – a 'buffoon'. A useful parallel can be drawn between the honours accepted on Pride and his purchase of the Worcester Park estate some years before: he readily acquired a Royal property, only to strip it of its assets. Honours and entitlement were only useful to Pride if they had a practical application: 1657 saw Pride steering a political course which he saw as the most expediential, strengthening the Protectorate by supporting the *Humble Petition and Advice*, but refusing to endorse a return to monarchy.

16

Thomas Pride in 17th century satire
'Oliver's Drayman'

From what we have seen of Thomas Pride's role in enforcing Protectorate rule – his military command, his association with the navy, the civic duties he undertook and his acceptance of honours – it is easy to see why he gained a reputation as a Cromwellian dogsbody. 'a useful man to Cromwell in all his projects,' was the view of the 18th century biographer, Mark Noble.[1] It was an aspect of Pride's character that was seized by the historians and commentators of later years, who regarded Cromwell's England as policed by dour, puritanical killjoys. They considered Pride a mere functionary, dutifully obeying orders and mindlessly carrying out the Protector's edicts.

It was a caricature drawn, firstly, by the satirists of the Restoration, who regarded Pride as a man who had furnished himself with the trappings of power and who had wielded an authority to which his birth had not entitled him. In 1679 a suitably parodic Thomas Pride appeared as an illustration in a set of playing cards. Entitled 'The Knavery of the Rump', each of the fifty-two cards in the deck lampooned some prominent figure of the Interregnum,[2] with the eight of clubs baring the legend 'Pride, Oliver's Drayman' below a caricature illustration. The cartoon depiction gives us a fair idea of how Pride was remembered some twenty years after his death. He stands with his horse and dray in front of a rustic cottage, his sword conspicuous and emblematic of his military background from where his authority supposedly derived. In his left hand he holds a brewer's sling, and is shabbily dressed in a labourer's crumpled hat and tattered coat. He has the has the open-mouthed, vacant look of a village simpleton – a Somerset yokel.

Pride's detractors cast him as a coarse, ill-educated man unsuited to a role in government. He was forever the brewer's drayman, carting Cromwell to fame and fortune, driving along the Protectorate government. In reality he was a successful businessman, but his opponents dearly loved to view him as a man from the provinces with a background in trade: low-born and therefore unfit to hold office. Even if the satirists had chanced to meet Pride this image might not have been dispelled, given his west-country heritage. The Somerset accent has been long-regarded as

Pride caricatured as a brewer's drayman in pack of Restoration playing cards entitled, 'The Knavery of the Rump'.

Pride Oliver.ᵉ Drayman

having done 'very heavy duty as representative of the clownish element in literature'[3] Accents may have altered since the 17th century, but the works of Jonson and Shakespeare are peppered with itinerants and country-dwellers commonly referred to as 'clowns', and familiar enough to Londoners who encountered them on the stage. We know that Pride was closely identified with his birthplace until his death, evidenced in the 1658 petition of the Glastonbury township who appealed to Pride for charity following a devastating fire, and he had been appointed as a commissioner of the peace in the county in 1652.[5] Given such close ties it is not beyond possibility that he retained something of the mummerset burr that set apart the clownish characters of the London stage from anything approaching respectability. With his speech littered with idiosyncrasies such as *thik* (the), *thee bist* (thou art) and *we'm* (we are), and with little oddities such as *wopse* (wasp), *zee'd* (saw), and *worze bin?* (where have you been?), it would have been difficult for Pride *not* to have been ridiculed as some sort of bumpkin. In the opinion of his Royalist and Presbyterian political opponents there existed a ludicrously wide gulf between the man and his elevated position in Cromwell's Upper House.

As to how Pride really looked, beyond his caricature, we only have the slimmest knowledge. The only extant likeness of him survives in the Sutherland Collection of the Ashmolean Museum in Oxford. In a grangerised version of Clarendon's *The True Historical Narrative of the Rebellion* there can be found a small (eight inches by six inches) illustration in a grey ink wash: a head and shoulders portrait of Colonel Thomas Pride in miniature. The face depicted has an air of quiet self-assurance, he has a neatly trimmed beard, carefully coiffured and slightly receding hair, and his burnished armour is topped off with a very respectable white collar: it is the image of middling-sort confidence, of hard-won and well-deserved privilege. The portrait is accompanied by a penned description: 'Colonel Pride. Commanded a Rear Guard at the Battle of Naseby, And likewise commanded the soldiers who assisted Cromwell in expelling the Members from the House.'[6]

The watercolour portrait is unsigned, but the words 'Colonel Pride' are recognisably the handwriting of the artist, Thomas Athow, who contributed several other watercolours to Sutherland's collection. The description below the sitter's name is in another hand, presumably that of Sutherland himself. Athow was active in London in the early nineteenth century and exhibited at the Royal Academy between 1806 and 1822.[7] The portrait of Pride must therefore be of this period, and certainly from before 1837 when the Sutherland Collection was presented to the Ashmolean. Athow specialised in watercolour copies of Tudor and Stuart portraits held in private collections. He usually identified the original paintings that he used as his source, but not it the case of the Pride portrait. However, the picture's grey wash suggests that Athow copied it from a monochrome engraving or print, not from a portrait in oils. The exact nature and whereabouts of the original painting, or even the engraving taken from it, is unknown. As such, it is quite impossible to tell whether this nineteenth century reproduction is in any way a true likeness of its subject.

Following the Restoration the general consensus was that Pride was an uncouth, low-born ignoramus who had achieved fame and fortune through rebellion and by murdering his King. The 1660 publication, *A New Meeting of Ghosts at Tyburn* stated that Pride acted in tandem with the other Regicides because he himself 'had not brains enough to plot'.[8] *The Court & Kitchin of Elizabeth, Commonly Known as Joan Cromwell* (1664) has Pride begin a food fight at a state banquet when he throws a milk pudding into a woman's lap:

> a Big Bellied Woman, a Spectator, neer *Cromwell's* table, upon the serving thereof with Sweatmeats, desiring a few dry Candies of Apricocks, Colonel *Pride* sitting at the same, instantly threw into her Apron a Conserve of Wet, with both his hands and stained it all over; when as if that had been

the Sign, *Oliver* catches up his Napkin and throwes it at *Pride*, he at him again, while all of that Table were engaged in the Scuffle[9]

Pride is oafish and imbecilic, portrayed as such to provide a contrast with the more refined and propitious majesty of a Stuart monarch (whose divine right to rule is the subtext of all these satires). It was a reputation that stuck, and it continued down the generations. By 1798, Noble felt able to state that Pride was incapable of acting without recourse to oppression and blind obedience, that he knew 'no law but the mandates of the general' and labelling him Cromwell's 'buffoon'.[10] By 1800, Pride was remembered merely as the jester at the Lord Protector's court.

Caricature is an art of simplifying and of exaggeration, it does away with the complexities of an individual's character and reduces them to a set of commonly accepted, readily understood 'myths'. The image of Pride as a rustic simpleton was such a useful device to satirists that it was repeated time and again, and thus endured. The caricature gained currency during the Restoration and by the time that Noble was writing, some one hundred and forty years after Pride's death, it was all that anyone knew of Pride. He was recognised and understood only through popularised caricature.

Not only was Pride of low, provincial stock, his very profession could be used against him. The term 'brewer' was a common rejoinder employed by Royalists to criticise prominent figures of the Parliament. It was often applied to Cromwell, whose father was said to have brewed his own ale. When the fighting in south Wales was believed to be going badly for the Parliament in 1648, a Royalist newspaper declared: 'their forces falling thick as *Hops*, it is even high time *Cromwell*, *Pride*, and *Horton*, the three *Brewers Generall* for the *State*, to return (if they can) and fall to their old *Trades* again.'[11] Samuel Butler's ballad of 1657, *As Close as a Goose*, refers to Pride in a similar vein. Pride had by this time been created a peer in Cromwell's upper house, and is portrayed as suitably attired in robes of state:

> In a robe of cow hide
> Sat yeasty Pride
> With his dagger and his sling;
> He was the pertinantest peer
> Of all that were there
> T'advise with such a king.[12]

The 'king' referred to was, of course Cromwell. Butler's ballad further develops and embellishes the caricature. The Protectorate peer retains the cow hide buff-coat of a soldier in place of a robe of office, indicative of the support Cromwell required of the army to keep him in power. Pride is armed not only with a brewer's sling (used for carrying beer barrels) but a dagger, which brings to mind the image of Caesar's assassins, and the notion that those who had put Cromwell in power were prepared to take it back by force if necessary.

Butler has the smell of yeast hanging around Pride like a cheap aftershave, and the unsavoury nature of the newly created peers was the subject of much punning and doggerel. Rumour had it that the Earl of Warwick refused to sit beside Pride in the new upper house because he would not tolerate being seated next to a brewer. 'OH, what a fine Trade is driven at *Westminster* with a *medley* of *Mechanicks* and *Politicks*!' exclaimed the Royalist news book, *Mercurius Pragmaticus.*[13] Those who believed in Divine Right majesty and ancient privilege could not conceive of a workable government led by an upstart brood of *nouveau riche*. 'King CHARLES the *Second* (in spight of all the Brewers and Bakers, Coblers, Pedlers, and Tinkers in the Parliament and Army) is rightful King',[14] wrote *Mercurius Elencticus,* another Royalist author. The criticism was that Pride had not been born into power but had risen through the ranks of Parliament's army, receiving promotion on merit. Others had risen further: Richard Mosse, who was to become colonel of the regiment following Pride's death, had been a private soldier fifteen years before;[15] Nicholas Andrews rose from private to lieutenant colonel in eleven years.[16] Conversely, no officer in the Royalists' Oxford Army was ever commissioned from the ranks.[17] The Royalist view was that an officer was a gentleman and, as such, was born into the position. This was the crime of which the Royalist satirists accused Pride: rising above his station.

Of all the trades, brewing was the one most often evoked in satirical writings. A brewer with political powers was not only an example of social inversion, it was a moral stigma. Beer and ale suggested drunkenness and impropriety, and it placed the Puritan government firmly (and hypocritically) in the alehouse. As the sketch of the food fight quoted above shows, the image of the crude and ill-educated brewer could be invoked to portray the Protectorate's elite as giddy rioters, drunk on their new-found powers. Pride, with 'his *froath*, his Yest-Tubb, [and] Hoggs-heads Barrel',[18] provided a ready target for scurrilous satire. As such, the caricature of the uncouth tradesman became more and more embellished: it was rumoured that when Pride was knighted by Cromwell, Pride insisted that the ceremony be carried out with a stick rather than the traditional – and distinctly regal – sword, as a snub to the peerage;[19] such was Pride's disdain for the legal profession that he was quoted as declaring that all "mercenary lawyers" should be ejected from their offices and their robes hung in Westminster Hall as trophies, alongside the Scottish colours captured at Dunbar;[20] that when Francis Acton, father-in-law of Cromwell's eldest son, Henry, was openly in favour of Cromwell being crowned, Pride jibed that Acton's true motive was to be known as the King of England's father-in-law.[21] Taken together, these anecdotes reveal a vein of contemptuous humour in the man. One begins to suspect the Pride may well have donned a buff coat in the robing room of the House of Lords, rather than suffer the traditional velvet and ermine.

Such anecdotal evidence may be difficult to corroborate, but it is a useful commentary on how Pride was viewed during the Protectorate and Restoration, at least by his opponents. Pride is invariably portrayed as an outspoken maverick, a gruff-old hand with an abrasive sense of humour who was not to be tamed by the good-living that he had managed to acquire for himself. Interestingly, these glimpses of his personality correspond with what *can* be substantiated of his character from contemporary records. It can be spotted in his brazen denial to the Commons of having any involvement in petition circulated among the troops in 1647; his protest against the levying of excise on beer in 1643, and his subsequent evasion of paying the excise on beer from his breweries; his offer to bail Cornet Joyce after reportedly threatening Cromwell. A further scuffle with authority comes to light in June 1658 when Oliver Vaughan (fellow brewer, militia officer and signatory of the 1643 brewer's petition) received a visit from the excise men after failing to pay £1,000 owing in tax. The excise had obtained a warrant to seize Vaughan's brewing vessels as recompense, but when they arrived at Vaughan's premises in Old Street they found the entrance barred by soldiers from Pride's regiment.[22] Pride was required to answer for his conduct in the matter, though what reason he may have offered for his actions is unrecorded. Another incident that hints at Pride over-reaching his authority occurred in August 1656 when he requested a warrant of arrest for a Dr. Savery for 'speaking troublesome words against his highness [Cromwell]'. Savery was later released without charge and the four soldiers who undertook the arrest on Pride's order were themselves committed to the gaol on Wood Street.[23] Pride may have been contemptuous of others' authority but he often seems to have prepared to use his own to his advantage or to aid his associates. The caricature of Pride in contemporary satire defines and reinforces what can be discerned of his character in the historical record.

The most biting, and offensive, of these character sketches is the anonymous 'On Colonel Pride', found in the 1662 publication *Rump*,[24] a twenty-two verse ballad which plumbs the depths in insult and defamation. As well as the typical labels of 'buffoon' and 'clown' Pride is forced to suffer accusations of being a bastard ('trucking with fame, to purchase a name / For 'tis said he had none of his own') and possessing the 'manners & features', and smell, of the pigs he had once supposedly reared. He is described as lecherous, having 'ever a mind to the Placket' (a placket being a petty-coat, but also a slang term for vagina), and a coward who flees the field of battle. His wife does not escape either, described a she-bear ('Ursula') and dismissed as a 'Trull', or whore. Gone are the mere exaggerations of character, replaced by insult and lie.

The most thorough rendering of Pride's caricature is found in the 1680 satire, *The Last Speech and Dying-Words of* Thomas (*Lord,* alias *Colonel*) Pride. This alleges to be the ruminations and final confessions of Pride on his deathbed. It is written in a kind of ironic, declamatory style and riddled with allusions and puns, the meanings of which are generally better understood by the reader that by the naïve narrator (the voice of Pride himself). *The Last Speech* begins with the sort of anecdote and hearsay that would have been familiar to readers: the first six pages are given over to Pride's extermination of the bears at the Hope Theatre, and the narrative has Pride dying in the royal palace ('at *Non-such.* 'Twas the Kings house, and Queen *Elizabeth* lov'd this above all her houses'),[25] both of which were common enough fabrications. Some parts of *The Last Speech* are lifted directly from other sources, Such as the popular 'turning [brewer's] slings to swords', which Samuel Butler used in his verse of 1657, and which was re-used by Winstanley in his *Loyal Martyrology* of 1663. The content and style affirms *The Last Speech* as a lampoon, rather than the true account it has sometimes been accepted to be by historians (see, for example, Temple, n.204). *The Last Speech* is valuable evidence that the memory of Pride was still vivid twenty years after his death, as the reader has to have a working knowledge of the man's life for the comedy to work. It seems an extraordinary length of time to wait to publish such a detailed piece, though. There seems to have been no event in 1680 to warrant resurrecting the figure of Pride in a satire, save perhaps the twentieth anniversary of the Restoration and the trial of Pride's fellow Regicides.

The Thomas Pride revealed in *The Last Speech* is a familiar fellow: none too bright, and who often finds himself a figure of fun. Among Pride's doomed-to-fail ventures includes a ploy to save money by using his dray horses to pull his lordly carriage. His clumsy attempts at rhetoric fail miserably as he tries to illustrate his rise from humble origins with a classical reference (as a scholar might) by suggesting that Julius Caesar himself started life as a lowly potato grower: Pride forgets Caesar's name and the whole anecdote collapses into a convoluted pun: 'Dig Tator ['dictator'], I think they called him'.

Perhaps the most revealing of these lengthy character sketches is one that purports to demonstrate Pride's feeble grasp of geography:

> I remember when I din'd with the *Florida* Embassadour at *Alderman Nowel's,* where we had *Florence*-Wines, I told the Alderman that when the Embasadour got home to his Country he'd send us more of that *Florida*-Wine. They all smil'd, but what car'd I? 'twere not two pence to me if *Florida* were in *Italy* and *Florence* in the Indies.[26]

What is interesting here is Pride's apparent attitude to his own ignorance. Pride may have muddled an Italian city with a Spanish colony, but he *does not care* that people find this risible, or that it makes him appear stupid. Pride's ability to brush aside embarrassment may well have been a character trait with which the readership was expected to be familiar, the stubborn fellow who knows his own mind. The country bumpkin and lout, which appear in other Royalist satires, are there in *The Last Speech,* but there is something more. Here is a portrait of someone who has risen in status but who had not been graced with the genteel airs of someone groomed for such a role. 'They all smil'd, but what car'd I?': by imbuing Pride with such a nonchalant disregard of what others may think of him, the author of *The Last Speech* inadvertently lends him some dignity. Like many of these satirical jibes, the anecdote concerning the ambassador was an embellishment of a real encounter: Pride had met the ambassador in London and apparently used the opportunity to promote his brewery business: 'When the Florida Ambassador was in London, Col. Pride being once at dinner with him, instead of propounding a question like a Statist [statesman], asked him, Whether there were not good vent for Beer and Ale in Florida?'[27] In a later age Pride may have been applauded for trying to encourage overseas trade, but for the Royalists it was just another example of how ill-bred the man was: talking of business when he should have been discussing more gentlemanly subjects, such as art or horse-rearing.

There was a rash side to Pride's character, shown in his attempts to avoid paying excise and his interfering in the case of fellow-brewer, Vaughan. It surfaced again in 1650 with Pride's support of a local government clique to gain control of the Somerset County Committee. Pride appears to have given tacit support to accusations of drunkenness and desultory conduct levelled at the governor of Bristol Castle, Latimer Sampson. The clique who brought about the accusations included George Sampson, a relation of the governor and a former captain in Barclay's Regiment. The Committee of Compounding that oversaw Latimer's subsequent dismissal was advised that Pride was man 'subject to passion and misinformation',[28] a man quick to act without first verifying the facts. It is a view reinforced by what we have seen of Pride's method of attack in the Second Civil War, and perhaps something of which Ireton was aware when he orchestrating the Purge in 1648.

Pride's bombastic and occasionally outspoken nature could leave him looking pompous and laughable, an obvious figure of fun to be exploited by the pamphleteers. As time went on he became the archetypal 'Roundhead', fitting seamlessly into the Victorian caricature of Cromwell's minions and lacking only the dour, puritanical religiosity. Curiously, religion is conspicuously absent in all of the contemporary biographical sketches of Pride. Perhaps, in an age of Ranters, Quakers, and Fifth Monarchists, Pride's separatism was unremarkable by comparison. There was a genuinely worthy side to Pride's character that stemmed from his religious faith, shown in his work with the London hospitals and the several public offices he held. It was a side that is sadly, and no doubt deliberately, missing from much that is written about him.

However great the distortion, the caricature retains at its heart a popularly accepted view of a public figure, a consensual agreement of known facts about the subject. In this way, the parody of Pride Royalist satire corroborates what we can glean of his personality from the historical record. Taken with caution, Royalist satires go some way to putting flesh on the bones of Pride's character. His idiotic and disdainful conduct is clearly a comic distortion of the manner in which often acted. He had a rash, simplistic attitude that perhaps betrays his provincial origins and trade background. He was a self-determined figure who followed his own moral guide. The Scottish divine, Bishop Burnet, looking back in the 1680s on the age in which he had lived, wrote of the 'Middle Sort' of people:

As for the men of trade and business, they are, generally speaking, the best body in the nation, generous, sober and charitable... There may be too much vanity, with too pompous an exterior, mixed with these in the capital city; but upon the whole they are the best we have.[29]

'an Ignorant, Illiterate Fellow ... yet being of a resolute Courage,' wrote Winstanley in 1664.[30] Such was the character of Colonel Thomas Pride that even his Royalist critics were obliged, occasionally, to acknowledge his qualities.

17

End of the Protectorate, 1658–1660

The men they couldn't hang

June 1658 saw Thomas Pride sitting on a High Court of Justice established to try Royalist sympathisers charged with plotting against the Protectorate. Illness forced him to withdraw from the proceedings. Elizabeth Carey, wife to one of the accused, wrote in her diary of the suddenness of Pride being taken sick: 'God's emedeate Hand … striking one of the Corte with an illnes, which forsed him to goe out'.[1] It was widely believed that Pride's absence from the courtroom allowed a verdict of not guilty to be secured for Carey's royalist husband, John Mordaunt, saving him from a death sentence.

'troubled with the Stone, and being long at Urine', were the symptoms of Pride's sickness.[2] Although he had remained active in his supervisory duties at the Ely House and the Savoy hospitals during the spring, Pride drops out of sight after June 1658, and almost nothing is recorded of his activities thereafter.[3] His symptoms were regarded at the time as 'his undoubted Fate', and it is reasonable to assume that this marks a decline in health that would eventually lead to his death in October. He was believed to have been suffering from some sickness of the bladder or urinary tract, but prostate cancer should not be ruled out. He would have been in his fiftieth year, or thereabouts. He may have been unaware that his life was drawing to a close because his preparation for the inevitable was hasty, his will being completed only on the 12 October, eleven days before he died. His reported final words, 'that he was very sorry for these three Nations, whom he saw in a most sad and deplorable Condition', are difficult to substantiate as they appeared in print one year after his death.[4]

On 23 October 1658 the Parliamentarian Richard Temple wrote to Sir Richard Leveson: 'Col. Pride is conceived to the be dead … he was very near it this morning';[5] a newsletter delivered to General Monck in Scotland some days later reported: 'Saturday last the Lord Pride dyed, whose death is heere much deplored'.[6] Both these sources, with their matter-of-fact tone, indicate that Pride's death was not unexpected. They also suggest that his passing would have political implications.

Despite indications of illness that June, Pride had been attentive to the changing political scene of his last months. On the day following Oliver Cromwell's death on 3 September, Pride signed the proclamation that made Richard Cromwell Lord Protector (which implies Pride was not wholly debilitated by his illness).[7] His name was accompanied by those of two of his former officers, Waldive Lagoe and William Goffe. A prominent figure in English politics for ten years, Pride's presence would have provided some stability during the transition of power from the older Protector to the younger, which is perhaps why news of his death was much 'deplored'. A testament to Pride's steadying influence can be seen in the way that the politics of his own regiment were to visibly shift following its colonel's death.

In the spring of 1659, Richard Cromwell recalled the Rump Parliament following conflict with army officers and the loss of their support. Many officers who had been supporters of Oliver Cromwell were subsequently removed from their regiments by a Rump eager to hold-on to its reinstated powers. Several of Pride's old officers lost their positions in a round of purges. Waldive Lagoe was appointed Adjutant General of the army in Ireland;[8] he was later posted to Scotland where he replaced his old comrade John Mason as the lieutenant colonel of Charles Fairfax's Regiment.[9] Mason himself appears to have earned the cautious approval of the Rump and was offered a choice of command: either a foot regiment of his own, the governorship of Inverness, or the governorship of Jersey.[10] Any of these would surely have removed him from London, and safely away from army politics, which may have been the Rump's true intention. Mason was a noted radical and never seems to have been wholly trusted by the establishment (as his removal to Caernarfon in 1650 following the near-riot in Newcastle has demonstrated). He accepted the governorship Jersey and colonelcy of the island's militia regiment.[11]

On Thomas Pride's death his regiment passed to the command of his lieutenant colonel, Richard Mosse. As his correspondence with Overton during the plot of 1654 showed, Mosse was an officer who had been suspected of harbouring republican sympathies. It says much for Pride's strength of character that it was only during his absences from the regiment (in Scotland in 1654, and now following his death) that the undercurrent of republicanism rise to the surface. Under Mosse's leadership the regiment underwent a deliberate and thorough restructuring by the Committee of Safety, following the ousting of Richard Cromwell and the army's support of a restored Rump Parliament. A new list of regimental officers approved by the Commons appeared in July 1659[12] and a notable omission from the list was Pride's eldest son, Thomas, who had held the rank of captain in the regiment for several years. Thomas absence cannot have been merely because of his family ties to the late colonel, as his younger brother William retained a company command until the eve of Charles II's return.[13] The decision was doubtless political, with Thomas viewed as untrustworthy by the republicans. Thomas would stubbornly continue to title himself 'captain' in the following months to come, which suggests that he had not given up his rank willingly.[14]

When in October 1659 the Rump cashiered Lambert, fearing him to be the focus of a rival power-base, Lambert was able to rally most of the troops quartered in London to his cause and he marched on Westminster. The result was a stand-off outside Parliament between Lambert, *en route* to forcibly dismiss the Rump, and Colonel Richard Mosse, whose own regiment was deployed to guard the House. It was a mirror image of Pride's Purge: Mosse preparing to defend with arms the legislative body Pride had created by force eleven years earlier. In spite of some defiant words, the MPs opposed to Lambert capitulated. Mosse gave way and the Rump was expelled.

Mosse's support for the republican Rump is indicative of how far the regiment's politics had shifted in the year since Pride, Goffe and Lagoe had declared their support for the new Lord Protector. In his summation of the political divisions among army officers at this time, Edmund Ludlow noted that, 'one party was known to be well affected to the Commonwealth', and he names both Mosse and Mason among its chief officers; in the Wallingford House, or army-party, he names Desborough; in yet a third party that remained loyal to Richard Cromwell he references Goffe.[15] The old political unity had fractured, and there remains the tantalising question of whether these factions would have remained united for longer if Pride had been there to help bind them. Certainly a firmer consensus can be observed two years earlier, when Pride was able to support Desborough's move against Cromwell's kingship with the loyalty of his own regiment.

A popular rising against the army officers during Christmas 1659 forced Lambert to flee London. The Rump was once more in power, but it was by this time a thoroughly unpopular institution. The re-establishment of the Long Parliament by General Monck in February 1660, re-admitting those members excluded for so long by the 1648 purge, saw Mosse's regiment reorganised further: three more captains were removed from command, including Ralph Prentice, who had been a private and regimental agitator during the mutinies of 1647.[16] It required a letter from Lieutenant Colonel Nicholas Andrews, writing to Monck from regimental headquarters in Canterbury, to assure the general of the men's compliance with the new government.[17] Monck does not seem to have been convinced, however. Mosse's support for the Rump and the evident political divisions among his officers meant that the regiment's loyalty to Charles II would have been, at best, questionable. Most of the army regiments quartered in England were disbanded within six months of the Restoration of May 1660; Mosse's regiment was unique in that it was requested to lay down its arms in April of that year – one month before the returning monarch even set foot in the country. Some of its officers continued to serve elsewhere. William Pride had already transferred to Ingoldsby's old regiment and would not leave the army until June. Henry Crispe, the officer who had conducted the convalescent soldiers to Bath in 1654, would serve in Sheffield's regiment until it disbanded that October.[18] But the politically dubious nature of Mosse's regiment convinced Monck that it must not be allowed to witness the return of the monarchy. The regiment was ordered to march up from Canterbury to the outskirts of London where, on Kennington Common in April 1660, it laid down its arms and was formally disbanded.

The Act of Indemnity and Oblivion, passed by Parliament in 1660, offered a general pardon to those who had acted against the Crown during the previous eighteen years of civil conflict. Of the handful of ex-parliamentarians exempted from this act were the Regicides, the forty-six signatories of Charles I's death warrant. Of these, eighteen were executed or condemned to life imprisonment in the months following Charles II's return. A further twenty men were either found guilty of involvement in the trial of Charles I, or of otherwise inciting regicide, and were similarly condemned.

Eighteen of the warrants' signatories had died in the intervening years, but this did not deter the Royalists from proclaiming that the four deceased Regicides considered to be most responsible Charles I's death were to be brought to account: Oliver Cromwell, as the figurehead of the Protectorate; his son-in-law, Henry Ireton, for being the driving force behind the move to try Charles I; John Bradshaw, who had presided over the court; and Thomas Pride, whose purge had paved the way for the Commons' vote that sanctioned the trial. Consequently, a bill was put in motion Commons on 15 May 1660, two weeks before Charles II's returned from exile, declaring that the four deceased Regicides were to be 'attainted of High Treason, for the Murthering of the Late King's Majesty'.[19] The attainder bill passed through Parliament in May, but it was not until December that the Commons decided what form the punishment would take. It was resolved that:

> the Carcases of Oliver Cromwell, Henry Ireton, John Bradshaw, and Thomas Pride, whether buried in Westminster Abbey, or elsewhere, be, with all Expedition, taken up, and drawn upon a Hurdle to Tiburne, and there hanged up in their Coffins for some time; and after that buried under the said Gallows.[20]

The seven month hiatus between the passing of the attainder and the sentence is significant: the exhumations and hangings were to be carried out on 30 January to coincide to with the twelfth anniversary of Charles I's execution. It was a carefully timed, stage-managed affair, and reveals the premeditated nature of the retribution that the Royalists were to exact. This had been at the back of their minds since the end of the Civil Wars. As early as May 1649, in fact, the Royalist news book *Mercurius Pragmaticus* had prescribed every detail of the Regicides' fates in doggerel:

> Then Tom and Nol. Ireton and Phill –
> The drayman Pryde shall drive
> Upon a sledge up Houle-bourne-Hill
> Till at Tyburne they arrive.
> – 'Nemo me impune lacessit' [21]

Here was Pride as the Royalists preferred to see him: the drayman driving along the apparatus of the Commonwealth, and in this case driving his accomplices to the gallows. Of those named in the above verse, 'Tom' (Fairfax) and 'Phil' (Skippon) were ultimately exonerated from their part in the Civil Wars, having taken no part in Charles I's trial. 'Nol' (Cromwell), Ireton and 'Pryde', were not.

For a first-hand account of the Regicides' execution we can turn to Samuel Pepys. On 28 January 1661, Pepys found himself in an ale-house near Fleet Street, 'where,' he noted, 'I met Mr. Davenport … some talk of Cromwell, Ireton, and Bradshaw's bodies being taken out of their graves to-day.'[22] But, it would seem, no talk of Thomas Pride.

The executions did not take place until two days after, when Pepys again noted the day's affairs in his diary: 'To my Lady Batten's; where my wife and she are lately come back again from being abroad, and seeing of Cromwell, Ireton, and Bradshaw, hanged and buried at Tyburne'.[23] In neither diary entry is there a reference to the body of Thomas Pride.

The exhumation of the other three leading Regicides was carried out by a man named John Lewis who, by his own account, was paid 'fifteen shillings, for the taking up the corpses of Cromwell, and Ireton, and Bradshaw.'[24] Again no reference to Pride's corpse, and if Lewis had recovered it from the Abbey he would surely have been paid for the job. Pepys' contemporary, John Evelyn, also witnessed the executions:

> the carcasses of those arch-rebels, Cromwell, Bradshawe (the judge who condemned his Majesty), and Ireton (son-in-law to the Usurper), dragged out of their superb tombs in Westminster among the Kings, to Tyburn, and hanged on the gallows there from nine in the morning till six at night, and then buried under that fatal and ignominious monument in a deep pit.[25]

In no contemporary account is there mention of a fourth corpse. Thomas Pride had evidently escaped his own execution. But why was Pride's body absent when the Royalists had taken such pains to carefully choreograph the executions; and if his body was not strung-up at Tyburn, then where was it?

Richard Smyth, a London clerk and bibliophile, penned the following entry in his Journal at the beginning of November: 'October 23 Coll. Tho. Pride (at first a drayman) died; his funeral at Nonsuch, Novem. 2'.[26] It is clear from this that Pride was buried outside London. There had been a full ten days between death and burial, plenty of time to arrange a lavish funeral at the Abbey or a London church and, if such an arrangement had been made, Smyth would surely have noted it. The order of exhumation passed by the Commons had decreed that the sentence be carried out on all four of the Regicides, 'whether buried in Westminster Abbey or elsewhere',[27] and as the bodies of Cromwell, Ireton and Bradshaw were all retrieved readily enough from the Abbey it is logical to assume that the body referred to as being 'elsewhere' must be that of Pride. Of the eighteen deceased Regicides, five had been interred at Westminster Abbey: Bradshaw, Cromwell and Ireton, together with Richard Deane and Sir William Constable. The latter two were also to be exhumed, together with a handful of Cromwell's associates who were buried there. As the Royalists seemed happy to disinter any parliamentarian interred at Westminster Abbey, we must deduce that that Pride's body never made its appearance at Tyburn because it had been laid to rest elsewhere. Fourteen other deceased Regicides, buried in places other than Westminster Abbey, were all left undisturbed. Buried elsewhere, it would seem that Pride's corpse was too trouble-some to go and find.

This leaves us with the puzzle of where Pride's body was buried and, presum-ably, where it is still. The notion that Pride had been interred in an unmarked grave, and his body therefore not exhumed because it could not be located, first occurs in the satire *The Last Speech*, written within living memory of the man's death. In this, Pride supposedly declaims: 'I prey ye vex not my corpse with a huge monument, which cannot protect itself, nor me; and many a man's bones had slept in quiet, if his prating tomb had not told where he lay.'[28] The purported facts of the *The Last Speech* are largely erroneous, however, the truth being tailored to suit a satirical purpose; the above lines could well be a swipe at Cromwell's hubris, whose fine monument in the Abbey had been easy for the Royalists to find. But given Pride's religious nonconformity, more eccentric that Cromwell's Calvinism, it would no surprise if he had been interred without ceremony. The Assembly of Divines at Westminster, which had policed religion in the 1640s during the absence of the Anglican bishops, gives some idea as to how a 'puritan' should be buried. Its Directory of Public Worship, published in 1654, stipulated:

> let the dead body … be decently attended from the house to the place appointed for publick burial, and there immediately interred without any ceremony … the custom of kneeling down and praying by or towards the dead corpse, and other such usages, in the place where it lies before it is carried to burial, are superstitious …praying, reading and singing, both in going to and at the grave, have been grossly abused, are no way benefi-cial to the dead … therefore let all such things be laid aside.[29]

Any person buried in this manner might easily vanish: there would be no one in attendance at the graveside to remember where in the churchyard the body may have been interred. Daniel Lysons's topographical history *The Environs of London* (1796) makes a passing reference to Pride's resting place, stating that Pride 'is said to have died at Nonsuch-palace in October 1658; but it is more likely that it was at Worcester-house in Nonsuch Great-park, which house he purchased in 1650'.[30] This is possibly Lysons' interpretation of the burial at 'Nonsuch' referred to by Smyth. Two years after Lysons, Mark Noble asserted that Pride died at Nonsuch and was buried there 'with baronial honours', although he does not disclose the source of this information.[31] By the beginning of the nineteenth century the distinction between Nonsuch Palace and Nonsuch Park was less distinct. An anonymous contributor to *Blackwood's Magazine* in 1829 claims to have penned a eulogy to Pride whilst sitting by his grave "at Nonsuch", but this was merely a rhetorical device for an article in which the writer turned to Pride as a symbol of Parliamentary reform.[32] Eighteenth century historians, then, had at least understood the rough approximation of Pride's grave. None of the parish churches in the area of Worcester Park has any record of Pride's burial and London's Nonconformist burial grounds were not designated as such until the Toleration Act of the 1680s.

Pride's being laid to rest in Surrey provides the clearest answer as to why his remains were left undisturbed in 1660, and his nonconformity the reason why they subsequently disappeared without trace. The order for exhumation was passed on the 10 January by the Lords, who clarified that the Sergeant of the House was to be responsible for putting the order into effect and that he was to be assisted 'by the Common Executioner for the County of Midd[lesex]. and all such others to whom it shall respectively appertain … And the Sheriff of Midd. is to give his Assistance herein.'[33] However, the order of exhumation did not stipulate that assistance was to be granted from any authority south of the Thames, and Pride's body appears to have remained undisturbed in Surrey because Parliament had sanctioned no one to carry out an exhumation there. Until further evidence comes to light it must be assumed that Pride was laid to rest somewhere on his Surrey estate, which is itself now buried under an expanse of Outer London conurbation.

If the mystery of Pride's bones is a curious footnote to the end of a remarkable life, the fate of his closest associates was just as bizarre. William Goffe fled to New England to escape the avenging Royalists with his father-in-law, and fellow Regicide, Edward Whalley. They arrived at Boston in July 1660 and were warmly welcomed by the governor of Massachusetts. All efforts by Royalist agents to arrest them were fruitless, as the colonists sympathised with the men's Independent faith and refused to reveal their whereabouts. Despite a royal proclamation warning that anyone harbouring the Regicides would be guilty of high treason, the authorities were told that both men had sailed for Holland not long after their arrival. Goffe's religious zeal won him many allies among the New Englanders, who had themselves left England to escape religious persecution, and the two Regicides were for a time sheltered by the followers of John Lathrop, the former leader of Pride's congregation who had fled to America after his release from prison in 1632. Aware that they were being pursued, Goffe and Whalley made their way to New Haven, Connecticut, 'a fiercely independent bastion of Calvinist zealotry.'[34] Here they spent a summer camped out in a cave, later moving into a house where they lived in seclusion for two years. Local settlers refused the agents of the Crown any assistance in apprehending the pair, for which they were labelled 'obstinate and pertinacious in their contempt of his Majesty'.[35]

'The Angel of Hadley' by Frederick Chapman, a depiction of William Goffe during his
New England exile in the 1670s.

By 1664 Goffe and Whalley had slipped away to Hadley, Massachusetts, a remote settlement some eighty miles distant on the border of native territory. There they sustained themselves through raising livestock and 'a little trade with the Indians'.[36] They held prayer meetings among the settlers, preached their millenarian convictions and were looked upon 'as men dropped down from heaven'.[37]

It was at Hadley that Goffe fought his last battle. In 1676 Wampanoag natives went to war with the encroaching English colonists, and Goffe emerged from seclusion to rally the settlers against a native raid on the Hadley settlement. He appeared as if heaven sent, entering local folk law as the 'Angel of Hadley', and no doubt making up for what he lacked in divine grace with skills acquired from his years in Parliament's army, organising a vigorous defence of Hadley and fighting off the attacks.[38]

Goffe's religious convictions remained unshaken by the failure of the Commonwealth. He never gave up his belief in the imminent return of Christ nor the chastisement of an irreligious English people: 'I cannot but tremble to think what may become of poor England whose sins are grown to a great Height', he wrote to his wife from exile. 'I am at a great distance, yet methinks I see the Lord shaking both your Earth & Heaven.'[39] The final letter written to his wife is dated April 1679. The last of Cromwell's major-generals was buried next to his

compensation from the Royal owners for the loss of his keepership as he had done from Pride.[6]

The land eventually passed out of Royal hands when Charles II bestowed the Great Park to one of his mistresses and Worcester House fell into disuse. By the 1930s the whole of the estate had been built on, but a substantial brick wall, believed to have surrounded the lodge's immediate grounds, survives along the east side of Delta Road – perhaps a last relic of Thomas Pride's house. Worcester Park itself is now a built-up area, a quiet corner of London commuter belt. The whereabouts of the long-lost park and lodge are revealed in local road names: Worcester Gardens, Parklands Way. Tucked away in suburbia, Worcester Park is now the leafy habitat of the London middle-classes, stockbrokers and City businessmen – people not dissimilar to Pride.

Appended to the narrative of the Great Park's demise is a curious tale: in the early 1900s workmen demolishing an old barn adjacent to Worcester House uncovered a store of barrels, apparently containing mead. The ancient brew was sampled and found to be so potent that it brought the day's work to a premature end. Clearly the ghost of a 17th century brewer was wishing the labourers a good health.[7]

From the beginning of the 1660s Pride's family were dogged by the debts inherited from the late colonel. Pride had in fact made arrangements for such financial straits in his will, stipulating that any land or tenements in his possession should be 'sold to the utmost value... towards the paying, satisfying and discharging of debts'.[8] Excluded from this were the most expensive properties of Worcester Park and the breweries at Kingston-upon-Thames, which he wished his family to retain. If this did not satisfy his creditors then the outstanding monies were to be paid out of the income in rents and timber from the park.

It soon transpired that Pride owed money to a great many people. Not long after his death his widow was approached by a Philip Pinchre, who had apparently credited Pride with £1,000 six years before and was still awaiting repayment. Elizabeth, in a plea for clemency, produced a comprehensive list of persons to whom her late husband owed money. Thirty creditors are named, including her son-in-law, Robert Walton, and the major of Pride's regiment, Nicholas Andrews. Another, a London shoe-maker named Jenkin Ellis, was awaiting payment for 3,000 pairs of shoes, the result of a business venture of Pride and Walton to supply clothing to the English army fighting in the Spanish Netherlands in 1658. The identities of others on the list are more vague, and with entries such as 'William Whonwood, £515 (but where he lives this defendant does not know)' and 'To a stranger, £500', it is doubtful if some of those on the list ever received their money. Totalling the debts listed in Chancery records, it is clear that Pride owed something in the region of £13,000 at the time of this death. Pinchre would have to wait in line.[9]

An atmosphere of fraudulence pervaded the Pride family finances in the late 1650s, revealed by the terms set out in Pride's will. He ensured that his widow would receive £400 a year out of the Surrey estate for her livelihood, but felt it necessary to add the codicil: 'I also further will and desire that my wife

Elizabeth Pride part not with any of the interest or portion that she shall have in my estate unto any person or persons whatsoever, unless it is unto my sonnes and daughter … And if it happen that she doth not performe this… she shall not have the least propriety in any of my lands or tenaments.' The expectation of an impending quarrel over money seems to have been uppermost in Pride's thoughts. Money and property bequeathed to his sons William and Samuel was to be 'equally and instantly divided between them, so that there may not be the least fraude or cousenage'.

Pride's youngest son, Joseph, was bequeathed £4,000 out of the Kingston breweries, to be held in trust by the eldest son, Thomas, until Joseph came of age, but a further clause in Pride's will read: 'if it shall happen that my sonne Thomas and Major Yates, my partners in those Brew-houses, shall refuse or deny forthwith to pay… then I give unto my sonne Joseph my full and whole share… in the said two Brew-houses.'[10] Pride was making a contingency in the likely event that Thomas would withhold payment. Clearly, Pride mistrusted his eldest son, shown not only by the wording of his will but by the fact that he appointed his wife and his son-in-law, Walton, to be his executors. Thomas was all but left out of the will entirely and bequeathed a token sum of five pounds, a common practice to ensure that his name appeared in the will and that he could not claim to have been omitted in error. He did however have the brewery business to run in partnership with Yates, a Kingston maltster.

Pride's daughter Elizabeth was also bequeathed only five pounds as she was provided for by her husband, Robert Walton. However, Walton's finances were also in a poor state. A tailor by trade, had been commissioned to provide the black cloth drapes for Oliver Cromwell's funeral but the Protectorate government, short of money, had never paid him in full. The newly-returned monarch had no intention of paying the debt and so the expense of the funeral cloth, calculated to be nearly £7,000, was never reimbursed.[11] A further loss for Walton is revealed in Samuel Pepys's diary on 28 January 1660: 'I went by appointment to my office and paid young Mr. Walton £500; it being very dark he took £300.'

The Walton estate at Great Stoughton, which had formed part of Robert and Elizabeths' marriage settlement, was sequestered by the Crown in 1660 as the property of a Regicide. Ownership was granted to the Walton's neighbour, the Earl of Manchester. Mounting debt eventually forced Robert and Elizabeth to leave the country and they settled in Virginia, where Robert invested what little money he had in a plantation. He died in 1669, after which Elizabeth continued to successfully manage the plantation, in much the same way her mother had managed Worcester Park.[12]

Meanwhile, the Pride family finances went from bad to worse. The Court of Chancery records nine separate cases in the 1660s concerning their debts. The younger Thomas Pride denied all knowledge of the money claimed by Phillip Pinchre. When it was suggested that his father's share in a brewery at St. Katharine's might be sold to pay off some of the debt, Thomas denied all knowledge of this too.[13]

In 1658 the younger Thomas Pride was living at Kingston-upon-Thames, over-seeing the breweries that had been left to him in his father's will. Prior to redevel-opment in 1998 the south bank of the Thames' riverside at Kingston was excavated and the remains of a brewery uncovered. Dating to c.1503, this could well have been one of the premises owned by Pride. Referred to in documents simply as the beer house, the property was leased with a garden, barn and a mill. Fresh water for the brewing process would have been drawn from the adjacent Hogsmill River, and the finished product shipped down the Thames to London. The whole area was in fact one large block of property split between various tenants, all of whom were connected in some way to the brewing trade. As well as the 'Berehouse', there were neighbouring timber-merchants, coopers and wheelwrights, across the alleyway was a large malt house that was still in use in the early 1900s. The Berehouse itself is now the site of The Ram public house.[14]

Thomas appears to have left Kingston not long after his father's death and moved with his own family to Kennington, Surrey. An associate, John Derbyshire, visited the family there and found Thomas in a pitiful financial state: 'his credit spent and wasted, many of his goods pawn'd or sold at alehouses … To an alehouse keeper who had formerly been Pryde's [sic] servant he had sold several quantities of linen, pewter and brass. And at the Lyon or some other alehouse in Kennington he had sold curtains and bedding.' Furthermore, 'a maide servant of his imbezziled and purloyn'd divers of said Prydes goods'.[15]

In November 1662 Thomas and his family moved into a house owned by Derbyshire in Holborn. Foreseeing trouble in collecting the rent from his new lodgers, Derbyshire came to arrangement whereby Thomas put up his entire estate in trust to his landlord for security. According to Thomas, the Prides still had lands in Surrey worth £7,200 and both parties agreed that these could be sold to pay off any debts if need be. What he neglected to tell Derbyshire was that his ownership of these lands was questionable.

Colonel Pride had acquired land at Rotherhithe, called 'Cuckold Corner', in the early 1650s from Sir John Wolstenhome. This was the property that Pride had settled on Elizabeth Monck when she had married the young Thomas in 1654.[16] Wolstenhome was a Royalist bankrupt who had lost £100,000 in funding Charles II's Worcester campaign of 1651. In 1660 he petitioned Charles II for money to buy back the property he had been forced to sell, including the land at Rotherhithe which Pride had bought for £8,200.[17] It is not known whether Wolstenhome's peti-tion was successful, but what is clear that by 1662 the Rotherhithe property was owned by Abraham Corsellis.

Corsellis was a London brewer of Dutch decent. He owned a brew-house called the Hartshorne in St. Katharine's parish, five minutes walk from the navy's Victualling Office, and it was most probably this brewery in which Colonel Pride had a share. The Hartshorne was the brewery that supplied beer to the navy, and from where Pride must have obtained a good deal of his supply during the Dutch War. Built in the reign of Henry VII its association with the Royal Navy lasted well into the 18th century, when it was commonly called 'his Majesty's brewhouse'.[18] Corsellis and Pride did a lot of business together. In 1656 Pride offered the lease of Worcester House to Corsellis, possibly as security for a loan or other venture. As well as being a fellow brewer, Corsellis had been a Parliamentarian during the Civil War. He had been the treasurer for the Tower Hamlets' Militia Committee[19] and, like Pride, he had protested at the levying of excise on beer in 1643.

By what agreement the property of Cuckhold Corner passed to Corsellis is uncertain, but the young Thomas Pride refused to accept that the sale had been lawful – which is why he must have thought it reasonable to put it up as security to John Derbyshire. When it became clear that Thomas's claim on the land was questionable at best, Derbyshire prosecuted. In court, Thomas acknowledged that he owed Derbyshire £1,750 but maintained that the Surrey property was good recompense. Derbyshire, for his part, complained that an estate in Pontefract, possibly part of the inheritance of Elizabeth Monck and which Thomas has also offered as security, had been neglected to the extent that the land was now worthless.[20] Thomas denied all knowledge. Soon after, the Prides vacated Derbyshire's house and went to live in Bow.

Thomas' conduct in these matters reveals him to be just the sort of shifty character that his father seems suspected he was. When removed from his father's old regiment in 1659 he had assumed the role of a 'reformado', continuing to title himself captain despite the fact that he longer held a commission. It rather perplexed others at the time: 'Captain Pride, of Kingston, we know not what title to give him', commented the parliamentary diarist Thomas Burton. He was recommissioned in February 1660 as captain in a newly constituted regiment that professed loyalty to Monck. He was still serving in July when command of the regiment passed to Viscount Mordaunt – the Royalist agent whose trial Colonel Pride had been involved with shortly before his death.[21] Whether Pride's captaincy lasted for very long after Mordaunt's arrival is hard to determine, and in any case the regiment was disbanded along with much of the Protectorate army in England in October that year.

Six months after the death of Colonel Pride, Thomas had fallen out with Yates, just as his father had foreseen. Owing money to the excise, Thomas began proceedings against his former business partner and suggested his creditors got their money directly from Yates, who himself had had his goods seized by the excise men in lieu of payment. Thomas' financial wrangling verged on the desperate – he even took his butcher to court in 1663 for what he considered an extortionate bill for meat.[22] the younger Thomas Pride was appallingly litigious and underhand, but is it very far removed from what we know of his father – flatly denying his involvement in the 1647 army petition and attempting to evade the excise? If the young Thomas was truculent and duplicitous, these were surely traits that he had inherited from his father.

A reference in Chancery papers for 1665 states: 'Elizabeth Pride, relict of Thomas Pride late of Oldford in the Parish of Bow, Middlesex',[23] indicating that Thomas was deceased by this date. It seems to have been something of a blessing for his family because his young daughter was now taken under the wing of her great uncle, George Monck, with whom she lived as his ward until his death in 1670.[24] The widowed Elizabeth continued to be supported in later years by her younger cousin Christopher Monck.

Christopher, George Monck's only son, was a notorious rake-hell and a friend of the young Duke of Marlborough. He would drink himself to death in Jamaica at the age of thirty-three, yet he provided well for his impoverished cousins. After the Lords finally declared Colonel Pride's lease of the lands at Rotherhithe null and void in 1666, Christopher attempted the same year to secure an inheritance for Elizabeth through Act of Parliament. But although the bill he introduced for 'Settling an Estate upon Mrs. *Elizabeth Pride* for the Benefit of her Children' was passed by both houses, it was not granted royal assent and never enacted.[25] It is likely that Charles II refused to pass a bill that would settle property on the heirs of a Regicide. Christopher himself seems to have guessed that if he did not legally settle some property on his cousin Elizabeth she would pursue him through the courts in order to obtain it. Writing to Lord Montague in January 1672, Christopher noted:

> Your Lordship's letter of the 6th instant came to me with an accompt of my cousin Bettey's intention of marriage and her desire of five hundred pounds from me to further her preferment ... I have nothing in my own power but the revenue of my estate ... I can spare nothing from my ordinary expenses; but something I owe her ... If I see she lives discreetly and well, I will make up that sum to be 500 pounds but as to my consent to her marriage, it's an affair too nice for me to be concern'd in ... The respect I have of the memory of her father induces me to wishe well to her ... though her demeanour towards me has not bin obliging [26]

Elizabeth apparently showed little respect to Christopher, and he thought her behaviour less than modest. Despite his misgivings, though, Christopher indicates a sense of duty felt towards his cousin.

When Christopher Monck died in 1688 he bequeathed £5,000 to Elizabeth and her son Thomas, one of the largest single sums in his will. Elizabeth was guaranteed an allowance of £40 a year out of the rents of the manor of Sutton upon Derwent, near York.[27] Christopher stipulated, however, that the £5,000 bequest to the Prides would be granted only on the condition that they relinquished any claim to the Monck family seat at Potheridge in Devon, revealing Christopher's determination to ensure that his cousins would not contest any further claim to the Monck estates. However, as Christopher had died without issue, Elizabeth believed herself to be the rightful claimant to the Duchy of Albemarle. She may well have felt that her fortunes had come full circle: born into West Country gentry in 1628, to losing her home in Kingston when she was thirty-one, to becoming heiress to a duchy thirty years later.

When the extinct Albemarle title had been resurrected in 1660 to be conferred on General Monck, Charles II had declared that should the Monck line die out the title would pass to John Grenville, Earl of Bath, another Royal favourite who deserved reward for loyal service in the Civil War. Although this Royal promise still stood, James II had instead conferred the dormant title on his own favourite, Henry Fitz-James, the youngest of five illegitimate children he sired with the Duke of Marlborough's sister. Just to complicate matters, England's new monarch, William of Orange, had bestowed the same title on one of his closest Dutch confidants, Van Keppel following the revolution of 1688. At the time of writing the Keppels retain the Albemarle title, notably as the directors of gentlemen's outfitter 'Albemarle of London' ('Fine shirts for the discerning gent').[28]

Following Christopher Monck's death, John Grenville was to spend the following seven years at the Court of Chancery contesting his right to the Monck estate in a legal tussle with Christopher's widow, whose second husband, the Earl of Montague, was pressing his own claim. Thomas Pride (the Regicide's grandson) felt that the estate was rightfully hers and argued his case before the House of Lords on 26 January 1694:

> That by the death of Christopher Monck, Duke of Albemarle, without issue, the real estate of George Duke of Albemarle did descend to the petitioner's mother (Elizabeth Monck) as right heir to George, and that her grace the Duchess of Albemarle, the Earl of Montague in her right, and the Earl of Bath, have possessed themselves of the said George's estate; and praying that he [Colonel Pride's grandson] may be permitted to procede at Law or Equity for the recovery of the said estate.[29]

The Pride family's claim to the Albemarle estate was founded on the testament of an illiterate woman, Anne Rowney, then aged 84. She claimed to have known George Monck's wife, Anne Clarges, when they had been girls. Clarges had worked as a maidservant and seamstress at the Tower of London where, as a Royalist officer, George Monck was held prisoner following his capture in 1644. In 1652 they were married at St. George's church, Southwark. It was rumoured, however, that George Monck was not Anne Clarges' first husband. She had been first married to a London farrier named Radford, and Anne Rowney claimed that although Radford and Anne had separated in 1649, and Radford afterwards disappeared, there was no proof that Anne had been a widow when she remarried.[30] On this evidence, the Prides argued, Christopher Monck had been the issue of a bigamous marriage and therefore should not have been allowed to inherit the Albemarle title and estates. Instead, the title ought to have passed at George Monck's death to his nearest living legitimate relative: his niece, Elizabeth Pride. The readiness with which the Prides were prepared to dismiss Christopher's legitimacy seems quite callous given the financial aid he had given them. It underscores Christopher's belief that Elizabeth had been 'less than congenial' toward him.

The Lords were not impressed by the Prides' evidence. Nevertheless, the family continued to press its claim to the title. Thomas, Colonel Pride's grandson, died in 1694 or 95 and thereafter the case was taken up by his widow Rebecca and their surviving daughters, Lucy and Elizabeth.[31]

The case concerning the Albemarle estate reads like something out of Dickens' *Bleak House* as 'Witnesses died sudden and mysterious deaths ... dark stories came to light.' An atmosphere of macabre melodrama pervaded the affair: it was rumoured that the Earl of Montague was keeping the Duchess of Albemarle under lock and key, enfeebled as she was by old-age and senility, and that he controlled the estate on her behalf; that the Duchess was quite mad, vowing she would only marry again to a powerful head of state, whereupon Montague had wooed and wed her in the guise of the Emperor of China; that the Duchess was in fact dead and the Earl was slyly living off her estates, Montague having to physically produce her before the House of Lords to prove this was not the case.[32] Eventually the court returned a verdict in favour of Montague, with Grenville's case collapsing amid charges of fraud and perjury. Costs amounted to £20,000, and were levied against Grenville, who died not long after. His son and heir, appalled by the debts that he had inherited, promptly shot himself.[33]

Still, the Prides were not deterred, in fact they appear to have made a good deal of money from settlements arrived at during the case: Grenville thought that he had secured the manor at Potheridge for himself after he paid Elizabeth Pride £8,500 to drop her claim to it. Her daughter arranged a similar settlement from Montague for land at Clitheroe,[34] which suggests that the Prides were playing off one side against the other. When the Chancery Court found against Grenville, the Pride family seem to have been buoyed by Montague's success: if Montague could claim a ducal estate through his marriage to Christopher's widow then the Prides were sure to have an even better claim, being blood relatives of the Moncks. The Prides were back and forth from court for ten years, pursuing the case with an obstinacy that appears to have been a family trait. The saga of *Montague versus Bath* dragged on. After Grenville's death in 1701 the case was retitled *Montague versus Sherwin*, which introduces a new character to the saga.

William Sherwin was an artist and engraver, reputed to have introduced the technique of mezzotint into England. His artistic output, however, was unremarkable: 'The quality of his work, although always competent, is not high, for he had no real ability of drawing.'[35] But in 1676 Sherwin had patented a method for printing designs on calico (he invented chintz) and enjoyed a virtual monopoly on his product for fourteen years. He employed upwards of two hundred people in a factory in West Ham, producing the first printed fabrics in the country. Calico printing would be that area's chief industry during the following century.

Sherwin's factory stood on the River Lea at Bow, and it is surely more than coincidence that this is where the Pride family had moved in 1660. Griffiths (2004) suggests that the capital Sherwin needed to establish his business came from his marriage to Pride's granddaughter.[36] This area of London produced the scarlet dye for soldier's coats (known as 'Bow-dye', so vivid it was said to make tailors and seamstresses go blind)[37] that Colonel Pride and Robert Walton were contracted to produce in the late 1650s. It was probably through the early textile industry, then, that Sherwin came into contact with the Prides, and perhaps also a similar background of religious dissent: Sherwin's father had been a nonconformist divine who was ejected from his ministry on the return of the Stuarts in 1662, after which he had devoted his time to writing apocalyptic prophesies and propounding the immanent return of Christ.[38]

Records of marriage licences reveal that the fifty year-old widower, Sherwin, married an Elizabeth Gibbs in November 1697.[39] Elizabeth's first husband (presumably that for whom she had sought Christopher's permission to marry), had been John Gibbs, a famed horse racer, gambler and, for a short time, governor of North Carolina. He left America in the early 1690s and returned to England with his wife and their two daughters.[40] Gibbs seems to have been enthused by the Prides' pursuit of the Albemarle estate and he entered a legal dispute to recover the disputed property at Rotherhithe which appears to have come to nothing.[41] His dedication to the Prides' claim, and his belief as Elizabeth to be a genuine heiress, is demonstrated by his inclusion of Elizabeth's arms on his gravestone.[42] He died in 1695 and Elizabeth married William Sherwin two years later.

At the time of her second marriage, Elizabeth was resident in Holborn, barely a stone's throw from Pye Corner and an area with which the Prides had been associated for sixty years. Sherwin himself owned a workshop in Well Yard, close to St. Bartholomew's Hospital.[43] The first mention of Sherwin's name in connection with the prolonged court case was in January 1700, when he was placed in custody of the Sergeant of Arms in the Lords after Grenville had complained of a 'breech of his privilege'. It followed Sherwin's ejection of William Clarges (Grenville's tenant and Duke Christopher's cousin on his mother's side) from property in Sussex bequeathed to Clarges in the Duke's will.[44] However, with the death of Grenville in 1701 this chapter of the court case closed. Thereafter there was a lull, but the case was re-opened at the end of 1709 when Sherwin again pressed his case as heir apparent to the Monck title and fortune. Elizabeth's name was by now absent from the records, and presumably she had died in the intervening years. Anyone confused by the number of Thomases and Elizabeths in the Pride family would do well to view the family tree engraved by Sherwin in the late 1600s, to illustrate the Prides' rightful claim to the Albemarle estate, and which is now held by the British Museum.[45]

Others as well as the Sherwins were willing to pursue the Albemarle title: Martin Bladen, an army officer serving under Marlborough on the continent, had married Elizabeth's daughter, Mary Gibbs. Their son was baptised George Monck Bladen, a nod to their claim to the Albemarle estate. Martin Bladen was later a commissioner for the Board of Trade and Plantations, administering the colonies in North America (There is a Bladen County in North Carolina named for him). Both Bladen's and Gibbs' interests in the Duchy of Albemarle must surely have been motivated by the fact that the title carried with it substantial lands in North Carolina.[46]

The Albemarle case closed in 1710, seventeen years after proceedings had first begun. The court concluded that while Christopher Monck had been living his legitimacy had never been questioned and had always been regarded by George Monck as his legitimate son. It was also remarked that while Christopher had been alive the Pride family had benefited from his patronage, implying that it had been indecent to have slighted his name following his death. Chancery ordered that a perpetual injunction be issued against Sherwin *et al.* to deter prevent them from making any further claims to the Albemarle estate and 'to quiet all questions touching the legitimacy of Duke Christopher'.[47] Sherwin is said to have retired from business in 1711 and died three or four years later.

In 1702 Rebecca Pride, the widow of Colonel Pride's grandson, petitioned Queen Anne for the renewal of a family pension: £200 per annum that had been awarded to her father by Charles II but which had ceased during the reign of William of Orange. Rebecca wrote of her 'anshont' family, her failing eyesight and her 'miserable condition', complaining that 'my heart is redey to breack for want of monney to by bred',[48] and demonstrating some very idiosyncratic spelling. Rebecca's petition was successful and she continued to receive money from the Crown until at least 1718, four years in to the reign of George I.[49] It is possible to trace one other branch of the family into the Georgian period: Elizabeth Gibbs' youngest daughter, Anne, was married to a Nathaniel Rice, and a further link to the American colonies. Land in North Carolina (Gibbs Marsh) came into his possession through the marriage.[50] Anne predeceased her husband, but if any of her children survived her then they would have continued to live in North Carolina where, presumably, their descendants live still.

Appendix I

Colonel Pride's Officers

This section contains details of the army establishments in which Thomas Pride served, together with additional biographical information of some of the officers and men that fought alongside him. What emerges is a collective portrait of men who had grown wealthy from London trade, but who were not Londoners by birth.

The company commanders of Barclay's Regiment as passed by the House of Lords, 18 March 1645:[1]
    Colonel Barclay
    Lieutenant Colonel Emmins [or Innes]
    Major Cowell
    Captain Goffe
    Captain Gregson
    Captain Ramsey
    Captain Jamson [or Sampson]
    Captain Leete
    Captain Goddard
    Captain Blagrave

The company commanders of Edward Harley's Regiment, April 1645:[2]
    Colonel Edward Harley
    Lieutenant Colonel Pride
    Major William Cowell
    Captain Goffe
    Captain Gregson
    Captain Sampson
    Captain Hender
    Captain Ferguson
    Captain Mason
    Captain Lagoe

William Cowell. A businessman of St. Augustine's parish, Hammersmith. He commanded a company under Barclay and was promoted to major of the regiment on the formation of the New Model. Along with Pride and Goffe, Cowell was prominent in the mutinies of summer 1647, after which he was promoted to lieutenant colonel of Fairfax's Regiment. He was severely wounded at the Battle of Preston in August 1648 and appears to have died in York shortly after. He left a wife, Mary, and three young children.[3]

William Goffe. From Haverfordwest, Pembrokeshire, the son of a nonconformist minister. Apprenticed as a young man to a London grocer, he was quartermaster in Harry Barclay's regiment before being given the command of a company. He sat as a judge at Charles I's trial and was a Regicide (his name appears on the death warrant above that of Pride's). As lieutenant colonel he commanded Cromwell's regiment of foot at Dunbar and, in recognition of his ability, was subsequently given the command of the regiment as full colonel. Under the Protectorate he became Major General of Berkshire, Sussex and Hampshire, and represented Yarmouth and Hampshire in the Protectorate Parliaments of 1654 and 1656 respectively. He served in the Upper House alongside Pride. He married Frances, the daughter of Cromwell's cousin and fellow regicide, General Whalley. At the Restoration he and his father-in-law escaped to Massachusetts where they were sheltered by Puritan settlers.[4]

George Gregson. Captain of a company under Barclay, he retained his command under the New Model. Wounded at Berkeley Castle in September 1645, he was promoted to major following the resignation of Harley in July 1647. Gregson was seriously wounded in the attack on Chepstow Castle in May 1648, and a reference of monies paid to his executors (dated August 1648) indicates that he died not long after.[5]

George Sampson. Captain who hailed from Kingsbury Episcopi, a village ten miles south of Ashcott, and who was therefore a Somerset man like Pride. His cousin or bother, Latimer Sampson, was also prominent in Somerset and was appointed governor of Bristol in 1647. There has been some confusion over which of these Sampsons served under Pride, not made any clearer by Fairfax's assertion that Latimer had 'been employed in the service of Parliament from the first advance of the army under [Fairfax's] command into the field', which intimates that Latimer had served in the New Model. George Sampson certainly served alongside Pride under Barclay, however, ar this is attested by army pay warrants. George (if it was he) was wounded during the assault on Bridgwater in July 1645 and he subsequently left the New Model to became an officer in the Somerset militia, a post which he secured through the influence of county commissioner Colonel John Pyne, with Pride's support. Latimer's governorship at Bristol, on the other hand, was dogged by accusations of embezzlement and Royalist sympathies levelled at him by the same clique headed by Pyne[6]

William Leete. One of the original company commanders commissioned in 1643 under Harry Barclay and, like Pride and Cowell, a prosperous London tradesman. He was wounded on more than one occasion and left disabled, forcing him to relinquish his command in April 1645.[7]

William Hender. A Cornishman. Captain of a company during the 1645 campaign, he was wounded in the storming of Bristol in September 1645 and subsequently retired from service, though he continued to serve as captain in the Cornish militia. Prior to the New Model he served as Lord Robartes' captain-lieutenant.[8]

John Ferguson. Formerly an officer in Colonel Davis's Regiment of Essex's army. He was the only captain of Harley's regiment willing to serve in Ireland in 1647, and may have been the 'most expert and best' Major Ferguson who was killed in the attack on San Domingo, Hispaniola, in 1655.[9]

Thomas Parsons, of Milverton, Warwickshire. The first reference to him in connection with the regiment is as lieutenant to George Gregson, and he was given the command of a company after the mutiny of 1647. By the time of the Dutch War in 1653 he was the regiment's major and replaced Waldive Lagoe as Lieutenant Colonel in 1656. On 31 July 1657 he was the victim of an attack by armed robbers, an account of which was given in the contemporary newspaper, *Mercurius Politicus*:

> Travelling on the road towards London, not far from Saint Albons, being somewhat before the coach wherein was his wife and another gentlewoman, he was set upon by some highway-men mounted, and double armed, who first rode up to him and justled him; afterwards coming up with him again, they demanded his sword, which he refusing to deliver, one of them immedeatly shot him in the knee, upon which he fell off his horse; of which shot, together with his fall, he dyed the Sunday following [two days later]. After they had acted this villany upon the Lieut. Colonell they staid the coach wherein his wife was and robb'd and rifled it.

On the evening of the 7 August, Thomas Parsons was interred at St Margaret's church, Westminster, 'after the military manner, all the officers of the regiment, and the whole regiment being present at the celibration of the funeral'.[10]

Richard Mosse. The officer who took command of the regiment following Pride's death. He began his service as a private soldier in Barclay's and rose through the ranks until he was ensign to Goffe. He was a captain during the regiment's service in Scotland in 1654 and replaced Thomas Parsons as Lieutenant Colonel after the latter's death in 1657. A republican, his name was linked to Overton's plot against the Protectorate in 1654. His later opposition to Richard Cromwell as Protector, and his support for the Rump, secured his command of the regiment at the Restoration until it was disbanded.[11]

William Pride. Younger son of the colonel. Unlike his elder brother, Thomas, he retained his Captain's commission after the fall of Richard Cromwell. He seems to have served with the army into the Restoration and could well be the same William Pride who took part in the campaign against French and Spanish privateers on the island of Tortuga between 1663 and 1665. He was almost certainly the William Pride who was imprisoned in the Tower of London in November 1666 for reputedly claiming he would 'raise as many men as he could and head them' in armed rebellion. The fact that by February the following year he had been released would imply that the accusation was unfounded.[12]

Joseph Salkeld. Originally Captain Lieutenant to Colonel Harley. Salkeld took over the colonel's company when Edward Harley resigned in 1647. Firth and Davies (1940) identify him with a Captain Sawkins, who faced a court martial at Edinburgh in November 1651 for 'severall offences in the nature of Buggery'. Salkeld disappears from the regimental lists after this date.[13]

The following four soldiers are named as those elected to represent Pride's Regiment at an Army Council convened in October 1647:

Waldive Lagoe. The officer who captured the Royalist colour at Bristol in 1645. He was baptised at Kingsbury, Warwickshire, in 1617, the youngest of six children. It is possible he was related to George Fox, founder of the Quakers, whose mother was Mary Lagoe and who grew up ten miles from Waldive's birthplace, at Fenny Drayton in Leicestershire. Lagoe's unusual first name may have been due to family connections. One other prominent 'Waldive' in this period was Waldive Willington of Hurley, who was a colonel in the Warwickshire militia. His home was in the same Parish as Kingsbury and there may be a link between these two Waldives and the Waldive family of Welch Hall at nearby Meriden. Waldive Willington was also a religious nonconformist, a Presbyterian whose house was licensed in the 1670s to hold Congregational services.

Lagoe was apprenticed to a London salter and began his military career as a corporal in Hammond's company of Barclay's regiment before being commissioned as ensign, and later lieutenant to William Cowell. He received his captaincy on the formation of the New Model and was raised to major soon after the Battle of Preston. It is likely that he became lieutenant colonel sometime after June 1651, commanding the regiment in the latter stages of the war with Scotland and during the 1654 Scottish campaign. It is reputed to have been Lagoe who took custody of the mace when Cromwell expelled the Rump in 1653. During the Commonwealth he involved himself in local government, being one of the commissioners conducting tax assessment in Essex in January 1655, and he was returned as MP for Weymouth in 1656. He married and settled at Romford in Essex. He was wealthy enough to have built three houses in Piccadilly which he rented out as quarters to officers of Fleetwood's regiment and, latterly, to Sir Robert Cary. His first wife died young, and when Major General Worsley died in 1656 Lagoe took his place as Lieutenant Colonel of Cromwell's regiment of foot and married Worsley's widow, Dorothy, in 1659. He supported Monck against the republicans, both in Scotland in 1654 and in London during 1660, indicating a political outlook than was less radical than other officers who had served under Pride. He transferred to Charles Fairfax's Regiment of Foot in 1659 (replacing John Mason as its Lieutenant Colonel) and was subsequently appointed Adjutant-General of the Irish Army. After the Restoration he enjoyed a life of quiet obscurity. He moved to Manchester in the early 1660s (his second wife's family owned land at Peel in Lancashire) where he was accorded the status of an esquire. He died in Manchester and was buried at Prestwich in February 1669.[14]

John Mason. Ensign, and later lieutenant, to Pride under Colonel Barclay. Apparently from Gainsborough, he was an Anabaptist and had been apprenticed to a London harness-maker. He took over from Gregson as major of the regiment when the latter was wounded in the action at Chepstow in 1648. He presented the petition to the Commons in 1657 in which the army officers protested at Cromwell's becoming King. Becoming governor of Jersey in 1659, he promptly dismissed those officers in the garrison of whom he disapproved 'for divers good reasons'. He may be the John Mason who was imprisoned without trial, along with other suspected Cromwellian plotters, at Windsor Castle from 1664 to 1667.[15]

Ralph Prentice. Of Isleworth, Middlesex. Listed as a private soldier in October 1647, in the following month he was promoted to ensign. By 1659 he had risen to the rank of captain but was removed the same year by the Rump.[16]

Nic Andrewes. Listed as a private soldier at the Council of the Army in October 1647, he was subsequently a sergeant under Captain Gregson. By 1659 he was the regiment's lieutenant colonel, a rank he held until the regiment was disbanded.[17]

Roger Alsop. The first reference to Alsop in Parliament's forces is as an ensign, and later a lieutenant, in Sir Anthony St. John's company of the Earl of Essex's regiment. By 1647 he was a captain under Pride. Appointed Marshal-General of the English army on the eve of the Dunbar campaign, he was responsible for army discipline. He served in this post for six years but grew disenchanted with it, complaining to Cromwell that he would have preferred to have retained his captaincy: 'my pay has been less than a foot captain's … and I am 500l poorer than when I took the employment'. He was consequently granted command of a foot regiment for service in Flanders against the Spanish and fought at the Battle of the Dunes in 1658. He remained in Flanders as senior colonel of the Dunkirk garrison, where he received censure for his moral attitudes and was described as: 'an active man as a souldier [but] an eniemie to religion and godliness'. Alsop was in fact an Independent who had little regard for organised religion: he refused to maintain a chaplain in his regiment and allowed the citizens of Dunkirk to hold their fish market on a Sunday.

Alsop remained with the Dunkirk garrison in 1660 and came under the command of his old colonel when Edward Harley (now Sir Edward) was appointed the town's governor. Lord Falkland took command of the regiment but Alsop was retained as Lieutenant Colonel. In October 1662 Charles II returned Dunkirk to the French and the garrison was disbanded, after which Alsop received a commission in the garrison at Tangiers.

Tangiers had become an English possession following Charles II's marriage to the Portuguese Infanta, and by the 1670s was under continual attack by the Moors. During one such assault Alsop, who had been confined to his bed for three weeks with a fever, organised a solid defence of Fort Royal and under his command the attack was repulsed. He received a medal from Charles II for his part in the defence of the port and accepted a lieutenant colonelcy in Sir Henry Northwood's Regiment there. In May 1676, he was commissioned deputy-governor of Tangier. The old veteran was evidently a figure of affection to the garrison as he hobbled around the town's defences: 'honest old Colonel Alsop, if his legs were answerable to his heart, would give convincing testimonies of his great worthiness'.

Honest, diligent and industrious, Alsop was a useful soldier for both the Protectorate and the Stuarts. It should be noted, however, that he never served in England under the restored monarchy, which may have preferred to confine this New Model veteran to foreign garrisons. Alsop died at Tangier on 26 November 1676. In the fullness of time the Tangier Regiment evolved to be the 2nd Foot (The Queen's Royal Regiment) and, later, the Princess of Wales' Royal Regiment. Roger Alsop thus establishes a link between Thomas Pride's Regiment and the modern British army.[18]

Appendix II

Thomas Pride's family tree.

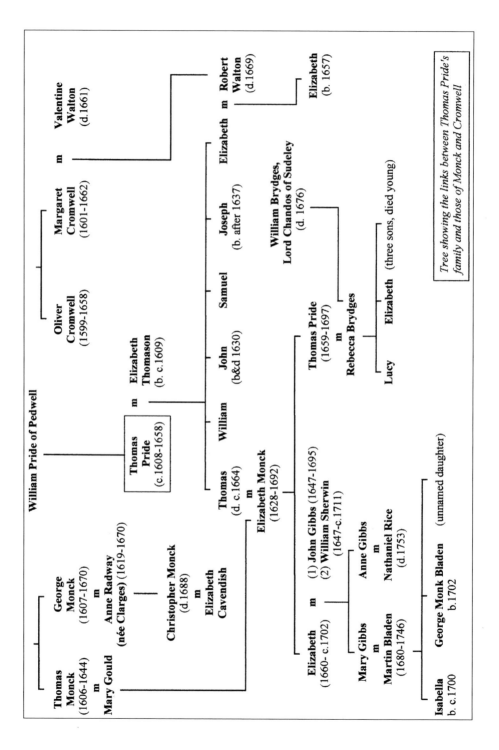

Tree showing the links between Thomas Pride's family and those of Monck and Cromwell

184

Abbreviations

Abbreviations:

BL	British Library
BM	British Museum
CJ	House of Commons Journal
CSPD	Calendar of State Papers, Domestic Series
ODNB	Oxford Dictionary of National Biography
GL	Guildhall Library
HMC	Historical Manuscripts Commission
LMA	London Metropolitan Archives
LRO	Lancashire Record Office
LJ	House of Lords Journal
TNA	The National Archives, London
SP	State Papers

The *Oxford Dictionary of National Biography* is cited from its online edition (2008-2016).

Notes

Introduction

1. Noble, M., *The Lives of the English Regicides* (2 vols) (London: J. Stockdale, 1798). p.132

1 Early Life, c.1608–29

1. Fynes Moryson, *Itinery*, cited in Wilson, J. D., *Life in Shakespeare's England* (London: Penguin, 1951), p. 17
2. Underdown, D. *Revel, Riot & Rebellion: Popular Politics and Culture in England, 1603-1660* (Oxford: Oxford University Press, 1985), p. 7
3. Guildhall Library (GL), Haberdashers Company, Apprenticeship Bindings 1610-1630, MS 15860/4, f. 173 v.
4. 'Etne', 'Col. Thomas Pride, A Somerset Native?', *The Somerset County Herald* (28 June 1958); Victoria County History of Somerset, vol. 9 Glastonbury and Street, Parishes: Meare
5. D. Bromwich, letter to the author, 2004
6. GL: Haberdashers Company, MS 15960/4, f. 173 v.; The National Archives (TNA), Chancery Proceedings C3/397/14
7. Palmer, A. and Palmer, P., *The Chronology of British History* (London: Century, 1992), p. 172
8. Palmer and Palmer, *Chronology*, ibid.
9. Barry, J. and Brooks, C. (eds.), *The Middling Sort of People: Culture, Socierty and Politics in England, 1550-*1800 (Basingstoke: Macmillan, 1984), p. 55
10. Winstanley, W., *The Loyal Martyrology* (London: Edward Thomas, 1665), p. 109
11. Barry and Brooks, *The Middling Sort*, p. 74
12. Barry and Brooks, *The Middling Sort, passim*
13. Greer, G., *Shakespeare's Wife* (London, Bloomsbury, 2007) p. 177
14. GL: Freedom Admissions 1526-1641, MS 15857/1, unfol. (24 April 1629)
15. London Metropolitan Archives (LMA) Registers of St. Anne's Blackfriars; Gentles, I. 'Pride, Thomas, appointed Lord under the Protectorate (*d.* 1658)', *Oxford Dictionary of National Biography*.
16. TNA: Exchequer Papers E133/141/23
17. TNA: C3/397/14
18. Usher, B. 'Gouge, William (1575–1653)', *ODNB*
19. TNA: C3/397/14

20. Bate, cited in Cockayne, G. E., *The Complete Peerage* (4 vols.) (London: St. Catherine Press, 1916), vol. 4, p. 630

21. *House of Lords Journal* (*LJ*) vol. 5, 308; *House of Commons Journal* (*CJ*) vol. 3, p. 522

22. Greer, *Shakespeare's Wife*, p.189; *Carpenters Company, Apprentices' Entry Books 1654-1694*, volume 1 (1913), p. 150, British History Online [online]

23. Dowing, T. and Millman, M. *Civil War* (London: Colins & Brown, 1992), p. 17

24. Will of Thomas Pride. The National Archives, Prerogative Court of Canterbury, 11/283/493

25. *Calendar of State Papers Domestic (Interregnum)*, vol. 183, 16 November 1658; vol. 202, 22 March 1659, Haberdashers Company, Apprenticeship Bindings

26. See Jeaffreson, J. C. (ed.) 'Middlesex Session Rolls', *Middlesex County Records, 1603*-1625 [online], vol. 2, *passim*

27. Underdown, *Revel, Riot and Rebellion*, pp.26-27

2 London, 1630–42

1. 'T. S.', 'The Last Speech and Dying Words of Thomas (Lord, Alias Colonel) Pride', *Harleian Miscellany*, vol. 3, (London: White and Murray, 1809), pp. 136-141

2. Henry IV Part 2, II, i, quoted in Williams, G. *A Glossary of Shakespeare's Sexual Language* (London The Althone Press, 1997), pp. 234-235

3. Ward, E.*, A Vade Mecum for Malt-Worms* (London: Bickerston, c.1718), p. 34

4. *CSPD (Interregnum)*, vol. 41, 3 October 1653

5. Burt, N., 'A New Years Gift for England', BL , E.684 (19); Harben, H. A., *A Dictionary of London* (London: Jenkins, 1918), entry for Windmill Court

6. Frazer, A. *Cromwell: Our Chief of Men* (third edition, St. Albans: Granada Publishing, 1973), p. 179

7. Weinreb, B. and Hibbert, C (eds.) *The London Encyclopaedia* (London: Macmillan, 1983), p. 284

8. ibid., p. 283

9. ibid., pp. 384-385

10. John Milton, *Areopagitica,* lines 600-601, quoted in: Davis, T. (ed.) *John Milton, Selected Shorter Poems and Prose* (London: Routledge,1988), p. 84

11. Greaves, R. L. and Zaller, R. (eds.) *The Biographical Dictionary of English Radicals* (Brighton: Harvester Press, 1984), entry for Chidley; Tolmie, M. *The Triumph of the Saints: The Separatist Churches of London, 1616-1649* (Cambridge: Cambridge University Press, 1977), p. 156ff.

12. Tolmie, ibid; 'Jacobites', *Exlibris.org* [online]

13. ibid.

14. ibid.

15. ibid.

16. Underdown, *Revel, Riot and Rebellion*, p. 141

17. Orme, W. (ed.) *Remarkable Passages in the Life of William Kiffin* (London: Burton & Smith, et al, 1823), p. 11

19. ibid., p. 12

19. ibid., p. 15

20. Greaves and Zaller, *Biographical Dictionary*, entry for Lathrop; Tolmie, *Triumph of the Saints*, op. cit.

21. Tolmie, *Triumph of the Saints*, p. 156 ff; Greaves and Zaller, *Biographically Dictionary*, entry for Duppa
22. Tolmie, *Triumph of the Saints*, ibid.
23. Haykin, M. A. G. 'Kiffin, William (1616-1701)', *ODNB*; 'Jacobites', exlibris.org [online]
24. Tolmie, *Triumph of the Saints*, op cit.; Haykin, 'Kiffin, William'; 'Baptists', *Exlibris.org* [online]
25. Tolmie, *Triumph of the Saints*, op. cit.
26. Watts, M. R. *The Dissenters: from Reformation to the French Revolution* (Oxford: Oxford University Press, 1978), passim
27. Greaves and Zaller, *Biographical Dictionary*, entry for Mason; Laurence, A. *Parliamentary Army Chaplains, 1642-1651* (Woodbridge: The Boydell Press, 1990), pp. 57-58
28. LMA: St. Gregory-by-Paul Parish Register
29. Prynne, W., *A Gospel Plea* (London: 1659)
30. Capp, B. 'Simpson, J. (1614/15-1622)', revised, *ODNB*.
31. LMA: St. Bride's Parish Register
32. ibid.
33. <http://en.wikipedia.org/wiki/Prides_Crossing_Beverly_Massachusetts>, (accessed 2015)
34. Barry and Brooks, *The Middling Sort*, passim
35. ibid, pp. 46-47
36. quoted in Richards, J., *Aristocrat and Regicide: The Life and Times of Thomas, Lord Grey of Groby* (London: New Millennium, 2003) p. 88

3 Service as a junior officer, 1643–44

1. Greaves and Zaller, *Biographical Dictionary*, entry for Samuel Eaton.
2. *see* Archer, I. W., *The History of the Haberdashers' Company* (Chichester: Phillimore,1991)
3. G. A. Raikes, *The Ancient Vellum Book*, cited in: Rees, J., *Leveller Organisation and the Dynamic of the English Revolution*, unpublished PhD thesis (Goldsmith's College London, 2014), p. 61
4. Nagel, L. C., *The Militia of London, 1641*-1649. Unpublished PhD thesis (King's College London, 1982), p. 21
5. Nagel, *Militia of London*, pp. 20-21
6. ibid, p. 20
7. British Library (BL) *Thomason Tracts* E669 F6 (10): 'The Names, Dignitie & Places of the Severall Colonells'
8. Nagel, *Militia of London*, p. 54
9. ibid, p. 13
10. BL, *Thomason Tracts*, E669 F6 (10) and ff.: 'The London Bands Alarm Places'
11. Gentiles, I (2004) 'Pride, Thomas'
12. TNA: State Papers SP28/262, part 3/448. Another of Barclay's captains commissioned at this date, Leete, is credited with raising '100 able and well affected young men at his own cost': TNA: SP28/265, part 2/212.
13. Scott, A. F. *Everyone a Witness: The Stuart Age* (London: White Lion, 1974) p. 21.
14. Greaves and Zaller, *Biographical Dictionary*, entry for Barclay; Roberts, K. *First Newbury 1643: The Turning Point* (London: Osprey, 2003), p. 23
15. Greaves and Zaller, *Biographical Dictionary*, entry for Gough
16. Cooper, T. 'Goffe, Stephen (1605-1681)', revised Bertram, J., *ODNB*.

17. Rogers, P. G. *The Fifth Monarchy Men* (London: Oxford University Press), p. 15
18. Rogers, *Fifth Monarchy Men*, p. 134
19. Greaves and Zaller, *Biographical Dictionary*, entry for Mason
20. Clarendon, quoted in Griffin, S. *The Siege of Redding* (Bristol: The Stuart Press, 1996), p. 30
21. see Archer, *History of the Haberdashers' Company*
22. *LJ*, vol. 6, p. 17
23. Griffin, *Siege of Redding*, passim
24. TNA SP28/266 part1/25; TNA PROB 11/283/493; *CSPD (Interregnum),* vol. 77, 1654 (undated)
25. Nagel, *Militia of London*, p. 82
26. ibid.
27. *Mercurius Aulicus*, quoted in Nagel, *Militia of London* p. 81
28. see Archer, *History of the Haberdashers' Company*
29. TNA SP28/266, part1/25
30. Peachey, S. and Turton, A. *Old Robin's foot: The Equipping and Campaigns of Essex's Infantry, 1642-1645* (Partizan Press, 1987), p. 58
31. Davis, G. 'The Parliamentary Army Under the Earl of Essex, 1642-45', *English Historical Review*, 49 (1934), pp.32-54.
32. Roberts, *First Newbury*, p. 89
33. '1643: The First Battle of Newbury', British-Civil-Wars.co.uk [online]
34. TNA SP28/266 part1/25; *Mercurius Britannicus*, 28 December-4 January 1643/44, cited in Davis, 'Parliamentary Army Under Essex', p. 42
35. TNA SP28/266 part1/27
36. Peachey and Turton, *Old Robin's Foot*, p. 58
37. TNA SP28/266 part1/25
38. Peachey and Turton, *Old Robin's Foot*, p. 58
39. TNA, ibid; Long, C. E. (ed.) *Richard Symonds's Diary of the Marches of the Royal Army* (1997 edition, Cambridge: Cambridge University Press, 1859), p. 7

4 Lostwithiel, 1644

1. TNA SP28/267 Part 3 (155)
2. The episode is recounted in Long, *Symonds's* Diary, pp. 48-49
3. Essex's Letter to Sir Philip Stapleton, in: 'Historical Collections: The Earl of Essex's March into the West, June 1644', Rushworth, J. *Historical Collections of Private Passages of State* (London: Browne, 1721), vol. 5, pp. 677-748 [online]
4. Long, *Symonds's* Diary, p. 53
5. ibid. p. 54
6. Rushworth, *Historical Collections*, vol. 5, pp. 677-748 [online]
7. Ibid.
8. ibid.
9. ibid.
10. Long, *Symonds's* Diary, p. 64
11. Rushworth, *Historical Collections*, vol. 5, pp. 677-748 [online]
12. Ibid.
13. 'Letter from the Earl of Essex to Major General Skippon', in: Rushworth, *Historical Collections*, ibid.

14. 'An Attestation of the Officers concerning their disaster in Cornwall', in: Rushworth, *Historical Collections*, ibid.
15. *Mercurius Aulicus*, cited in: Rushworth, op. cit.
16. *CJ*. vol. 3, pp. 641, 642, 645
17. 'Examination of Major General Skippon', in: Rushworth, *Historical Collections*, vol. 5, pp. 677-748 [online]
18. 'Essex's letter to Sir Philip Stapleton', Rushworth, *Historical Collections*, ibid.
19. Historical Manuscripts Commission (HMC), *6th Report*, part 1, p. 37
20. ibid.
21. ibid.
22. *CJ* vol. 4, p. 162
23. 'Major-General Skippon's Speech to the Field-Officers', in: Rushworth, *Historical Collections*, vol. 5, pp. 677-748 [online]
24. *Mercurius Aulicus*, cited in: Rushworth, *Historical Collections*, ibid.
25. Long, *Symonds's Diary*, pp. 66-67
26. ibid.
27. ibid.
28. 'Articles made with Parliament's Foot on Cornwall', in: Rushworth, *Historical Collections*, vol. 5, pp. 677-748 [online]
29. 'Essex's letter to Sir Philip Stapleton', Rushworth, *Historical Collections*, ibid.
30. TNA SP28/267 Part 3 (155)
31. For this and other details of the Second Battle of Newbury I have referred to Wanklyn, M. and Jones, F. *A Military History of the English Civil War, 1642-1646* (Harlow: Pearson/ Longman, 2005), pp. 204-209 and *passim*.
32. TNA, op. cit.
33. 'Skippon's letter to the Earl of Essex', in: Rushworth, *Historical Collections*, vol. 5, pp. 677-748 [online]
34. Wanklyn and Jones, *A Military History*, pp. 204-209
35. 'Letter from Skippon to the Committee of Both Kingdoms', Rushworth, *Historical Collections*, vol. 5, pp. 677-748 [online]
36. ibid.
37. Wanklyn, M., 'Oliver Cromwell and the Performance of Parliament's Armies in the Newbury Campaign, 20 October – 21 November 1644', *Journal of the Historical Association*, vol. 96, issue 321 (January 2011), pp. 3-25

5 Reading, December 1644–April 1645

1. Wanklyn and Jones, *A Military History*, pp. 213-214
2. *LJ* vol. 7, pp. 106-107
3. Guilding, J. M. (ed.) *Reading Records: Diary of the Corporation* (London: James Parker, 1892-1896), vol. 4, p. 129
4. Ditchfield, P. H. and Page, W. (eds.) *History of the County of Berkshire* (1925) [online], vol. 3, pp. 342-364, n. 349
5. Wanklyn and Jones, *A Military History*, p. 227
6. *CJ*, vol. 4, p. 26
7. *LJ*, vol. 7, p. 277

8. Temple, R., 'Officer Lists of the New Model Army', *Bulletin of the Institute of Historical Research*, 59:139 (1986), pp. 50-77
9. Temple, 'Officer Lists', p 71, n. 171
10. ibid.
11. Foard, G. *Naseby: The Decisive Campaign* (2004 edition, Barnsley: Pen and Sword, 1995), pp. 74-75
12. TNA SP28/29, part 2, f. 327
13. Denton, B. *Cromwell's Soldiers: The Moulding of the New Model Army, 1644-1651* (Cambridge: Denton Dare Publishing, 2004), *passim*.
14. Temple, 'Officer Lists', p. 71
15. ibid.
16. ibid, p. 53; 'The Posthumous Works of Samuel Butler', in Goodwin, vol. 3, pp. 345-346
17. Gardiner, S. R. (ed.) *The Constitutional Documents of the Puritan Revolution, 1625-1660* (Oxford: Clarendon Press, 1899), p. 269
18. ibid, p. 133
19. Denton, *Cromwell's Soldiers*, pp. 164-165
20. *CJ* vol. 4, p. 98
21. ibid.
22. Temple, 'Officer Lists', p. 53
23. Davis, G. 'The Formation of the New Model Army', *English Historical Review*, 56 (1941), pp. 103-105.
24. Lady Brilliana Harley to Edward Harley, cited in Scott, *The Stuart Age*, p. 78
25. TNA SP 28/265, part 2, f. 212
26. Laurence, *Parliamentary Army Chaplains*, p. 140
27. ibid. p. 154
28. ibid. p. 183
29. ibid. p. 134; HMC, *7th Report*, vol. 1, p. 114
30. ibid. p. 157; Langley, A. S. 'Some Notable Names in Midland Baptist History', *Baptist Quarterly*, 3:6 (1927), pp. 280-286
31. Redmayne, S. *The History of King-Killers, or the 30th January Commemorated* (London: S. Redmayne, *et al*, 1719), vol. 3, p. 56
32. TNA E121/4/8
33. Denton, *Cromwell's Soldiers*, pp. 157-163; Temple, 'Officer Lists', pp. 60, 71
34. TNA SP 28/266, part 1, f. 25
35. Wanklyn and Jones, *A Military History*, p. 233
36. This company appears to have been commanded by Lieutenant William Wills, TNA SP28/31 part 1, f. 21

6 Naseby

1. Sprigg, J. *Anglia Rediviva: England's Recovery* (Oxford: Oxford University Press, 1854), pp. 38-39
2. George Bishop, 'A More Exact and Perfect Relation', quoted in: Foard, *Naseby*, p. 405
3. Sprigg, *Anglia Rediviva*, pp. 105, 149
4. Foard, *Naseby*, p. 237
5. Sprigg, *Anglia Rediviva*, p. 42; Foard, Naseby, p. 240, 294 n. 69
6. see for example The Battlefield Trust [online]

7.   Roberts, K. *Pike and Shot Tactics, 1590-1660* (London: Osprey, 2010), p. 57
8.   Foard, *Naseby*, pp. 249, 263
9.   Sprigg, *Anglia Rediviva*, p. 39
10. Walker, Historical Discourses (1705), quoted in Adair, J. 'By the Sword Divided: Eyewitnesses of the English Civil War (London: Book Club Associates, 1983), pp. 194-95
11. Sprigg, *Anglia Rediviva*, *p.* 41
12. TNA SP28/173, part 1 (unfoliated)
13. Sprigg, *Anglia Rediviva*, p.41
14. TNA, op. cit.
15. '1645: The Storming of Leicester and the Battle of Naseby', British-Civil-Wars.com [online]
16. Sprigg, *Anglia Rediviva*, p. 42
17. TNA op. cit.; Sprigg, p. 328
18. 'Battle of Naseby', UK Battlefields Resource Centre [online]

7   Campaigns in the West, 1645–46

1.   *CSPD (Charles I)*, vol. 507, 20 June 1645
2.   TNA E121/4/8 pt 106; Sprigg, *Anglia Rediviva*, p. 333
3.   TNA ibid.; CJ, vol. 4, p. 615
4.   Sprigg, *Anglia Rediviva*, p. 75
5.   ibid.
6.   ibid., p. 76
7.   see for example *CSPD (Interregnum)*, vol. 181, 18 May 1658
8.   Sprigg. *Anglia Rediviva*, p. 78
9.   ibid., p. 77
10. Nichols, J. F. and Taylor, J. *Bristol Past and Present* (Bristol, Arrowsmith, 1862), vol. 3, p. 4
11. Sprigg, *Anglia Rediviva*, p. 104
12. Bernard de Gomme, quoted in Harrington, P. *English Civil War Fortifications, 1642-1651* (London: Osprey Books, 2003), p. 18
13. Rushworth, *Historical Collections*, vol. 6, pp. 23-89 [online]
14. ibid.
15. Sprigg, *Anglia Rediviva*, p. 116
16. Colonel Thomas Rainsborough, quoted in Lynch, p. 155
17. ibid.
18. Sprigg, *Anglia Rediviva*, p. 105; Roberts, *Pike and Shot Tactics, passim.*
19. Nichols and Taylor, *Bristol Past and* Present, vol. 3, p. 9
20. Carlyle, T. *Oliver Cromwell's Letters and Speeches* (London: Routledge, 1885), vol. 1, p. 228
21. ibid.
22. Sprigg, *Anglia Rediviva*, p. 116
23. Nichols and Taylor, *Bristol past and Present, vol.* 3, p. 9-10
24. Although the only reference for this appears to be in the Victorian romance, *Herbert Tresham*, by John Mason Neale.
25. Carlyle, *Cromwell's Letters and Speeches*, op. cit.
26. Sprigg, *Anglia Rediviva*, p. 117
27. ibid.; Heath, J., *A Chronicle of the Late Intestine War in the Three Kingdoms of England, Scotland and Ireland* (London: 1676), p.86
28. Long, *Symonds's* Diary, p. 211

29. Lancashire Record Office, DDKE/9/38/18; Fearn, J. *Discovering Heraldry* (Aylesbury: Shire Publications, 1980), p. 40
30. Carlyle, *Cromwell's Letters and Speeches*, vol. 1, pp. 228-229
31. Carlyle, ibid, vol. 1, p. 228
32. Sprigg, *Anglia Rediviva*, pp. 132-137
33. *CSPD (Charles I)* vol. 511, 6 October 1645
34. Sprigg, *Anglia Rediviva*, p. 136
35. ibid., p. 176
36. ibid., p. 181
37. ibid., p. 200
38. TNA SP28/265, part 2, f. 210
39. Peters, H., *Mr. Peters Last Report of the English Warres* (London: 1646), p.4
40. Gentles, I. 'The New Model Officer Corps in 1647: a collective portrait', *Social History*, 22:2 (1997), pp. 111-129
41. Corrigan, G., *Mud, Blood and Poppycock: Britain and the First World War* (London: Cassell, 2003), p. 10
42. Harrison, vol. 3, p. 179
43. Rutt, J. T. (ed.), *The Diary of Thomas Burton Esq.*, 1828 [online], vol. 4, pp. 388-389, n. 8
44. ibid.

8 Army Mutiny, 1647

1. Underdown, D. *Pride's Purge: Politics in the Puritan Revolution* (Oxford: Oxford University Press,1971), pp. 1-2
2. Pearl, V., 'London's Counter-Revolution', Aylmer, G. E. (ed.), *The Interregnum: The Quest for Settlement, 1646-1660'*, (London: Macmillan, 1983), pp. 29-57
3. ibid.
4. ibid.
5. Sprigg, *Anglia* Rediviva, pp. 244, 283
6. *LJ*, vol. 9, p. 520
7. Eales, J. *Puritans and Roundheads: The Harleys of Brampton Bryan and the Outbreak of the English Civil War* (Cambridge: Cambridge University Press, 1990), p. 186
8. *LJ*, vol. 9, p. 112; *A Perfect and True Copy of the grievances of the Army*, BL, E.390 (3)
9. ibid, p. 115
10. ibid.
11. Rushworth, *Historical Collections*, vol. 6, pp. 444-475
12. *LJ*, vol. 9, p. 114
13. ibid.
14. 'Heads of the Petition', ibid.
15. 'Declaration of Dislike of both Houses', ibid; *The Declaration of the Army Printed by the officers subscribed*, BL, E.390 (26)
16. Frazer, *Cromwell*, p. 188
17. *LJ*, vol. 9, p. 208
18. *CJ*, vol. 5, p. 132
19. Whitelock, B. *Memorials of the English Affairs* (Oxford: Oxford University Press, 1853), vol. 2, p. 128
20. Rushworth, *Historical Collections*, vol. 6, pp. 444-475

21. *CJ*, vol. 5, p. 132
22. Lindley, K. and Scott, D. *The Journal of Thomas Juxon, 1644-1647* (Cambridge: Royal Historical Society), p.152
23. *LJ*, vol. 9, p. 115
24. Firth, C. H. and David, G. *The Regimental History of Cromwell's Army* (Oxford: Oxford University Press, 1940), pp. 360-64
25. Ibid.
26. ibid.
27. ibid.
28. Rushworth, *Historical Collections*, vol. 6, pp. 444-475
29. *LJ*, vol. 9, p. 153
30. ibid., p. 208
31. Firth and Davis, *Cromwell's Army*, p. 360
32. *LJ*, vol. 9, p. 153
33. Redmayne, *King-Killers*, vol. 3, p. 55; Rushworth, *Historical* Collections, vol. 6, pp. 604-657
34. Firth, C. H. (ed.) *The Clarke Papers: Selections of the Papers of William Clarke, Secretary to the Council of the Army 1647-1649, and to General Monck and the Commanders of the Army in Scotland 1651-1660* (London: The Camden Society, 1894), vol. 1, p. 217
35. Eales, *Puritans and* Roundheads, p. 188
36. Firth, *The Clarke Papers*, p.217
37. *CJ*, vol. 5, pp. 255-257
38. ibid,, p. 259
39. ibid, p. 261
40. *LJ*, vol. 9, p. 360
41. ibid.
42. Rushworth, *Historical Collections*, vol. 7, pp. 731-800
43. ibid.
44. ibid.
45. ibid.
46. quoted in Frazer, *Cromwell*, p. 214
47. 'London Brewers' Petition', *LJ*, vol. 9, pp. 402-403
48. ibid.
49. Firth, *The Clarke Papers*, vol. 2, pp. 274-277
50. Holdisworth, 'An Answer Without a Question' (London: 1649)
51. Fraser, *Cromwell*, pp. 190-191

9 The Second Civil War, 1648

1. Whitelock, B., *Memorials of the English Affairs* (Oxford: Oxford University Press, 1853), vol. 2, p. 314
2. Rushworth, *Historical Affairs*, vol. 7., pp. 1097-1134 [online]
3. ibid.; TNA SP28/56, f.387
4. Nelson, C., *Cromwell in Pembroke* (revised edition, Pembroke: Pembroke Civil Trust Society, 1974), p. 8
5. Phillips, J., 'William Goffe the Regicide', *English Historical Review*, 7 (1892), pp. 717-720
6. ibid., p.719
7. Nelson, *Cromwell in Pembroke*, p. 16

8. *The Moderate Intelligencer*, cited in Robbins, p. 109
9. *CSPD (Charles I)*, vol. 516, 3 August 1648
10. Firth and Davis, *Regimental History*, p. 366
11. Carlyle, *Cromwell's Letters and Speeches*, vol. 1, p. 211, Letter XLI
12. ibid. p. 220, Letter XLIII
13. ibid.
14. ibid.
15. TNA, PROB/11/205
16. *CJ*, vol. 6, p. 298
17. Carlyle, *Cromwell's Letters and Speeches*, vol. 1, p. 220, Letter XLIII
18. ibid; *CJ*, vol. 6, p. 237
19. Heath, *A Chronicle*, p. 178
20. Carlyle, *Cromwell's Letters and* Speeches, vol. 1, p. 212, Letter XLI
21. Health, ibid.
22. 'The Preston Campaign, 1648', *BCW Project* [online]. Heath's account of the fight at Winwick (printed in 1678) is longer and more detailed than the author's description of the Battle of Preston, indicating the size and importance of the battle outside Warrington on 19 August 1648.
23. Rushworth, *Historical Affairs*, vol. 9, pp. 1281-1314 [online]

10 Pride's Purge

1. Edwards, G. *The Last Days of Charles I* (Stroud: Sutton Publishing, 1999), p. 74
2. quoted in Deane, J. B. *The Life of Richard Deane* (London: Longman, 1870) pp. 323-326
3. ibid.
4. ibid.
5. ibid.
6. ibid.
7. ibid.
8. Firth, C. H. (ed.) *The Memoirs of Edmund Ludlow, Lieutenant General of the Horse in the Army of the Commonwealth of England* (Oxford: Clarendon Press, 1894), vol. 1, pp. 203-204
8. Edwards, *Last Days of Charles* I, p. 79 ff.
10. Underdown, *Pride's Purge*, p. 132
11. Edwards, *Last Days of Charles I*, p. 82
12. Underdown, *Pride's Purge*, p. 127
13. ibid. pp.117-118
14. Edwards, *Last Days of Charles I*, p. 82
15. Frazer, *Cromwell*, p. 268; Underdown, *Pride's Purge*, p. 134
16. Edwards, *Last Days of Charles I*, p. 82
17. ibid.
18. Underdown, *Pride's Purge*, p. 139
19. Edwards, *Last Days of Charles I*, p. 82
20. Firth, *Ludlow's Memoirs*, vol. 1, p. 206
21. ibid.
22. ibid, p. 210
23. ibid.
24. ibid. pp. 209-210

25. Underdown, *Pride's Purge*, p. 141
26. ibid.
27. ibid.
28. see Greaves and Zaller, *Biographical Dictionary*, entry for Pride.
29. Underdown, *Pride's Purge*, p.141
30. ibid.
31. ibid. p. 143
32. *CJ*, vol. 6, p. 93
33. ibid.
34. Cobbett, W. *Parliamentary History of England* (London: Hansard, 1808), vol. 3, p. 1249
35. Underdown, *Pride's Purge*, p. 144; Prynne, W., *Mr. Prynne's Demand of His Liberty to the Generall* (London: 1648), p. 1; Prynne, W., *A True and Perfect Narrative* (London: 1659), p .49
36. ibid., p. 147
37. Rutt, *Burton's Diary*, 7 February 1658
38. Fritze, R. H. & Robinson, W. B. (eds.) *Historical Dictionary of Stewart England, 1603-1677* (California: Stanford University Press, 1990), entry for Pride's Purge; Underdown, *Pride's Purge*, p. 212
39. Underdown, *Pride's Purge*, p.212
40. Wheatley, H. B. *London Past and Present* (London: John Murray, 1891), vol. 2, p. 201
41. *Mercurius Pragmaticus*, 21-28 November 1648, quoted in Gentles, I., *The New Model Army in England, Ireland and Scotland*, (Oxford: Blackwell Books, 1992), p.278; Richards, *Aristocrat and Regicide*, p. 289
42. Bradley, E. T., 'Grey, Thomas, Baron Grey of Groby (1622–1657)', revised Kelsey, S., *ODNB*
43. Underdown, *Pride's Purge*, pp. 145-146
44. ibid.
45. Harris, W., *The Lives and Writings of James I and Charles I, and the Lives of Oliver Cromwell and Charles II* (London: F. C. and J. Rivington, *et al.*, 1814), vol. 3, p. 182
46. ibid.
47. ibid. p. 183
48. ibid. p. 181
49. Underdown, *Pride's Purge*, p. 141
50. ibid. p. 151
51. ibid. p. 152
52. ibid. p. 153
53. ibid.
54. ibid. p. 153-154
55. ibid. p. 159
56. ibid. p. 160
57. ibid. p. 167
58. ibid. p. 160
59. Edwards, *Last Days of Charles I*, p. 98
60. ibid. p. 99
61. ibid.
62. Gardiner, *Constitutional Documents*, pp. 357-358; *CJ*, vol. 6, p. 113

11 London, 1649–50

1. Edwards, *Last Days of Charles I*, p. 114
2. ibid. p. 126
3. Gardiner, *Constitutional* Documents, pp. 372, 374
4. 'The Sentence of the High Court of Justice', Gardiner, *Constitutional Documents*, p. 380
5. Edwards, *Last Days of Charles I*, p. 163-164
6. ibid. pp. 160-163
7. Underdown, *Pride's Purge*, p. 188
8. ibid. p. 187
9. Noble, *English Regicides*, p. 132
10. Underdown, *Pride's Purge*, p. 189
11. details of the Regicides' educational backgrounds are taken from individuals' entries in the *Oxford Dictionary of National Biography*.
12. Winstanley, *Loyal Martyrology*, pp. 108-109
13. Noble, M., *The Memoirs of the Protectoral-House of Cromwell* (second edition, London: G. G. J. and J. Robinson, 1797), p. 418
14. TNA SP28/267 part 3, f. 160; BL Add Ms 63788B, ff.114-155
15. GL, Haberdashers Company, Apprenticeship Bindings 1610-1630, MS 15860/4, f. 173 v.
16. Cockayne, *Complete Peerage*, vol. 4, p.630; Burke, B., *General Armoury of England, Ireland, Scotland and Wales* (1969 edition, London: Hanson and sons,1842), p. 824
17. BL Add MS 26758 f.37
18. Cockayne, *Complete Peerage*, op. cit.
19. Farrar, E., *Church Heraldry in Norfolk* (Norwich: Goose, 1887-1893), vol. 1, p. 53; Blomefield, F., *An Essay Towards a Biographical Dictionary of Norfolk*, (London: William-Miller, 1805-1811, vol. 1, p. 532
20. Edwards, *Last Days of Charles I*, pp. 176, 178
21. quoted in: *Dunfermline Saturday Press*, 2 July 1864, *British Newspaper Archive* [online]
22. Edwards, *Last Days of Charles I*, p. 186
23. ibid. p. 189
24. 'An Act Abolishing the House of Lords', Gardiner, *Constitutional Documents*, p. 387
25. 'An Act Declaring England to be a Commonwealth', ibid, p. 388
26. Rees, *Leveller Organisation*, pp. 148, 149 n. 112
27. Jeaffreson, J. C. (ed.) 'Middlesex Session Rolls', *Middlesex County Records, 1603-1625* (1888) [online], vol. 3, pp. 188-193
28. *CSPD (Interregnum)*, vol. 1, 1 Feb 1649
29. ibid. 'warrants', 4 July 1649; 8 Aug 1649
30. ibid, 4 Jan 1650
31. ibid, 9 May 1649
32. ibid, 11 May 1649
33. ibid, vol. 3, 23 Oct 1649; warrants, 5 November 1649; anon., 'Death of the Duke of Hamilton', *The Christian Observer*, vol ii, January-December 1803, p. 263
34. *Calendar of State Papers Venetian* (CSPV), vol. 28: 11 January 1650
35. *CSPD (Interregnum)*, vol. 5, 1 Feb 1650
36. ibid, vol. 2, 25 July 1649; 25 August 1649
37. ibid, 'Warrants of the Council of State', 27 July 1649
38. Moore, N., *The History of St. Bartholomew's Hospital* (London: Pearson, 1918), vol. 2, p. 308

39. Burford, E. J., *Royal St. James's: Being a Story of Kings, Clubmen and Courtesans* (London: Hale, 1988), p. 15
40. quoted in Firth, C. H. *Cromwell's Army* (London: Methuen, 1902), pp. 289-290
41. *CSPD (Interregnum)*, vol. 2, 31 August 1649
42. ibid, 'Warrants of the Council of State', 31 July 1649
43. ibid, 'Warrants from the Council of State, Admiralty Committee', 16 and 26 March 1649
44. Weinreb and Hibbert, *London Encyclopaedia*, p. 809
45. ibid.
46. *The Man in the Moon*, 21, 5-12 September 1649, quoted in: Raymond, J. *Making the News: An Anthology ODF the Newsbooks of Revolutionary England* (Witney: Windrush Press, 1987), pp. 149-150
47. *Mercurius Elencticus 27 August-3 September 1649*, BL Thomason Tracts, E572/15, pp. 147-8
48. Ashcott Parish Registers, familysearch.org [online]
49. *Mercurius Elencticus 27 August-3 September 1649*, BL Thomason Tracts, E572/15, pp. 147-8
50. Whitelock, *Memorials*, vol. 3, p. 87
51. ibid, p. 88
52. Chidley, 'A Cry Against A Crying Sin', quoted in Park, T. (ed.), *The Harleian Miscellany*, (London: Robert Dutton, 1810), vol. 6, p. 272, ff.
53. Ibid.
54. Rushworth, *Historical Collections*, vol. vii, p. 1274 [online]
55. Hosea, 8:12; Park, *Harleian Miscellany*, vol. 6, p. 272, ff.
56. Park, *Harleian Miscellany*, ibid.
57. GL, Brewers' Company, Wardens' Accounts 1501/2-1692 (MS 5442/1-8)
58. Raymond, *Making the News*, p. 150
59. see Pearl, V., 'London's Counter-Revolution', Aylmer, *The Interregnum*, pp. 30, 41

12 The War with Scotland, 1650–51

1. Cited in *The Morpeth Herald*, 12 July 1879. British Newspaper Archive [online]
2. Whitelock, *Memorials*, vol. 3, p. 202
3. Long, *Symonds's Diary*, pp. 31, 41, 154
4. Whitelock, *Memorials*, vol. 3, p. 199
5. For this and other details of the Dunbar campaign, see: Reid, S., *Dunbar 1650: Cromwell's Victory* (Oxford: Osprey, 2004)
6. Scott, W. (ed.), *Original Memorials Written During the Civil War* (Edinburgh: Constable & Co, 1806), p. 134
7. ibid., p. 278
8. Carlyle, *Cromwell's Letters and Speeches*, vol. 1, pp. 107-108; Scott, *Original* Memorials, pp. 278-279
9. quoted in Firth, *Cromwell's Army*, p. 387
10. Scott, *Original Memorials*, p. 142
11. Ibid.
12. quoted in Morley, J. *Oliver Cromwell* (London: Macmillan, 1900), p. 321
13. Scott, *Original Memorials*, ibid.
14. '1650: The Battle of Dunbar', British-Civil-Wars.co.uk [online]
15. *CSPD (Interregnum)*, vol. 11, 12 October 1650

16. *Perfect Diurnall*, 21 September-8 October 1650, p. 577, quoted in: Kelsey, S. *Inventing a Republic* (Manchester: Manchester University Press, 1997), p. 72

17. see Medvei, V. C. and Thornton, J. L. (eds.) *The Hospital of Saint Bartholomew*, 1123-1973 (London: Pearson, 1974); *CSPD (Interregnum)*, 31 December 1651

18. Oppenheim, M., *A History of the Administration of the Royal Navy* (London: Bodley Head, 1896), p. 324

19. ibid., p. 325

20. *CSPD (Interregnum)*, 'Orders of the Navy Committee', 11 November 1650

21. *CJ*, vol. 6, p. 469; *CJ*, vol. 7, pp. 258-259

22. *CSPD (Interregnum)*, vol. 123, p. 619

23. Burnet, G. *History of His Own Time* (London: Orr & Co., 1850), vol. 1, p. 318; de Krey, 'Bethel, Slingsby (*bap.*1617, *d.*1697)', revised Kelsey, S., *ODNB*

24. Burnet, *History*, vol. 1, p.318

25. *CJ*, vol. 6, p. 619

26. *CSPD (Interregnum)*, vol. 125, March 1656

27. Atkinson C. T., *Letters and Papers Relating to the Dutch War, 1652-1654* (London: Naval Records Society, 1899-1930), vol. 3, p. 430

28. *CSPD (Interregnum)*, 31 December 1651

29. *CSPD (Interregnum)*, 'Warrants of the Council of State, Generals of the Fleet, &t.', 17 December 1651 and *passim*

30. *CJ*, vol. 7, 11 February

31. Grant, J. *Old and New Edinburgh* (6 vols) (London: Cassell, 1883), vol. 3, p. 187.

32. Greaves and Zaller, *Biographical Dictionary*, entry for Mason

33. *A Perfect Diurnal, 5-12 August, 1651*, BL, E.786 (31)

34. Cary, H. (ed.), *Memorials of the Great Civil War in England, from 1646-1652* (London: Henry Colburn, 1842), vol. 2, p. 358

35. ibid.

13 The Dutch War, 1652–54

1. 'T.S.', *The Last Speech*, p. 385

2. TNA E317/Surrey/39, cited in Dent, J., *The Quest for Nonsuch* (second edition, London: Hutchinson), pp. 295-298

3. Dent, *Nonsuch*, p. 196

4. Benedict, J. 'Mayo, Richard (c.1630-1695)', *Oxford Dictionary of National Biography*; Burroughs, E. *The Memorable Works of a Son of Thunder and Consolation* (London:1672)

5. An inventory of the contents of Worcester Park at Pride's death can be found in Court of Chancery records, TNA C5/402/121

6. TNA E317/Surrey/39, ibid.

7. Holman Hunt, cited in Dent, *Nonsuch*, p. 219; Ordnance Survey 1:10,560 Epoch 1, British History Online [online]

8. Barber, W. *The Storming and Totall Routing of Tythes* (London: 1651); Baker, P. R. S., 'Barber, Edward (*d.* 1663), *ODNB*

9. 'The Beacon Quenched', BL E.678 (3)

10. ibid.

11. 'The Beacon Flameing', BL E.683 (30)

12. Greaves and Zaller, *Biographical Dictionary*, entry for Pride

13. *CJ*, vol. 7, pp.129-130; Richards, *Aristocrat and Regicide*, p. 388
14. *CSPD (Interregnum)*, vol. 36, 31 May 1653. Another of the hospitals' governors was the Baptist, Samuel Richardson (*see* Shaw, W. A., 'Richardson, Samuel (*fl.* 1637-1658)', rev. Sean Kelsey, *ODNB*)
15. accounts of the Savoy and Ely House hospitals are found in TNA, SP28 104/1
16. *CSPD (Interregnum)*, vol. 36 11 May 1653
17. ibid, vol. 36, 20 May 1653; Atkinson, *The Dutch War*, vol. 5, p. 291
18. TNA, SP28 104/1, f. 134
19. ibid. f. 101
20. *CSPD (Interregnum)*, vol. 36, 12 May 1653
21. *A Schedule, or List of the Prisoners in the Fleet*, BL, E.968 (13); *A List of All the Prisoners in the Upper Bench Prison*, BL, E.213 (8); *CJ*, vol. 7, pp.293, 302-303; Firth, C. H. and Rait, R. S. (eds.) *Acts and Ordinances of the Interregnum* (London: 1911), pp.753-754
22. *CSPD (Interregnum)*, vol. 69, 14 April 1654
23. ibid., vol. 37, 1 June 1653
24. ibid., vol. 34, 25 March 1653
25. *CSPD (Interregnum)*,1653-54, 'Warrants by the Council of State for Payment of Money', 20th October 1653; ibid, 'Warrants of the Council of State, General of the Fleet, &c', 20th October 1653.
26. Atkinson, *The Dutch* War, vol. 4, p. 236
27. ibid., p. 237
28. *CSPD (Interregnum)*, vol. 39, 6 August 1653
29. *CSPD (Interregnum)*, 1653-54, *Warrants of the Council of State, General of the Fleet, &c.*, 19 September 1653.
30. Oppenheim, *Administration of the Royal Navy*, vol. 1, p. 325
31. TNA C5/24/62
32. ibid.
33. Oppenheim, *Administration of the Royal Navy*, p. 326
34. *CSPD (Interregnum)*, vol. 38, 6 July 1653
35. ibid., vol. 77, (undated) 1654
36. Oppenheim, *Administration of the Royal Navy*, p. 326
37. Atkinson, *The Dutch War*, vol. 5, p. 257
38. ibid., p. 279; Cornel, M., 'The Three-Threads Mystery and the Birth of Porter: the answer is ...', *Zythophile*, 2015 [online]
39. Atkinson, *The Dutch War*, p. 279
40. *CSPD (Interregnum)*, vol. 76, 17 Oct 1654
41. Oppenheim, *Administration of the Royal Navy*, p. 320
42. *see* Cornell, op. cit., for a fuller discussion of 'three-threads'
43. *CSPD (Interregnum)*, 1656-1657, 'Letters and Papers Relating to the Navy, &c.', February 1657, ref.31
44. Atkinson, *The Dutch* War, vol. 4, p. 291
45. Backhouse, T. (2016) 'Members of the Town Council of Portsmouth, 1531-1835' [online] available: HTTP <http://www.history.inportsmouth.co.uk/people/town-council>, (accessed 2011)
46. TNA E317/Surrey/39, ibid.
47. *CSPD (Interregnum)*, vol. 162, *Letters and Papers Relating to the Navy*, ref. 31

48. *CSPD (Interregnum),* 'Warrants for the Council of State for Payment of Money', 1653-54, pp. 450-460
49. *CSPD (Interregnum)*, vol. 66, f. 7
50. ibid., vol. 70, April 20-20 1654
51. ibid., vol. 69, 14 April 1654
52. ibid.
53. Macray, W. D. (ed.) *A Calendar of the Clarendon Papers State Papers Preserved in the Bodleian* Library (Oxford: Clarendon Press, 1864), vol. 2, p. 379
54. Firth, C. H., *Scotland and the Protectorate: Letters Relating to the Military Government in Scotland from January 1654 to June 1659* (Edinburgh: University Press,1899), p. xix.
55. Macray, *Clarendon* Papers, vol.2, p. 380

14 Instruments of Government, 1654–56

1. *CSPD (Interregnum)*, vol. 69, 14 April 1654
2. ibid.
3. Ashley, M., Cromwell's Generals (London: Jonathan Cape, 1951), p. 205
4. Birch, T. (ed.), *A Collection of the Papers of John Thurloe* (London: Fletcher Gyles, 1742), vol. 2, p. 414
5. Macray, *Clarendon Papers*, vol. 2, p. 380
6. ibid. vol. 2, pp. 304-305
7. ibid. vol. 2, p. 260
8. Firth, *Scotland and the Protectorate*, p. xx
9. Birch, *Thurloe* Papers, vol. 2, p. 526
10. Ashley, *Cromwell's* Generals, p. 205
11. Nickolls, J., *Original Letters and Papers of State Addressed to Oliver Cromwell* (London: Bowyer, 1743), p. 132
12. Firth, *Scotland and the Protectorate*, p. 252
13. Birch, *Thurloe Papers*, vol. 3, pp. 185-195
14. Frazer, *Cromwell*, p. 514
15. Birch, *Thurloe Papers*, vol. 3, pp. 134-139
16. ibid. p. 56; *Mercurius Politicus 11-18 January 1655*, BL Thomason Tracts E.825 (4)
17. Greaves and Zaller, *Biographical Dictionary*, entry for Mason
18. Firth, *Scotland and the Protectorate*, p. 306
19. HMC, *Report on Leyborne-Popham Manuscripts*, p. 172
20. Firth, *Scotland and the Protectorate*, vol. 3, p. 7
21. Birch, *Thurloe Papers*, vol. 2, p. 526
22. Macray, *Clarendon Papers*, vol. 2, pp. 405-406
23. Warner, G. F., *Correspondence of Sir Edward Nicholas, Secretary of State* (London: Camden Society, 1897), vol. 3, pp. 263-264
24. Firth, *Scotland and the Protectorate*, pp. 272, 280, 282
25. *CSPD (Interregnum)*, vol. 166, 'Letters and Papers relating to the Navy &c.', 26 May 1657
26. *CSPD (Interregnum)*, vol. 77, 1654 (undated), f. 98
27. ibid.
28. ibid.
29. ibid, f. 99

30. *CSPD (Interregnum),* vol. 70, April 26 1654; ibid., 'Addenda', 15 August; ibid., 'Warrants of the Protector and Council of Payment of Money', 16 August
31. *CSPD (Interregnum),* vol. 72, 13 June 1654
32. 'Minute Book: 10 September 1661', in, Shaw, W. A., *Calendar of Treasury Books, Volume 1: 1660-1667* (1909) [online]
33. Nagel, *Militia of London,* p. 52, n. 5
34. Thomas Monck family tree, UK Geneaology Archives [online]
35. Greer, *Shakespeare's Wife,* pp. 42, 44
36. LMA, Registers of St. Botolph's Aldgate
37. TNA C5/19/81
38. ibid.
39. ibid.
40. LMA, Registers of St. Botolph's Aldgate
41. *CJ,* vol. 7, p. 747
42. *CSPD (Interregnum),* vol. 179, 25 Feb 1658
43. TNA E214/318
44. TNA PROB 11/240
45. Ashley, *Cromwell's Generals,* pp.151-152
46. *CSPD (Interregnum),* vol. 125, 25 March 1656; vol. 127, 13 May 1656
47. Macauley, T. B., *The History of England from the Accession of James II* (Boston: Philips, Sampson and Co., 1854), vol. 1, p. 126
48. Hotson, J. L. 'Bear Gardens and Bear Baiting in the Commonwealth', *PMLA: Proceedings of the Modern Language Association,* 40:2 (1945), pp.276-288
49. Hotson, 'Bear Gardens', p. 278; *CSPD (Interregnum),* vol. 36, 5 May 1653
50. *The Diary of Henry Townsend,* quoted in Hotson, 'Bear Gardens', p. 286
51. ibid.
52. ibid, p. 278
53. Hotson, 'Bear Gardens', p. 285
54. Macray, *Clarendon Papers,* vol. 3, p. 415
55. Anon., *Rump Songs,* p. 300
56. Winstanley, *Loyal Martyrology,* p. 109
57. Hotson, 'Bear Gardens', pp. 286-287
58. quoted in Hotson, 'Bear Gardens', p. 286; Macray, *Clarendon Papers,* ibid.
59. Hotson, 'Bear Gardens', p. 283, and *passim*
60. BL E.683 (30), 'The Beacon Flameing'
61. ibid.
62. ibid.

15 London, 1656–57

1. Ludlow, *Memoirs,* vol. 2, p. 25
2. Greaves, R. L. (2004) 'Owen, John (1616-1683)', *ODNB*
3. Ludlow, *Memoirs,* ibid; Birch, *Thurloe Papers,* vol. 4, p. 621
4. Birch, *Thurloe Papers,* vol.6, p. 281
5. Burnet, *History,* vol. 1, p. 130
6. Redmayne, *King-Killers,* part 3, p. 54
7. Firth, *Clarke Papers,* vol.2, pp. xxv-xxvi

8. ibid, pp.133-134
9. ibid.
10. Birch, *Thurloe Papers*, vol. 6, p. 310
11. Frazer, *Cromwell*, pp. 612-613
12. Cobbett, *Parliamentary History*, vol.3, p.1482
13. Rutt, *Burton's Diary*, vol. 1, p. 127
14. ibid., vol. 2, p. 20
15. Birch, *Thurloe Papers*, vol. 6, p. 281; Firth, *Clarke Papers*, vol. 2, p. 25, n. 8
16. Rutt, *Burton's Diary*, vol. 2, p. 118; *CJ* vol. 7, p. 535
17. references to the committees on which Pride sat are found in: *CJ*, vol. 7, pp.526-573
18. *CJ*, p. 568
19. ibid., p. 573
20. ibid., pp. 832-833
21. TNA PROB 11/240

16 Oliver's Drayman

1. Noble, *English Regicides*, p. 132
2. 'Knavery of the Rump', Guildhall Library (1978)
3. Time Out, *Time Out: South West England* (London: Penguin, 2003), p. 111
4. Greaves and Zaller, Biographical Dictionary; Calendar for the Committee of Compounding, vols. G251 and G253 *passim*
5. Time Out, *South west England*, p. 111
6. Portrait of Colonel Pride (C.III.374), Sutherland Collection, Ashmolean Museum.
7. Battista, K. (ed.) *Benezit Dictionary of Artists* (14 vols) (Oxford: Oxford University Press), entry for Thomas Athow, p. 792
8. BL E.1985 (7), 'A New Meeting of Ghosts at Tyburn'
9. Knoppers, p. 47
10. Noble, *English* Regicides, vol. 2, pp. 132-133
11. Knoppers, 'Sing Old Noll the Brewer', p. 33
12. Mackay, p. 118
13. Knoppers, 'Sing Old Noll the Brewer', p. 36
14. ibid., p. 37
15. TNA E121/4/8, part 106, 'Sale of Crown Properties'
16. ibid.
17. Gentles, 'New Model Officer Corps', p. 143
18. Knoppers, 'Sing Old Noll the Brewer', p. 39
19. Ludlow, *Memoirs*, vol. 2, p. 25
20. *A New Year's Gift for England* (1653), p. 15, quoted in: Worden, B. *The Rump Parliament 1648-53* (Cambridge: Cambridge University Press,1974), p. 117
21. Rutt, *Burton's Diary*, vol. 2, p. 117, n. 1
22. *CSPD (Interregnum)*, vol. 181, 15 June 1658
23. ibid, vol. 129, 5 August 1656
24. Anon., *Rump*, pp. 299-302
25. Park, *Harleian Miscellany*, vol.8, p. 385
26. ibid.
27. Wharton, G., *Select and Choice Poems* (London:1651), p.54

28. British History Online [online], Calendar for the Committee of Compounding, 14 May 1650
29. Barry and Brooks, *The Middling Sort*, p. 15
30. Winstanley, *Loyal Martyrology*, p. 109

17 End of the Protectorate, 1658–1660

1. 'The Private Diarie of Elizabeth Viscountess Mordaunt', quoted in Kouffman, p. 97
2. Heath, *A Chronical,* p. 405
3. Stater, V. 'Mordaunt, John, first Viscount Mordaunt of Avalon (1626–1675)', *ODNB*; CSPD (Interregnum) vol. 180, 8 April 1658
4. TNA, PROB 11/240; *The Weekly Intelligencer of the Commonwealth* (1-8 November 1659), BL, E.1005 (3)
5. HMC, *5th Report*, p. 172
6. Firth, *Clarke Papers*, vol. 3, p. 167
7. Whitelocke, *Memorials*, vol. 4, pp. 335-336
8. *CJ*, vol. 7, p. 743
9. *CJ*, vol. 7, p. 722
10. *CSPD (Interregnum),* vol. 203, 16 June 1659
11. *CJ*, vol.7, p. 696
12. ibid, vol.7, p. 700
13. ibid, vol.7, p. 829
14. Rutt, *Burton's Diary*,11 and 13 April 1659, vol.4, pp. 396, 419
15. Ludlow, *Memoirs*, vol. 2, p. 61
16. *CJ*, vol. 7, p. 830; Firth (1891) vol. 2, p. 437
17. HMC, *Report on the Manuscripts of F. W. Leyborne-Popham, Esq.*, p. 172.
18. 'The Regicides', British Civil Wars [online]
19. *CJ*, vol. 8, p. 27
20. ibid, p. 202
21. *CSPD (Charles I),* 'newspapers for the years January 1648 – January 1649'
22. Latham, R. and Mathews, W. (eds.), *The Diary of Samuel Pepys* (London: Bell and Hyman, 1970-73), vol. 2, p. 24
23. ibid, vol. 2, p. 27.
24. *CJ*, vol. 8, p. 27
25. Bray, W. (ed.), *The Diary of John Evelyn* (London: M. W. Dunne, 1901), vol. 1, p. 340
26. Ellkis, H. (ed.), *The Obituary of Richard Smyth,* (London: Camden Society, 1849), p. 48
27. *CJ*, vol. 8, p. 200
28. 'T. S.', *The Last Speech*, p. 139
29. *Directory of Public Worship* (1656), cited in: Neal, vol. 3 appendix
30. Lysons, D., *The Environs of London* (1796), British History Online [online], vol. 4, pp. 577-617
31. Noble, *English Regicides*, p. 132
32. Anon. 'A Panegyric on Pride', *Blackwood's Magazine*, 26:160 (July-December 1829), pp. 914-917
33. *LJ*, vol.11, p. 205
34. Jordan, D. and Walsh, M., *The King's Revenge* (London: Abacus, 2013), p. 257
35. ibid, p. 259

36. ibid, p. 309
37. Durston, 'Gough, William (*d.*1679?)', *ODNB*.
38. ibid.
39. ibid.
40. Jordan and Walsh, *The King's Revenge*, p. 319
41. *CSPD (Interregnum)*, Warrants of Council of State, 19 April 1660; *CPSD (Charles II)*, 1670, with addenda 1660-1670
42. *CSPD (Charles II)*, vol. 96, April 1-17 1664; Zook, M. 'Holmes, Abraham (*d.* 1685)', *ODNB*
43. *CSPD (Charles II)*, vol. 217, September 12-26 1667

18 Epilogue: Debtors and Duchesses

1. Ammussen, S. D. (1988) *An Ordered Society: Gender and Class in Early Modern England,* cited in Foyster, 'Gender Relations', Coward, B. (ed.) *A Companion to Stuart Britain*, 2003 (Chichester: Wiley-Blackwell), pp. 111-129.
2. *CSPD (Charles II)*, vol. 26, undated
3. British History Online [online], *Calendar of Treasury Books*, vol. 6, pp. 545-562
4. TNA E133/141/23.
5. *CSPD (Charles II)*, vol. 71, 9 April 1663; vol. 88, undated, 1663
6. Dent, *Nonsuch*, p. 201
7. ibid, p. 220
8. TNA PROB 11/283/493
9. TNA C5/402/121
10. TNA PROB, op. cit.
11. *CJ*. Vol. 7, p. 833
12. Latham and Mathews, *Pepys Diary*, 28 Jan 1660; British History Online [online], *Calendar of Treasury Books*, vol. 8, Entry Book, September 1688; *CSP Colonial*, America and West Indies, vol. 7, 2 Jan 1673; Acts of the Privy Council of England (vol.1, 1613-1680), pp.586-587
13. TNA C9/243/152, Pincher v. Pride
14. Andrews, P., *et al.*, *Charter Quay, The Spirit of Change: The Archaeology of Kingston's Riverside* (Salisbury: Wessex Archaeology, 2003), *passim;* Phillpots, C., 'The Charter Quay Site, Kingston, Documentary Research Report', p. 9 , http://www.wessexarch.co.uk/projects/london/charter_quay/spirit/reports.html [online]; McCarthy, J., *Secret Kingston Upon Thames.*
15. TNA C9/31/45, Derbyshire v. Pride
16. TNA C10/19/30
17. *CSPD (Charles II)*, vol. 19, 19 October 1661
18. Greenstreet, C., 'What did the brewers clerk tell us?' http://marinelives-theshippingnews.org/blog/2012/12/10 [online]; Atkinson, C., *The Case of Christopher Atkinson, Esq. Stated Large* (London: Almon *et al,* 1785), p. 74
19. *LJ*, vol. 6, p. 489
20. TNA C9/31/45
21. Rutt, *Burton's Diary*, 11 and 13 April 1659, vol.4 [online]; Wanklyn, M. *Reconstructing the New Model Army* (Solihull: Helion, 2015-16), ii, p. 166; *The Parliamentary Intelligencer, 30 July–8 August 1660*, BL, E.186 (25); *The Humble Remonstrance* (London: 1660), BL, E.1021 (1)

22. TNA C5/64/87, Pride v. Wood
23. TNA C9/409/189, Pride v. Derbyshire
24. Ward, E. F., *Christopher Monck, Duke of Albemarle* (London: John Murray, 1915), p. 51
25. 'An Act for Settling an Estate in Trust for the Benefit of Mrs. Elizabeth Pride and her Children', *Statutes of the Realm*, vol. 5, pp.89-90; 646-647
26. Ward, *Christopher Monck*, pp. 51-52
27. Copy of the Last Will and Testament of Christopher Monck, Nottinghamshire Archives, DD/4P/41/24; Ward, *Christopher Monck*, pp. 50-51; Sherwin, W. 'The Pedigree of the Monkes of Potheridge', British Museum (BM), 1864, 0813.293
28. http://www.albemarleoflondon.com [online] (accessed 2013)
29. *LJ*. vol.15, p. 352
30. Ward, *Christopher Monck*, p. 50
31. *LJ*. vol.19, p. 39
32. Ward, *Christopher Monck*, p.347
33. Stater, V. 'Grenville, John, First Earl of Bath (1628-1701)', *ODNB*
34. Ward, *Christopher Monck*, ibid.
35. Griffiths, A. 'Sherwin, William, (*b. c.* 1645, *d.* in or after 1709)', *ODNB*
36. ibid.
37. History of the County of Middlesex, vol.2, pp. 121-132; History of the County of Essex, vol.6, pp. 76-89; Griffiths, 'Sherwin, William'
38. Johnston, W. 'Sherwin, William (1607-1690)', *ODNB*
39. Armytage, G. T., (ed.), *Allegations for Marriage Licences Issued by the Bishop of London, 1611 to 1828* (London: Wardour Press,1887), vol.2, p.322
40. North Carolina Genealogy Forum, 2009 [online], Brown, D. 'Nathaniel Rice (d.1753), Colonial Governor of North Carolina'
41. TNA C10/19/30
42. Blomfield, *Biographical Dictionary of Norfolk*, p. 332
43. Trustees of the British Museum, 'William Sherwin (Biographical Details)' [online] Available: HTTP <http://www.britishmuseum.org/research/search_the_collection_database/term_details.aspx?bioId=107588> (accessed, July 2016)
44. *LJ* vol.16, p. 494
45. BM, 1864, 0813.293
46. Brown, 'Nathaniel Rice', *passim*
47. House of Lords Manuscripts, vol. 8, p. 316
48. *CSPD (Anne),* 1702-1703, 7 Sept. 1702
49. British History Online [online], *Calendar of Treasury Books*, vol. 32, p. 554
50. Brown, 'Nathaniel Rice', *passim*

Appendix I: Colonel Pride's Officers

1. *LJ*, vol. 7, p. 279
2. Sprigg, *Anglia Rediviva*, p. 329
3. TNA Prob 11/205/425; Sprigg, *Anglia Rediviva*, p. 79 and *passim*; Carlyle, *Cromwell's Letters and Speeches*, vol.1, p. 220; Firth and Davies, *Regimental History*, p. 359, ff.
4. Durston, 'Goffe, William', *ODNB*; Greaves and Zaller, *Biographical Dictionary*
5. Sprigg, *Anglia Rediviva*, p. 329; Rushworth, *Historical Collections*, vol. 7, pp. 1097-1134 [online]; TNA SP28/56, f. 387

6. Temple, 'Officer Lists', p. 60, n. 76; British History Online, *Calendar Committee for Compounding,* part 1, 6 Sept. 1650; ibid. parts 3 and 9, September 1650; Sprigg, *Anglia Rediviva*, p. 329; Rushworth, *Historical Collections*, vol. 6, pp. 475-500; TNA SP 28/301, f.612

7. TNA SP28/265, part 2, f.212

8. Sprigg, *Anglia Rediviva*, p. 329; *CJ* vol. 4, p. 98; Temple, 'Officer Lists', p. 75; CPSD (Interregnum), 'Commissions Granted by the Council of State to Officers of the Militia'

9. *CJ*, vol 4, p. 98; Firth and Davies, *Regimental History*, p. 360; Birch, *Thurloe Papers*, vol. 3, pp. 596, 510

10. Burke, A. M., *Memorials of St. Margaret's Church, Westminster* (London: Eyre & Spottiswoode, 1914) p. 648, n. 4; *CSPD (Interregnum)*, vol. 43, *passim*; *Mercurius Politicus*, 6-13 August 1657, quoted in Firth and Davies, *Regimental History*, p. 369

11. TNA E121/4/8, 'Sale of Crown Properties', f. 58; Birch, *Thurloe Papers*, vol. 3, p. 56; *CJ.* vol.7, p. 829

12. *CJ.* ibid; HMC, *Heathcote Manuscripts*, p. 136; *CSPD (Charles II)*, vol. 162, 12 July 1666; ibid. vol. 168, August 1666; ibid. vol. 177, 2 November 1666; ibid. vol. 192, 25 February 1667

13. *Mercurius Politicus, 7-14 November 1650* BL Thomason Tracts E.616 (1); Wanklyn, i, p. 90; ibid, ii, p. 47, n. 50

14. Sprigg, *Anglia Rediviva*, p. 117; Gentles, 'New Model Officer Corps', *passim*; Pickvance, p. 28, n. 2; *CSPD (Interregnum)*, 1650, vol. 11, 'Militia Papers'; Duignan, p. 121; Turner, p. 273; TNA E121/4/8, 'Sale of Crown Properties', f.59; Greaves and Zaller, *Biographical Dictionary*; Firth and Davies, p.330ff; *CSPD (Interregnum)* 'Warrants for Payments for the Council of State', July 1659; TNA PROB 11/326, 'Last Will and Testament of Waldive Lagoe'; LRO Kenyon correspondence, DDKE 9

15. Greaves and Zaller, *Biographical Dictionary*; *CSPD (Charles II)*, vol. 82, October 1663; *CJ* vol. 7, p. 531; *CPSD (Interregnum)*, vol. 203, 30 June 1659; HMC, *Report on the Manuscripts of Leyborne-Popham of Littlecote*, p.173; *CSPD (Interregnum)*, 'Warrants of the Council of State', 19 April 1660; *CJ* vol. 8, p. 34; *CSPD (Charles II)*, vol. 96, April 1-17 1664; ibid. vol. 217, September 12-26 1667; Zook, M. 'Holmes, Abraham (*d. 1685*)'

16. TNA PROB 11/301; Firth, *Clarke Papers*, vol.1, p. 437; *CJ* vol.7, pp.700, 830

17. Firth, *Clarke Papers*, ibid; HMC, *Leyborne-Popham Manuscripts*, p. 172

18. Firth and Davies, *Regimental History*, p.678 ff; *CSPD (Interregnum)*, 3 Sept 1656

Bibliography and Sources

Primary Sources

The National Archives, Kew

Chancery Proceedings:
  C3/397/14; C5/19/81, 24/62, 64/87; 402/121; 9/31/45, 243/152, 409/189; 10/19/30
State Papers:
  SP 28/29, 28/31, 28/56; 28/104, part 1; 28/173, part 1; 28/262, part 3, f.448; 28/265, part 2, f.210, 212; 28/266, part 1, f.25; 28/266, part1, f.27; 28/267, part 3, f.155, 160
Exchequer Papers:
  E121/4/8; 133/141/23; 214/318
Prerogative Court of Canterbury:
  PROB 11/205; 11/240; 11/326

The British Library

Thomason Tracts:
  E.572/15, pp.147-8; E.213 (8); E.390 (3, 26); E.616 (1); E.669 F6(10); E.786 (31); E.825 (4); E.968 (13); E.1005 (3); E.1985 (7)
Additional Manuscripts:
  Add MS 26758

Guildhall Library

Brewers Company, Wardens' Accounts 1501/2-1692 MS 5442/1-8
Haberdashers Company, Apprenticeship Bindings 1610-35, 15860/4, f. 173 v
Haberdashers Company, Freedom Admissions 1526-1641, MS 15857/1, unfol. (24 April 1629)

Historical Manuscripts Commission

Heathcote Manuscripts (1899) Norwich: HMSO
Leyborne-Popham Manuscripts (1899) Norwich: HMSO

Fifth Report (1876) London: HMSO
Sixth Report (1877) London: HMSO
Seventh Report (1879) London: HMSO

London Metropolitan Archives

Parish registers:
St. Anne's Blackfriars; St. Botolph's Aldgate; St. Bride's; St. Gregory-by-Paul

Lancashire Records Office

Kenyon correspondence:
  DDKE/9/38/18

Nottinghamshire Archives

Deposited Documents:
  DD/4P/41/24

Surrey History Centre

Parish Registers of St. Mary's, Kingston-upon-Thames

State Papers

Calendar of State Papers Domestic, Charles I, W. D. Hamilton (ed.), London,
    HMSO, 1891: vols 511, 516
Calendar of State Papers Domestic, Interregnum, M. A. E. Green (ed.), London,
    HMSO, 1875-1886: vols 1, 5, 11, 16, 36, 38, 41, 43, 66, 69, 70, 72, 76, 77, 123, 125,
    130, 162, 166, 179, 180, 181, 183, 302
Calendar of State Papers Domestic, Charles II, M. A. E. Green (ed.), London,
    HMSO, 1860: vols 19, 26, 71, 82, 84, 162, 168, 177, 192, 217
Calendar of State Papers Domestic, Anne, R. P. Mahaffy (ed.), London, HMSO,
    1916: vol. 1
Calendar of State Papers, Venice, A. B. Hinds (ed.), London, HMSO, 1927: vol. 28

Parliamentary Publications:

House of Commons Journal, London, HMSO, 1802-1803: vols 4-8
House of Lords Journal, London, HMSO, 1767-1830: vols 5, 6, 7, 9, 11, 15, 16, 19

Contemporary Accounts:

Acts of the Privy Council of England (volume 1), 1613-1680 (Hereford: Brothers).
Anon., *Rump, or an exact collection of the Choycest Poems and Songs relating to the
    late times* (London: Brome and Marsh, 1662).

Armytage, G. T., (ed.), *Allegations for Marriage Licences Issued by the Bishop of London 1611 to 1828* (2 vols) (London: Wardour Press,1887).

Atkinson, C., *The Case of Christopher Atkinson, Esq. Stated Large* (London: Almon et al, 1785).

Atkinson, C. T., (ed.), *Letters and Papers Relating to the Dutch War, 1652-1654* (6 volumes) (London: Navy Records Society, 1899-1930).

Barber, E., *The Storming and Totall Routing of Tythes* (London: 1651).

Birch, T. (ed.), *A Collection of the Papers of John Thurloe Esq.* (7 vols) (London: Fletcher Gyles, 1742).

Bray, W. (ed.), *The Diary of John Evelyn* (2 vols) (London: M. W. Dunne, 1901).

Burroughs, E. *The Memorable Works of a Son of Thunder and Consolation* (London: 1672).

Carlyle, T., *Oliver Cromwell's Letters and Speeches* (3 vols) (London: Routledge, 1885).

Cary, H. (ed.), *Memorials of the Great Civil War in England, from 1646-1652* (2 vols) (London: Henry Colburn, 1842).

Ellkis, H. (ed.), *The Obituary of Richard Smyth,* (London: Camden Society, 1849).

Firth, C. H. (ed.), *The Clarke Papers: Selections of the Papers of William Clarke, Secretary to the Council of the Army 1647-1649, and to General Monck and the Commanders of the Army in Scotland 1651-1660.* (4 vols) (London: The Camden Society, 1894).

Firth, C. H. (ed.), *The Memoirs of Edmund Ludlow, Lieutenant General of the Horse in the Army of the Commonwealth of England* (2 vols) (Oxford: Clarendon Press, 1894).

Firth, C. H. and Rait, R. S. (eds.) *Acts and Ordinances of the Interregnum* (London: 1911).

Gardiner, S. R. (ed.),*The Constitutional Documents of the Puritan Revolution, 1625-1660* (Oxford: Clarendon Press, 1899).

Guilding, J. M., *Reading Records: Diary of the Corporation* (4 vols) (London: James Parker, 1892-1896).

Heath, J., *A Chronicle of the Late Intestine War in the Three Kingdoms of England, Scotland and Ireland* (London: 1676)

Latham, R. and Mathews, W. (eds.), *The Diary of Samuel Pepys* (London: Bell and Hyman, 1970-73).

Lindley, K. and Scott, D. (eds.), *The Journal of Thomas Juxon, 1644-1647* (Cambridge: Royal Historical Society, 1999).

Long, C. E. (ed.), *Richard Symonds's Diary of the Marches of the Royal Army* (1997 edition, Cambridge: Cambridge University Press, 1859).

Mackay, C. (ed.), *The Cavalier Songs and Ballads of England from 1642 to 1684* (London: Griffen Bohn and Co., 1863).

Macray, W. D. (ed.), *A Calendar of the Clarendon State Papers preserved in the Bodleian Library* (2 vols) (Oxford: Clarendon Press, 1864).

Nickolls, J., *Original Letters and Papers of State Addressed to Oliver Cromwell* (London: Bowyer, 1743).

Orme, W. (ed.), *Remarkable Passages in the Life of William Kiffin* (London: Burton & Smith, *et al*, 1823).

Park, T. (ed.), *The Harleian Miscellany* (London: Robert Dutton, 1810).

Peters, H., *Mr. Peters Last Report of the English Warres* (London: 1646).

Prynne, W., *A True and Perfect Narrative* (London: 1659).

Rushworth, J., *Historical Collections of Private Passages of State* (8 vols) (London: Browne, 1721).

Rutt, J. T. (ed.), *The Diary of Thomas Burton Esq.*, 1828 [online] British History Online, available <http://www.british-history.ac.uk/catalogue.aspx? gid=45& type=2> (accessed 2014).

Scott, W. (ed.), *Original Memorials Written During the Civil War* (Edinburgh: Constable & Co, 1806).

Sprigg, J., *Anglia Rediviva: England's Recovery* (Oxford: Oxford University Press, 1854).

The Statutes of the Realm (1908 edition, London: Dawsons, 1819)

Warner, G. F. (ed.), *Correspondence of Sir Edward Nicholas, Secretary of State* (London: Camden Society, 1897).

Wharton, G., *Select and Choice Poems* (London: 1661).

Whitelock, B., *Memorials of the English Affairs*, (4 vols) (Oxford: Oxford University Press, 1853).

Winstanley, W., *The Loyal Martyrology* (London: Edward Thomas, 1665).

Secondary Sources

Published Books

Adair, J., *By the Sword Divided: Eyewitness Accounts of the English Civil War* (London: Book Club Associates).

Andrews, P., *et al.*, *Charter Quay, The Spirit of Change: The Archaeology of Kingston's Riverside* (Salisbury: Wessex Archaeology, 2003).

Archer, I. W., *The History of the Haberdashers' Company* (Chichester: Phillimore, 1991).

Archer, I. W., *The Haberdashers' Company in the Later Twentieth Century* (Chichester, Phillimore, 2004).

Ashley, M., *Cromwell's Generals* (London: Jonathan Cape, 1951).

Barry, J. and Brooks, C. (eds), *The Middling Sort of People: Culture, Society and Politics in England, 1550-1800* (Basingstoke: Macmillan, 1994).

Battista, K. (ed.) *Benezit Dictionary of Artists* (14 vols) (Oxford: Oxford University Press, 2010).

Blomefield, F., *An Essay Towards a Biographical Dictionary of Norfolk* (11 vols) (London: William Miller, 1805-1811).

Burford, E. J., *Royal St. James's: Being a Story of Kings, Clubmen and Courtesans* (London: Hale, 1988).

Burke, A. M., *Memorials of St. Margaret's Church, Westminster* (London: Eyre & Spottiswoode, 1914).

Burke, B., *General Armoury of England, Ireland, Scotland and Wales* (1969 edition, London: Hanson and Sons, 1842).

Burnet, G., *History of his Own Time* (London: Orr & Co, 1850).

Cobbett, W., *Parliamentary History of England* (36 vols) (London: Hansard, 1808).

Cockayne, G. E., *The Complete Peerage* (4 vols) (London: St. Catherine Press, 1916).

Corrigan, G., *Mud, Blood and Poppycock: Britain and the First World War* (London: Cassell, 2003)

Davis, T. (ed.), *John Milton, Selected Shorter Poems and Prose* (London: Routledge, 1988).

Deane, J. B., *The Life of Richard Deane* (London: Longman, 1870).

Dent, J., *The Quest for Nonsuch* (Second edition, London: Hutchinson, 1970).

Denton, B., *Cromwell's Soldiers: The Moulding of the New Model Army, 1644-1651* (Cambridge: Denton Dare Publishing, 2004).

Ditchfield, P. H. and Page, W. (eds.), *History of the County of Berkshire* (4 vols) 1925, [online] British History Online, available <http://www.british-history.ac.uk/catalogue.aspx?gid=3&type=1> (accessed 2012)

Downing T. and Millman, M., *Civil War* (London: Colins & Brown, 1992).

Duignan, W. H., *Warwickshire Place Names* (Oxford: Oxford University Press, 1912).

Dunning, R. (ed.), *A History of the Country of Somerset: Volume 8 – The Poldens and the Levels* (2004) [online] British History Online, available, <http://www.british-history.ac.uk/source.aspx?pubid=62> (accessed 2015)

Eales, J., *Puritans and Roundheads: The Harleys of Brampton Bryan and the Outbreak of the English Civil War* (Cambridge: Cambridge University Press, 1990).

Ede-Borrett, S., *Lostwithiel 1644: The Campaign and the Battles* (Surrey: The Pike and Shot Society, 2004).

Edwards, G., *The Last Days of Charles I* (Stroud: Sutton Publishing, 1999).

Farrar, E., *Church Heraldry in Norfolk* (3 vols) (Norwich: Goose, 1887-1893).

Fearn, J., *Discovering Heraldry* (Aylesbury: Shire Publications, 1980).

Firth, C. H., *Scotland and the Protectorate: Letters Relating to the Military Government of Scotland from January 1654 to June 1659* (Edinburgh: University Press, 1899).

Firth, C. H., *Cromwell's Army* (London: Methuen, 1902).

Firth, C. H. and Davis, G., *The Regimental History of Cromwell's Army* (Oxford: Oxford University Press, 1940).

Foard, G., *Naseby: The Decisive Campaign* (Barnsley: Pen and Sword, 1904).

Frazer, A., *Cromwell: Our Chief of Men* (Third edition, St. Albans: Granada Publishing, 1973).

Fritze, R. H., and W. B. Robinson (eds), *Historical Dictionary of Stuart England 1603-1689* (Connecticut, Greenwood Press, 1996).

Gentles, I., *The New Model Army in England, Ireland and Scotland, 1645-1653* (Oxford: Blackwell Books, 1992).

Goodwin, W. *History of the Commonwealth of England* (4 vols) (London: Colburn, 1824-1828)

Grant, J., *Old and New Edinburgh*(6 vols) (London: Cassell, 1883).

Greaves, R. L., *Enemies under his feet: Radicals and Nonconformists in Britain: 1664-1677* (California: Stanford University Press, 1990).

Greaves, R. L. and Zaller, R. (eds), *The Biographical Dictionary of English Radicals in the Seventeenth Century* (3 vols) (Brighton: Harvester Press, 1984).

Greer, G. *Shakespeare's Wife* (London: Bloomsbury, 2007).

Griffin, S. *The Siege of Redding,* (Bristol: The Stuart Press, 1996).

Harrington, P. *English Civil War Fortifications 1642-1651* (Oxford: Osprey Books, 2003).

Harris, W. *The Lives and Writings of James I and Charles I, and the Lives of Oliver Cromwell and Charles II* (3 vols) (London: F. C and J. Rivington, *et al.*, 1814).

Hotson, L. *The Commonwealth and Restoration Stage* (Cambridge: Cambridge University Press, 1928).

Jeaffreson, J. C. (ed.), 'Middlesex Session Rolls' (4 vols), *Middlesex County Records 1603-1625,* 1888 [online] British History Online, available <http://www. british-history.ac.uk/catalogue.aspx?gid=114&type=2> (accessed 2012).

Jordan, D. and Walsh, M., *The King's Revenge* (London: Abacus, 2013).

Kelsey, S., *Inventing a Republic* (Manchester: Manchester University Press, 1997).

Laurence, A., *Parliamentary Army Chaplains 1642-1651* (Woodbridge: The Boydell Press, 1990).

Lysons, D., *The Environs of London* (4 vols), 1796 [online] British History Online, available   <http://www.british-history.ac.uk/catalogue.aspx?gid=80&type=2 (accessed 2012).

Macauley, B., *The History of England from the Accession of James II* (4 vols) (Boston: Philips, Sampson and Co., 1854)

Medvei, V. C. and Thornton, J. L. (eds), *The Hospital of Saint Bartholomew, 1123-1973* (London, 1974).

Moore, N., *The History of St. Bartholomew's Hospital* (2 vols) (London: Pearson, 1918).

Morley, J., *Oliver Cromwell* (London: Macmillan, 1900).

Neal, D., *The History of the Puritans in London* (London: Tegg & son, 1837).

Neale, J. M., *Herbert Tresham: a Tale of the Great Rebellion*, Anglican History, 1843 [online] available <http://anglicanhistory.org/neale/htresham.html> (accessed 2015).

Nelson, C., *Cromwell in Pembroke* (revised edition, Pembroke: Pembroke Civil Trust Society, 1974).

Nichols, J. F. and Taylor, J., *Bristol Past and Present* (3 vols) (Bristol: Arrowsmith, 1862).

Noble, M., *The Lives of the English Regicides* (2 vols) (London: J. Stockdale, 1798).

Noble, M., *The Memoires of the Protectoral-House of Cromwell* (Second edition, London: G. G. J. and J. Robinson, 1797).

Oppenheim, M., *A History of the Administration of the Royal Navy* (2 vols) (London: Bodley Head, 1896).

McCarthy, J., *Secret Kingston Upon Thames* (Stroud: Amberley, 2014)

Palmer, A. and Palmer, P., *The Chronology of British History* (London: Century, 1992).

Peachey, S. and Turton, A., *Old Robin's Foot: The Equipping and Campaigns of Essex's Infantry, 1642-1645* (Partizan Press, 1987).

Pickvance, T. J., *George Fox and the Purefeys: A Study of the Puritan Background in Fenny Drayton in the 16th and 17th Centuries* (London: Friends' Historical Society, 1970)

Raymond, J., *Making the News: An Anthology of the Newsbooks of Revolutionary England* (Witney: Windrush Press, 1993).

Redmayne, S., *The History of King-Killers: Or, the 30th of January Commemorated* (Second edition, London: S. Redmayne, *et al.*, 1719).

Reid, S., *Dunbar 1650: Cromwell's Victory* (Oxford: Osprey, 2004).

Richards, J., *Aristocrat and Regicide: the Life and Times of Thomas, Lord Grey of Groby* (London: New Millennium, 2003).

Roberts, K., *First Newbury 1643: The Turning Point* (London: Osprey, 2003).

Roberts, K., *Pike and Shot Tactics, 1590-1660* (London: Osprey, 2010).

Rogers, P. G.,*The Fifth Monarchy Men* (London: Oxford University Press, 1966).

Scott, A. F., *Everyone A Witness: The Stuart Age* (London: White Lion Publishers, 1974).

Shaw, W. A., *Calendar of Treasury Books, Volume 1: 1660-1667* (1909) [online] British History Online, available <http://www.british-history.ac.uk/report.aspx?compid=80021> (accessed 2015).

Time Out, *Time Out: South West England* (London: Penguin, 2003).

Tolmie, M., *The Triumph of the Saints: The Separatist Churches of London, 1616-1649* (Cambridge: Cambridge University Press, 1977).

Turner, G. L.,*Original Records of Early Nonconformity and Persecution Under Indulgence* (London, Unwin, 1911).

Underdown, D., *Pride's Purge: Politics in the Puritan Revolution* (Oxford: Oxford University Press, 1971).

Underdown, D., *Somerset in the Civil War and Interregnum* (Newton Abbot: David & Charles, 1973).

Underdown, D., *Revel, Riot & Rebellion: Popular Politics and Culture in England 1603-1660* (Oxford: Oxford University Press, 1985).

Wanklyn, M. *Reconstructing the New Model Army* (2 Vols.) (Solihull: Helion and Company, 2015-2016)

Wanklyn, M. and Jones, F., *A Military History of the English Civil War, 1642-1646* (Harlow: Pearson/Longman, 2005).

Ward, E., *A Vade Mecum for Malt-Worms* (London: Bickerston, c.1718)

Ward, E. F., *Christopher Monck, Duke of Albemarle* (London: John Murray, 1915).

Watts, M. R., *The Dissenters: from the Reformation to the French Revolution* (Oxford: Oxford University Press, 1978).

Weinreb, B. and Hibbert, C. (eds), *The London Encyclopaedia* (London: Macmillan, 1983).

Wheatley, H. B., *London Past and Present* (3 vols) (London: John Murray, 1891).

Williams, G., *A Glossary of Shakespeare's Sexual Language* (London: The Althone Press, 1997).

Wilson, J. D., *Life in Shakespeare's England* (London: Penguin, 1951).

Worden, B., *The Rump Parliament 1648-53* (Cambridge: Cambridge University Press, 1974).

Articles and papers

Anon., 'A Panegyric on Pride', *Blackwood's Magazine*, 26:160 (July-December 1829), pp. 914-917.

Anon., 'Death of the Duke of Hamilton', *The Christian Observer*, vol ii (Janurary-December 1803), pp. 262-265.

Baker, P. R. S., 'Barber, Edward (*d.* 1663),*Oxford Dictionary of National Biography* (Oxford: Oxford University Press, 2004).

Benedict, J., 'Mayo, Richard (c.1630-1695)', *Oxford Dictionary of National Biography* (Oxford: Oxford University Press, 2004).

Bradley, E. T., 'Grey, Thomas, Baron Grey of Groby (1622-1657)', *The Oxford Dictionary of National Biography* (Oxford: Oxford University Press, 2004)

Brown, D., 'Nathaniel Rice (d.1753), Colonial Governor of North Carolina', North Carolina Genealogy Forum, 2009 [online] available, <http://genforumgenealogy.com> (accessed 2013).

Capp, B., 'Simpson, John (1614/15-1662)', revised, *Oxford Dictionary of National Biography* (Oxford: Oxford University Press, 2004).

Cooper, T., 'Goffe, Stephen (1605-1681)', revised, Bertram, J., *Oxford Dictionary of National Biography* (Oxford: Oxford University Press, 2004).

Cornel, M., 'The Three-Threads Mystery and the Birth of Porter: the answer is …', *Zythophile*, 2015 [online] available <https:zythophile.wordpress.com> (accessed 2015).

Davis, G., 'The Parliamentary Army Under the Earl of Essex, 1642-45', *English Historical Review*, 49 (1934), pp.32-54.

Davis, G., 'The Formation of the New Model Army', *English Historical Review*, 56 (1941), pp.103-105.

De Krey, G. S., 'Bethel, Slingsby (*bap.* 1617, *d.* 1697)', revised Kelsey, S., *Oxford Dictionary of National Biography* (Oxford: Oxford University Press, 2004).

Durston, C., 'Goffe, William (d. 1679?)', *The Oxford Dictionary of National Biography* (Oxford: Oxford University Press, 2004).

'Etne', 'Col. Thomas Pride, A Somerset County Native?', *The Somerset County Herald* (28 June 1958).

Firth, C. H., 'Thomas Pride', *The Oxford Dictionary of National* Biography (Oxford, Oxford University Press, 1896).

Foyster, E., 'Gender Relations', Coward, B. (ed.) *A Companion to Stuart Britain* (2009 edition, Chichester: Wiley-Blackwell, 2003), pp.111-129.

Gentles, I., 'The New Model Officer Corps in 1647: a collective portrait', *Social History*, 22:2 (1997), pp.127-144.

Gentles, I., 'Pride, Thomas, appointed Lord under the Protectorate (*d.* 1658)', *Oxford Dictionary of National Biography* (Oxford: Oxford University Press, 2004).

Greaves, R. L., 'Owen, John (1616-1683)', *Oxford Dictionary of National Biography* (Oxford: Oxford University Press, 2004).

Greenstreet, C., 'What did the brewers clerk tell us?', *Marine Lives – The Shipping News* [online]

Griffiths, A., 'William Sherwin, (*b. c.* 1645, *d.* in or after 1709)', *Oxford Dictionary of National Biography* (Oxford: Oxford University Press, 2004).

Haykin, M. A. G., 'Kiffin, William (1616-1701)', *Oxford Dictionary of National Biography* (Oxford: Oxford University Press, 2004).

Hotson, J. L., 'Bear Gardens and Bear Baiting in the Commonwealth', *PMLA: Proceedings of the Modern Language Association*, 40:2 (1945), pp.276-288.

Johnston, W., 'Sherwin, William (1607-1690)', *Oxford Dictionary of National Biography* (Oxford: Oxford University Press, 2004).

Knoppers, L. L., ''Sing Old Noll the Brewer: Royalist Satire and Social Inversion, 1648-64', *The Seventeenth Century*, 15:1 (2000), pp.35-52

Langley, A. S., 'Some Notable Names in Midland Baptist History', *Baptist Quarterly*, 3:6 (1927), pp.280-286.

Pearl, V., 'London's Counter-Revolution', Aylmer, G. E. (ed.), *The Interregnum: The Quest for Settlement 1646-1660*, pp. 29-57 (London: Macmillan, 1983).

Phillips, J., 'William Goffe the Regicide', *English Historical Review*, 7 (1892), pp.717-720.

Phillpots, C., 'The Charter Quay Site, Kingston, Documentary Research Report', *Wessex Archaeology Online* [online] available HTTP <http://www.wessexarch.co.uk/projects/london/charter_quay/spirit/reports.html> (accessed 2016).

Shaw, W. A., 'Richardson, Samuel (*fl.* 1637-1658)', rev. Sean Kelsey, *Oxford Dictionary of National Biography* (Oxford: Oxford University Press, 2004).

Stater, V., 'Grenville, John, first Earl of Bath (1628-1701)', *Oxford Dictionary of National Biography* (Oxford: Oxford University Press, 2004).

Stater, V., 'Mordaunt, John, first Viscount Mordaunt of Avalon (1626-1675)', *Oxford Dictionary of National Biography* (Oxford: Oxford University Press, 2004).

'T. S.', 'The Last Speech and Dying Words of Thomas (Lord, Alias Colonel) Pride', *The Harleian Miscellany,* 3, pp.136-141 (London: White and Murray, 1809).

Temple, R., 'Officer Lists of the New Model Army', *Bulletin of the Institute of Historical Research*, 59:139 (1986) [online] available HTTP <http://www.robert-temple.com/papers/Offprint-OfficerList.pdf> (accessed 2012).

Trustees of the British Museum, 'William Sherwin (Biographical Details)' [online] available: HTTP <http://www.britishmuseum.org/research/search_the_collection_database/term_details.aspx?bioId=107588> (accessed, July 2016)

Usher, B., 'Gouge, William (1575-1653)', *Oxford Dictionary of National Biography* (Oxford: Oxford University Press, 2004).

Wanklyn, M., 'Oliver Cromwell and the Performance of Parliament's Armies in the Newbury Campaign, 20 October – 21 November 1644', *Journal of the Historical Association*, vol. 69, issue 321 (January 2011), pp.3-25.

Zook, M., 'Holmes, Abraham (*d.* 1685)', *Oxford Dictionary of National Biography* (Oxford: Oxford University Press, 2004).

Unpublished PhD Theses

Kouffman, A. *The Cultural Work of Stuart Women's Diaries* (University of Arizona, 2000).

Nagel, L. C., *The Militia of London, 1641-1649* (King's College London, 1982) [Online] Available <https://kclpure.kcl.ac.uk/portal/files/2927314/403590.pdf> (accessed 2013).

Rees, J., *Leveller Organisation and the Dynamic of the English Revolution.* (Goldsmith's College London, 2014.)

Internet

Backhouse, T. (2016) *History in Portsmouth* [online] available: HTTP <http://www.historyinportsmouth.co.uk/index.htm> (accessed 2016)

Battlefield Trust, *UK Battlefields Resource Centre* [online] available: HTTP <http://www.battlefieldstrust.com/resource-centre/civil-war/battleview.asp?BattleFieldId=51> (accessed 2013).

Cornell, M., *Zythophile: Beer Now and Then* [online] available: HTTP <http://zythophile.co.uk> (accessed 2016).

Family Search, *familysearch.org* [online] available: HTTP <https://familysearch.org/learn/wiki/en/Ashcott,_Somerset_Genealogy> (accessed 2015).

Findmypast Newspaper Archive Limited (2015) [online] available: HTTP <http://www.britishnewspaperarchive.co.uk> (accessed 2015).

M Library Digital Collections, University of Michigan (2016) *Early English Books Online* [online] available: HTTP <http://quod.lib.umich.edu/e/eebogroup> (accessed 2016).

Oxford University Press (2016) *Oxford Dictionary of National Biography* [online] available: HTTP <http://www.oxforddnb.com/index.jsp> (accessed 2016).

Plant., D. (2012) *British Civil Wars, Commonwealth and Protectorate, 1638-1660* [online] available: HTTP <http://www.british-civil-wars.co.uk > (accessed 2013).

QuelleNet (1997-2008) *Exlibris* [online] available: HTTP <http://www.exlibris.org> (accessed 2013).

United States Army Combined Arms Centre, Fort Leavenworth, Kansas [online] available: HTTP <http://www.cgsc.edu> (accessed 2015).

University of London (2014) *British History Online* [online] available: HTTP <http://www.british-history.ac.uk> (accessed 2016).

Index

Index of People

Andrews, Nicholas 153, 160, 168

Barclay, Colonel Harry 28-33, 35, 37, 39-41, 43, 45-54, 56, 58, 112, 156, 177-181, 188
Bath, John Grenville, Earl of, 173-175, 206, 216
Bethel, Slingsby 118-119, 199, 215
Blake, Admiral Robert 11, 129, 131
Bradshaw, John 101, 161-163
Bradway, Thomas 12, 14-15, 18
Burton, Thomas 98, 146, 171, 187, 193, 196, 203-205, 211
Butler, Colonel John 40-42, 60, 152-153, 155, 191
Butler, Samuel 152, 155, 191

Carlyle, Thomas 89, 192-193, 195, 198, 206, 210
Charles I i, vi, viii-ix, 15-16, 21, 24, 26-30, 35, 37, 39, 42-43, 46-47, 50, 55, 59, 66, 75, 77, 79, 81, 83, 86-87, 92-95, 98-99, 100-109, 111-113, 122-123, 127, 132, 142, 146, 153, 161-162, 167, 178, 192-193, 195-197, 204-205, 213
Charles II 105, 112, 119-120, 132, 159-161, 166, 168, 170, 172-173, 176, 182, 196, 205, 207, 209, 213
Chidley, Daniel 19-20, 22, 110, 113, 187, 198
Cockayne, G. E. 104, 187, 197, 212
Cowell, Major William 29, 47-48, 65, 69, 78, 80, 89-90, 93, 177-180
Cromwell, Oliver i, iii, ix, 18, 43, 45, 48, 70-71, 79, 81-82, 85-93, 97, 103, 106, 110, 112-114, 116-117, 120, 124, 132-134, 136-139, 142-149, 151-154, 156, 159-163, 165, 169, 178, 180-181, 187, 190-198, 201-203, 206, 210-214, 217, 220
Cromwell, Richard 159-160, 180

Deane, Colonel Richard 89, 93, 163, 195, 212

Desborough, Major John 143-146, 160
Duppa, John 19, 21-23, 49, 53, 188

Eaton, Samuel 22, 188
Emmins, Lieutenant-Colonel 48, 52, 177
Essex, Robert Devereux, Earl of 27-33, 35-37, 39-43, 45-51, 53, 74, 76, 179, 189-190, 206, 214-215
Evelyn, John 162, 204, 210

Fairfax, Charles 89, 136, 159, 181
Fairfax, Sir Thomas vi-vii, 47-48, 50-51, 54-63, 65-75, 78-80, 82-83, 89, 92, 94-95, 99-100, 103, 106, 108, 136, 159, 162, 178, 181
Ferguson, Captain John 51, 81, 177, 179
Firth, C.H ix, 113, 145, 180, 194-195, 198, 200-204, 206-207, 210, 212, 216
Fleetwood, Colonel Charles 62, 124, 181

Gentles, Ian 75, 186, 193, 196, 203, 207, 213, 216
Gibbs, Elizabeth 175-176
Gibbs, John 104-105, 175-176
Glencairne, Earl of 132-133, 137
Goddard, Captain Vincent 47, 51-52, 55, 177
Goffe, Captain William vi, 28-29, 47, 49, 78, 82, 84, 87, 109, 112, 119, 125, 146, 159-160, 164-165, 177-179, 188, 194, 206, 215-216
Goring, Lord George 40, 62-63, 66
Gregson, Captain George 47, 72, 86, 177-179, 181
Grey of Groby, Lord ii, 96, 98, 103, 188, 214

Hamilton, Duke of 88-90, 106, 197, 209, 215
Hammond, Colonel Robert 56, 58, 60-61, 68, 70-71, 73-75, 86, 180
Harley, Colonel Edward vi, 51-56, 58, 60-63, 65, 70, 72-76, 78, 80-82, 84, 98, 100-101, 124, 134, 177-180, 182, 191

Index of Places

Index of General & Miscellaneous Terms

The Century of the Soldier series – Warfare c 1618-1721

www.helion.co.uk/centuryofthesoldier

'This is the Century of the Soldier', Falvio Testir, Poet, 1641

The 'Century of the Soldier' series will cover the period of military history c. 1618–1721, the 'golden era' of Pike and Shot warfare. This time frame has been seen by many historians as a period of not only great social change, but of fundamental developments within military matters. This is the period of the 'military revolution', the development of standing armies, the widespread introduction of black powder weapons and a greater professionalism within the culture of military personnel.

The series will examine the period in a greater degree of detail than has hitherto been attempted, and has a very wide brief, with the intention of covering all aspects of the period from the battles, campaigns, logistics and tactics, to the personalities, armies, uniforms and equipment.

Submissions

The publishers would be pleased to receive submissions for this series. Please contact us via email (info@helion.co.uk), or in writing to Helion & Company Limited, 26 Willow Road, Solihull, West Midlands, B91 1UE.

Titles

Books within the series are published in two formats: 'Falconets' are paperbacks, page size 248mm × 180mm, with high visual content including colour plates; 'Culverins' are hardback monographs, page size 234mm × 156mm. Books marked with * in the list above are Falconets, all others are Culverins.